Garfield takes up space

BY JIM DAVIS

Ballantine Books • New York

2010 Ballantine Books Trade Paperback Edition

Published in the United States by Ballantine Books, an imprint of The Random House Publishing Group,
a division of Random House, Inc., New York.

BALLANTINE and colophon are registered trademarks of Random House, Inc.

Originally published in slightly different form in the United States by Ballantine Books, an imprint of
The Random House Publishing Group, a division of Random House, Inc., in 1990.

ISBN 978-0-345-49178-7

Printed in China

www.ballantinebooks.com

9 8 7 6 5 4 3 2

Ask a cat.

Q: Why does a cat always land on its feet?
A: Because it beats landing on its face.

Q: Can cats see in the dark?
A: Yes. They see a whole lot of dark.

Q: Is there more than one way to skin a cat?
A: I have given your name to the authorities.

Q: Why do cats eat plants?
A: To get rid of that mouse aftertaste.

Q: How often should I take my cat to the vet?
A: As often as you would like to have your lips ripped off.

Q: Should I have my cat fixed?
A: Why? Is it broken?

Q: Why do cats spend so much time napping?
A: To rest up for bedtime.

Q: How much food should my cat eat?
A: How much have you got?

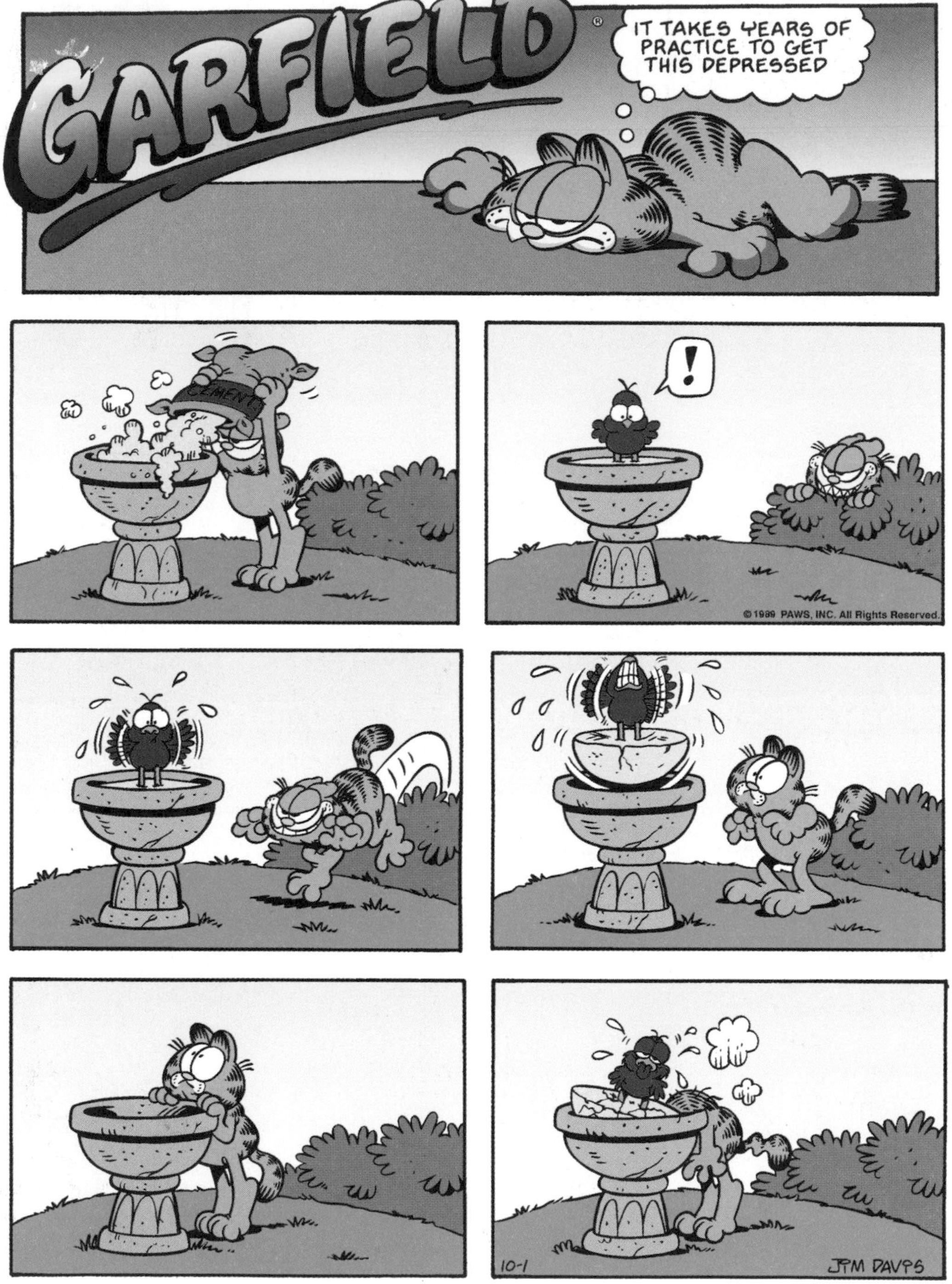
GARFIELD
IT TAKES YEARS OF PRACTICE TO GET THIS DEPRESSED
CEMENT
!
©1989 PAWS, INC. All Rights Reserved.
10-1
JIM DAVIS

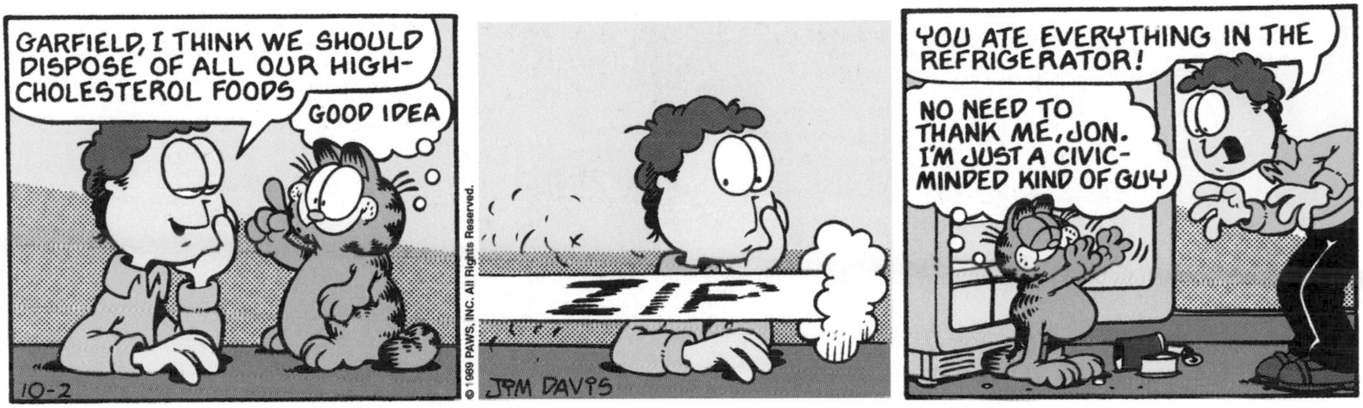
GARFIELD, I THINK WE SHOULD DISPOSE OF ALL OUR HIGH-CHOLESTEROL FOODS
GOOD IDEA
10-2
© 1989 PAWS, INC. All Rights Reserved.
ZIP
JIM DAVIS
YOU ATE EVERYTHING IN THE REFRIGERATOR!
NO NEED TO THANK ME, JON. I'M JUST A CIVIC-MINDED KIND OF GUY

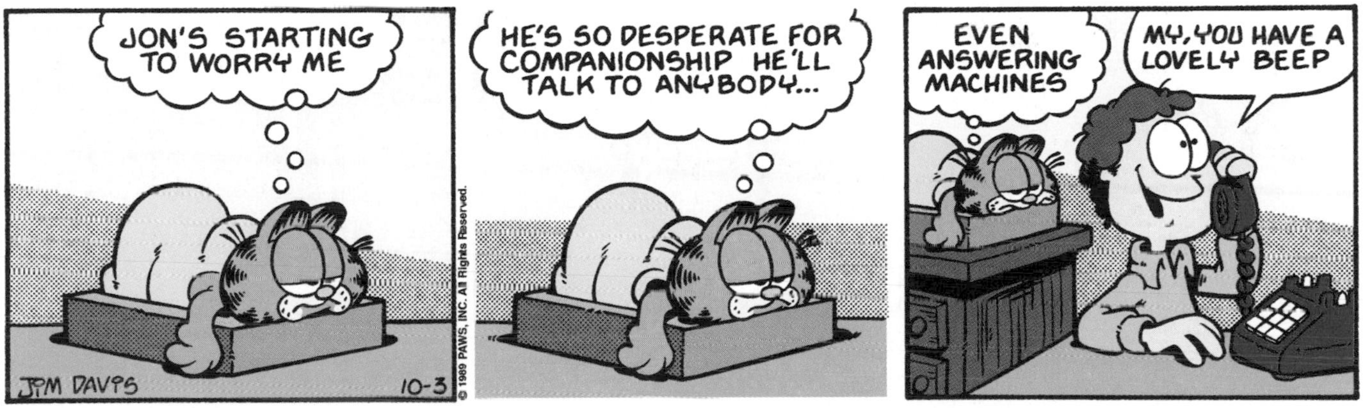
JON'S STARTING TO WORRY ME
JIM DAVIS
10-3
© 1989 PAWS, INC. All Rights Reserved.
HE'S SO DESPERATE FOR COMPANIONSHIP HE'LL TALK TO ANYBODY...
EVEN ANSWERING MACHINES
MY, YOU HAVE A LOVELY BEEP

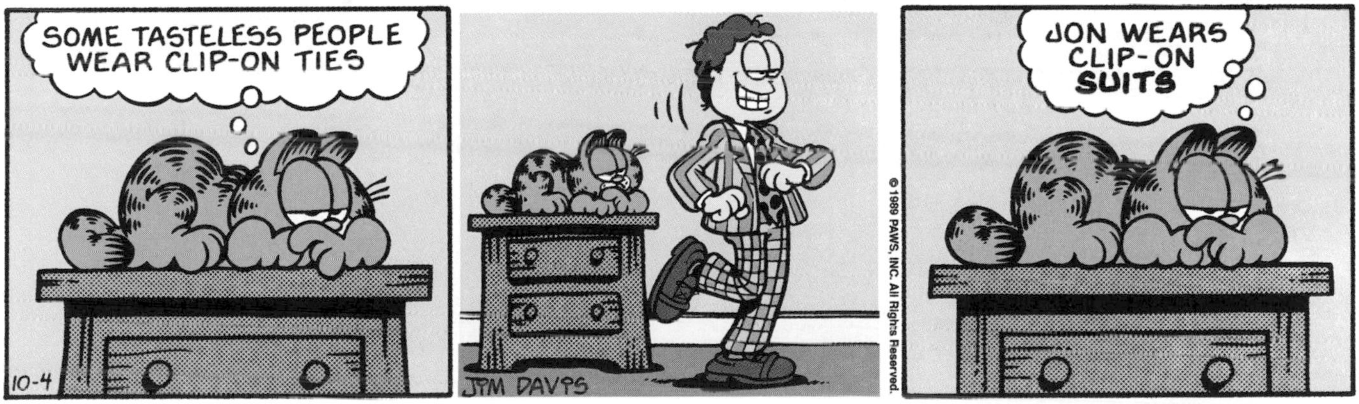
SOME TASTELESS PEOPLE WEAR CLIP-ON TIES
10-4
JIM DAVIS
© 1989 PAWS, INC. All Rights Reserved.
JON WEARS CLIP-ON SUITS

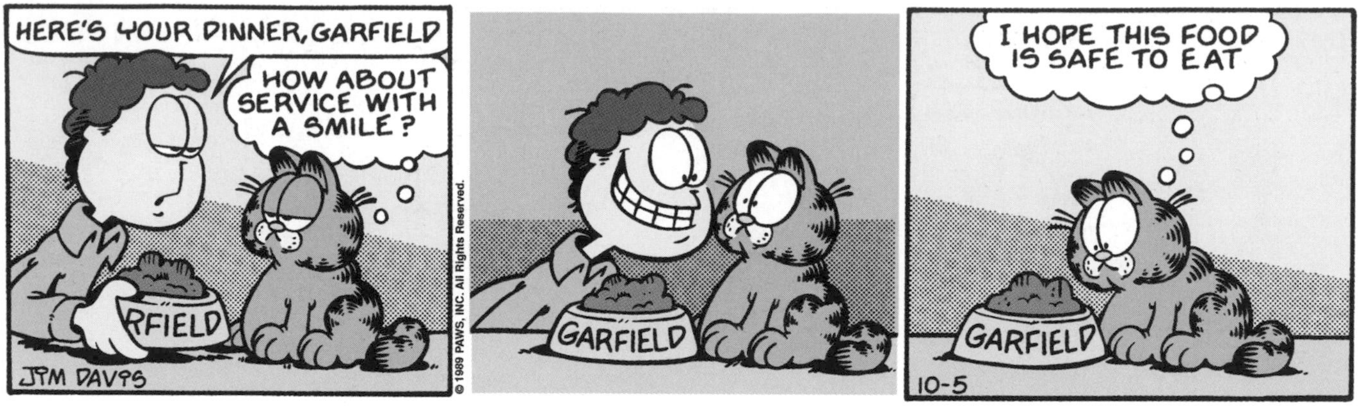
HERE'S YOUR DINNER, GARFIELD
HOW ABOUT SERVICE WITH A SMILE?
RFIELD
JIM DAVIS
© 1989 PAWS, INC. All Rights Reserved.
GARFIELD
I HOPE THIS FOOD IS SAFE TO EAT
GARFIELD
10-5

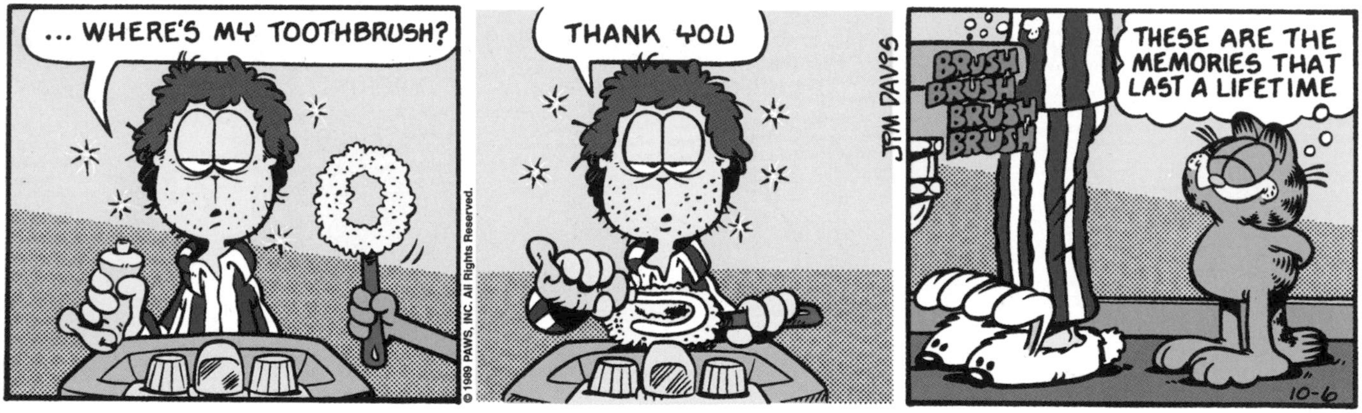
... WHERE'S MY TOOTHBRUSH?
© 1989 PAWS, INC. All Rights Reserved.
THANK YOU
JIM DAVIS
BRUSH BRUSH BRUSH BRUSH
THESE ARE THE MEMORIES THAT LAST A LIFETIME
10-6

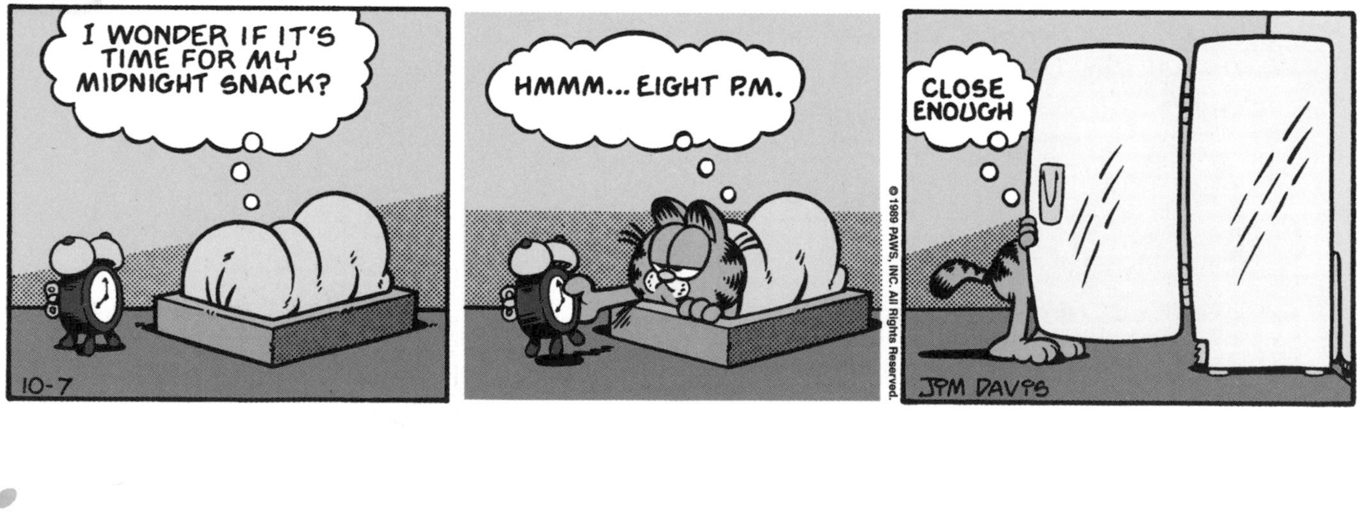
I WONDER IF IT'S TIME FOR MY MIDNIGHT SNACK?
10-7
HMMM... EIGHT P.M.
© 1989 PAWS, INC. All Rights Reserved.
CLOSE ENOUGH
JIM DAVIS

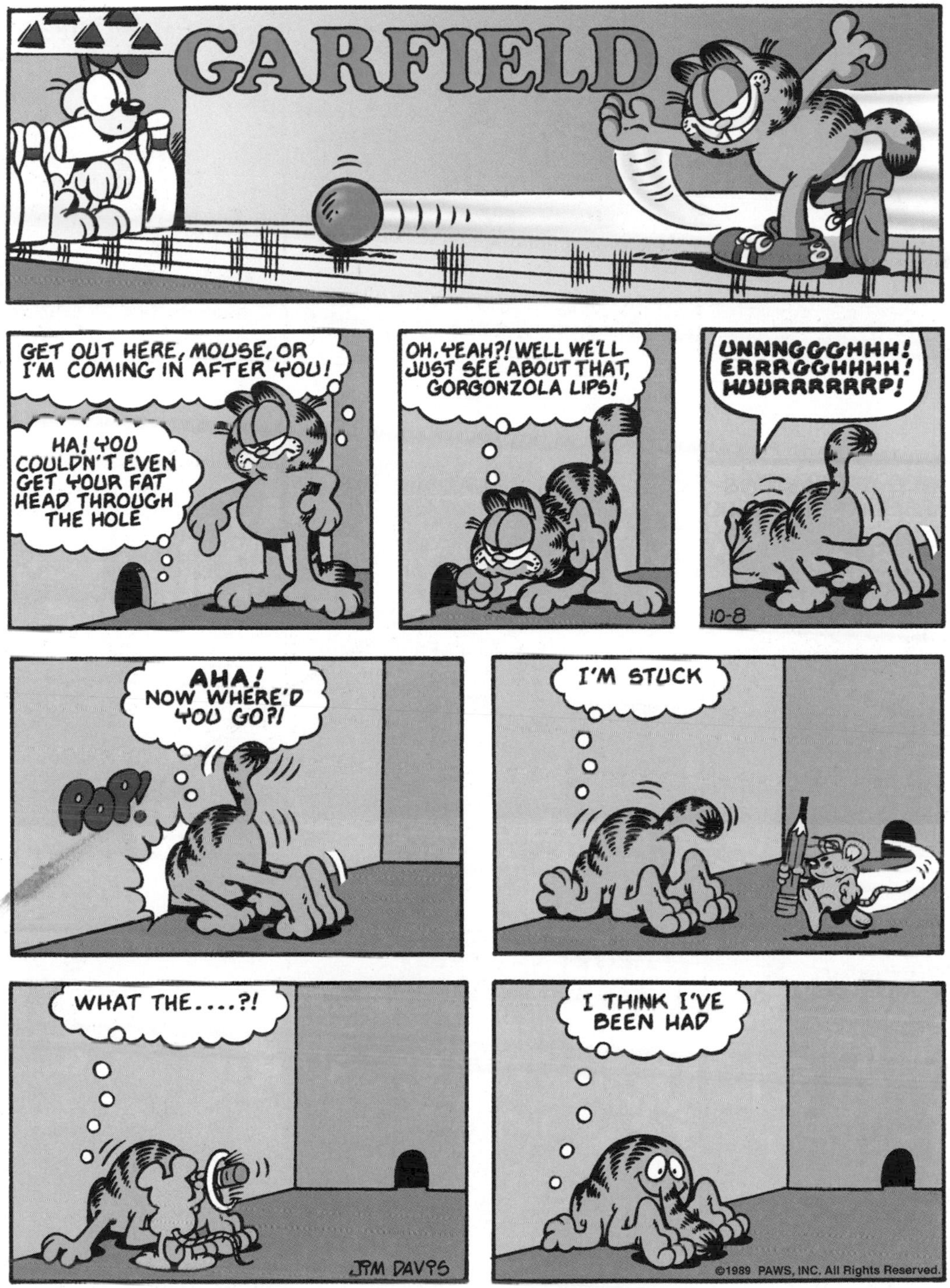
GARFIELD
GET OUT HERE, MOUSE, OR I'M COMING IN AFTER YOU!
HA! YOU COULDN'T EVEN GET YOUR FAT HEAD THROUGH THE HOLE
OH, YEAH?! WELL WE'LL JUST SEE ABOUT THAT, GORGONZOLA LIPS!
UNNNGGGHHH! ERRRGGHHHH! HUURRRRRRP!
10-8
POP!
AHA! NOW WHERE'D YOU GO?!
I'M STUCK
WHAT THE....?!
JIM DAVIS
I THINK I'VE BEEN HAD
©1989 PAWS, INC. All Rights Reserved.

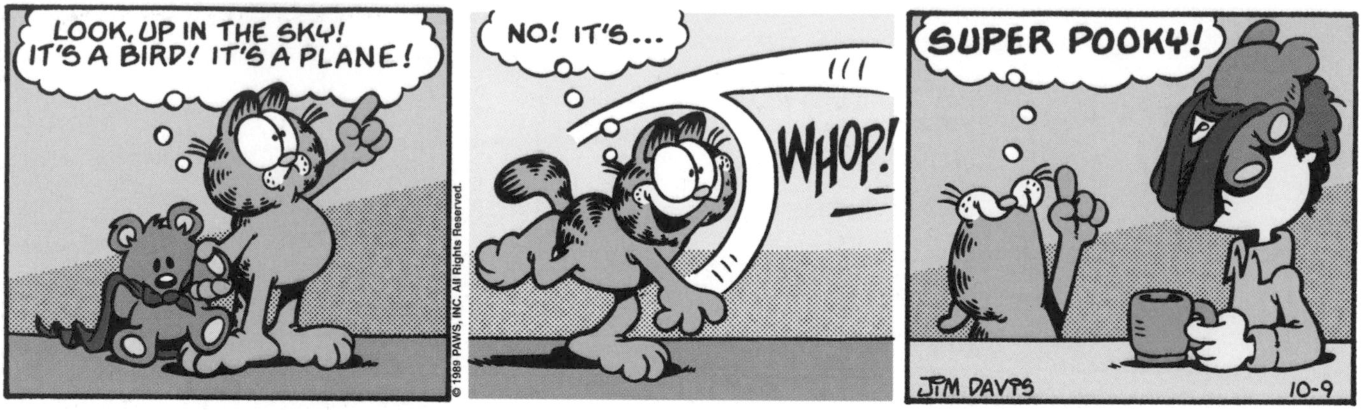
LOOK, UP IN THE SKY! IT'S A BIRD! IT'S A PLANE!
© 1989 PAWS, INC. All Rights Reserved.
NO! IT'S...
WHOP!
SUPER POOKY!
JIM DAVIS
10-9

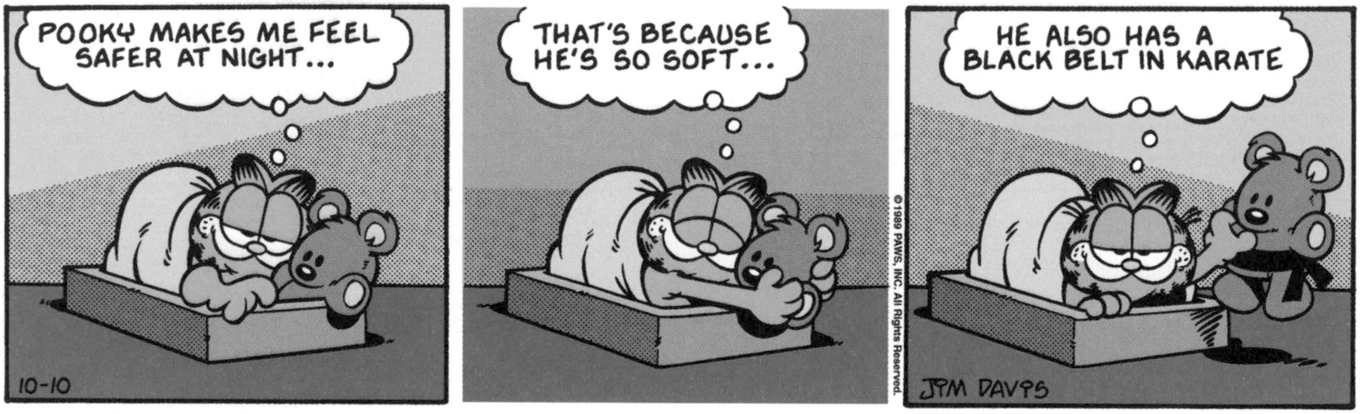
POOKY MAKES ME FEEL SAFER AT NIGHT...
10-10
THAT'S BECAUSE HE'S SO SOFT...
© 1989 PAWS, INC. All Rights Reserved.
HE ALSO HAS A BLACK BELT IN KARATE
JIM DAVIS

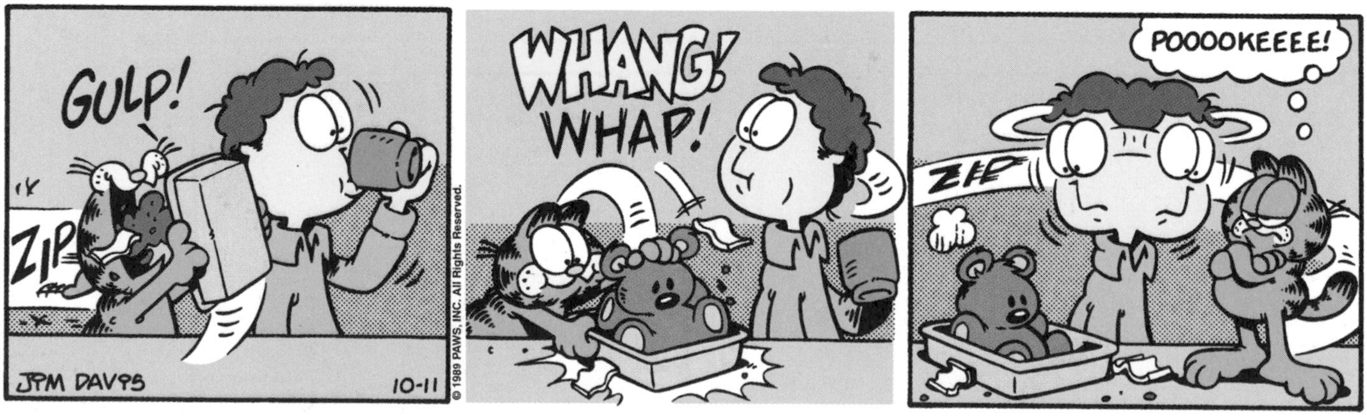
GULP!
ZIP
JIM DAVIS
10-11
© 1989 PAWS, INC. All Rights Reserved.
WHANG!
WHAP!
POOOOKEEEE!
ZIP

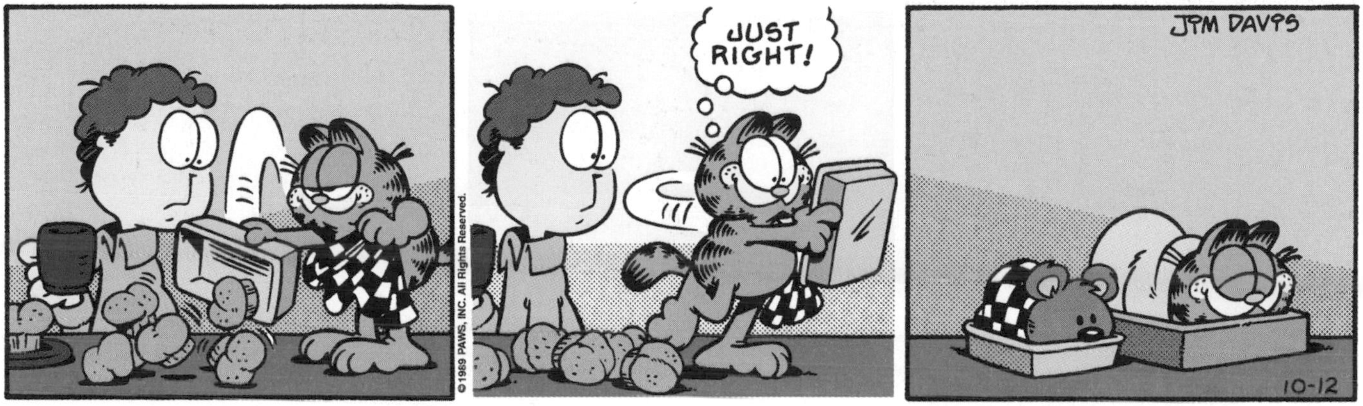
© 1989 PAWS, INC. All Rights Reserved.
JUST RIGHT!
JIM DAVIS
10-12

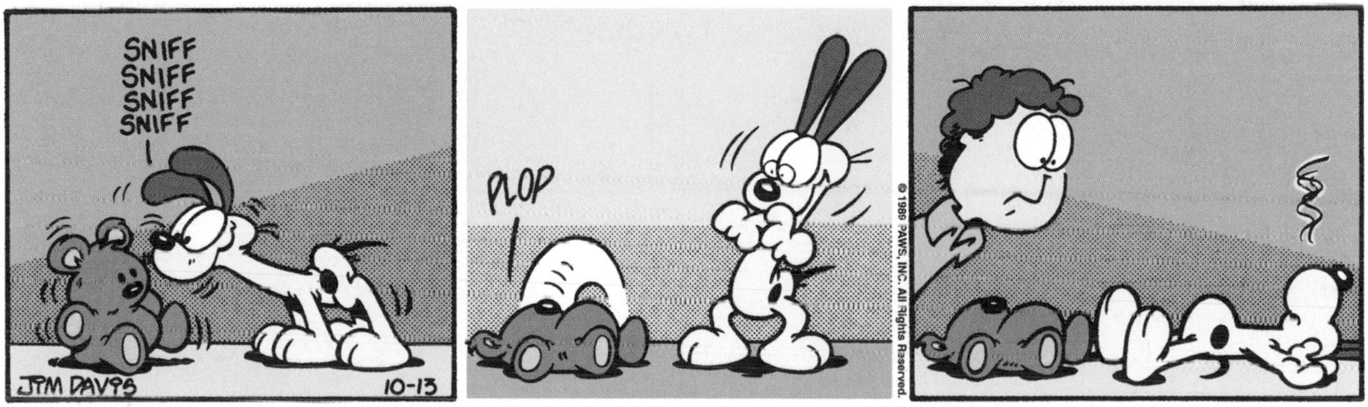
SNIFF SNIFF SNIFF SNIFF
JIM DAVIS
10-13
PLOP
© 1989 PAWS, INC. All Rights Reserved.

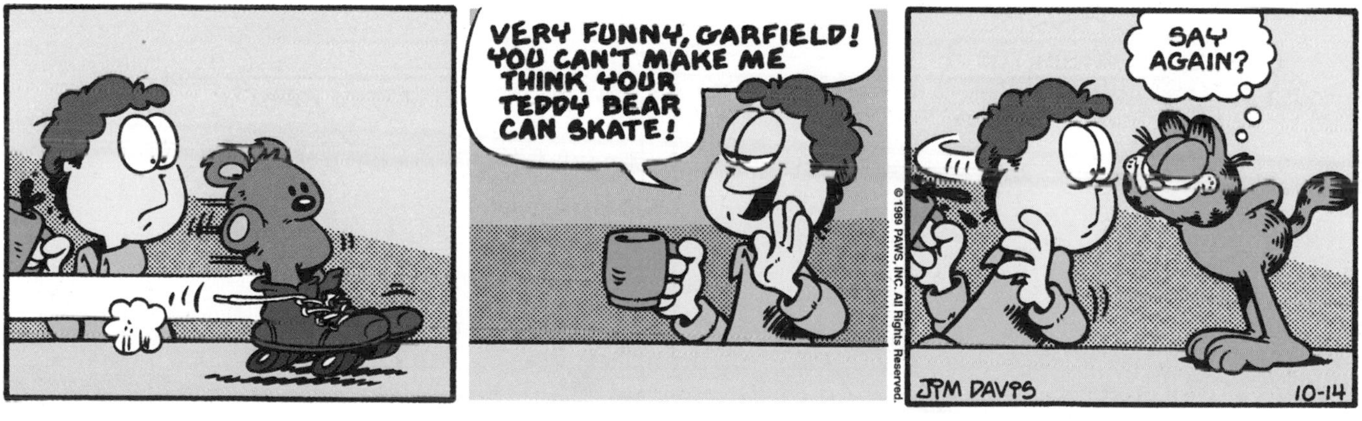
VERY FUNNY, GARFIELD! YOU CAN'T MAKE ME THINK YOUR TEDDY BEAR CAN SKATE!
© 1989 PAWS, INC. All Rights Reserved.
SAY AGAIN?
JIM DAVIS
10-14

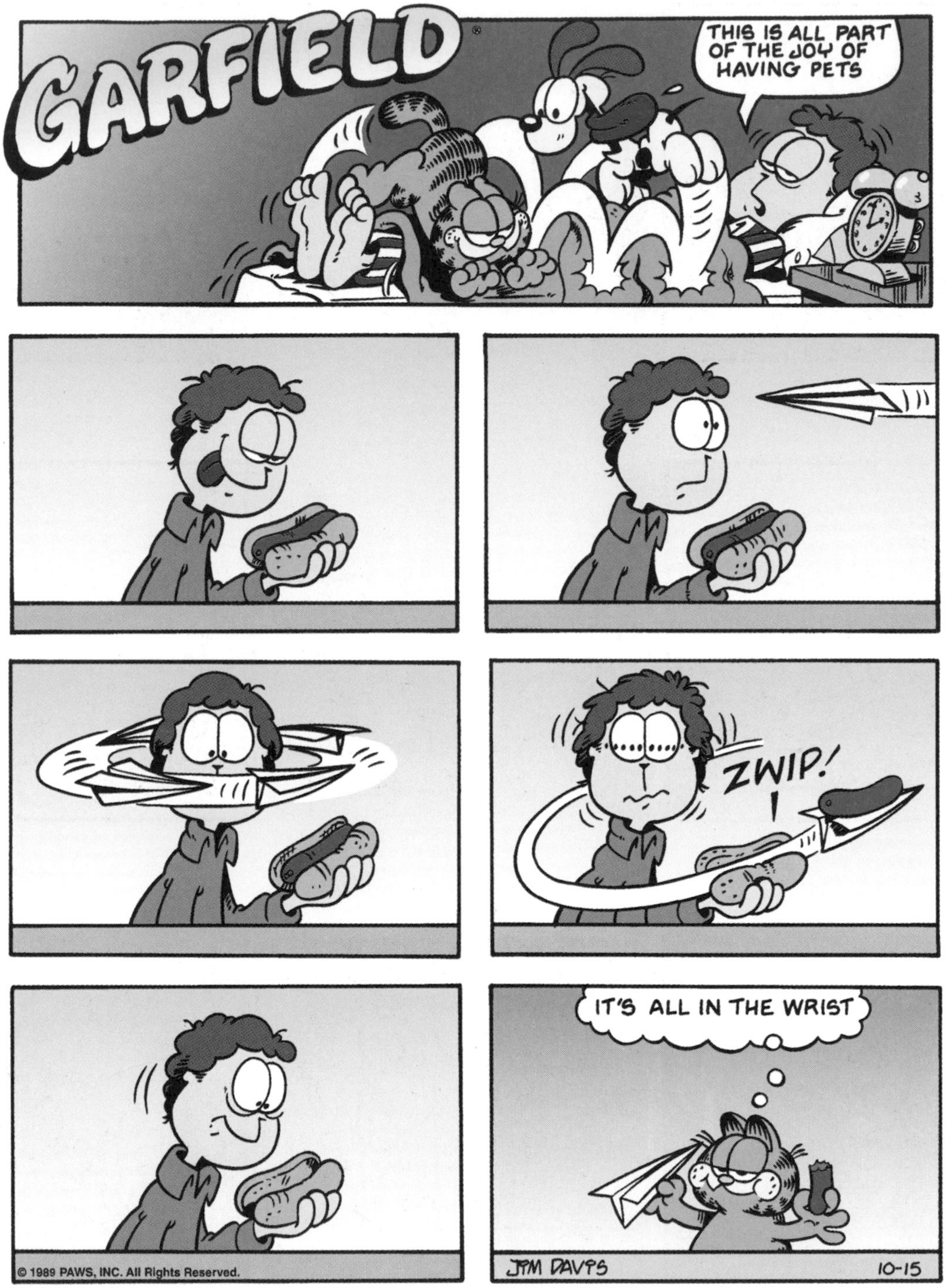
GARFIELD
THIS IS ALL PART OF THE JOY OF HAVING PETS
ZWIP!
IT'S ALL IN THE WRIST
JIM DAVIS
10-15

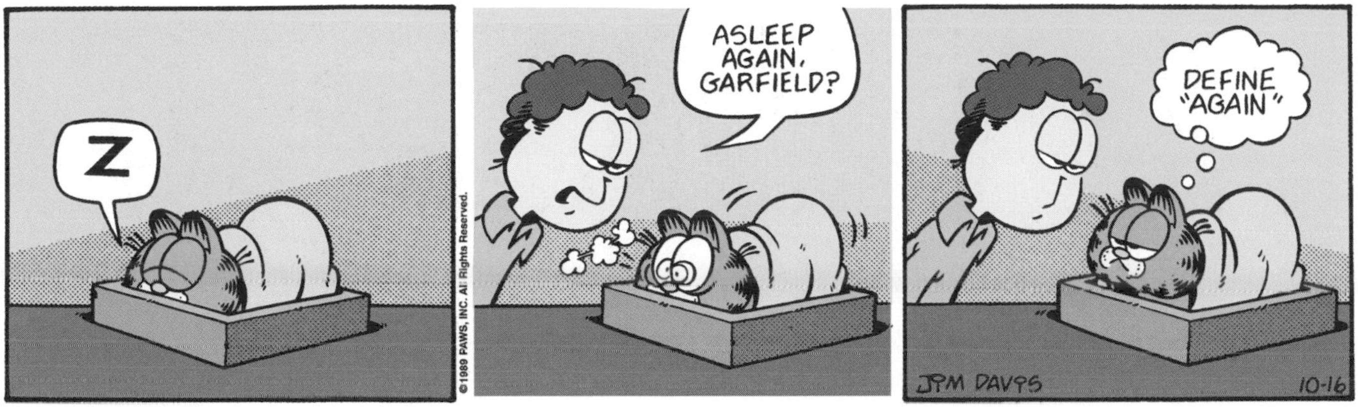
Z
ASLEEP AGAIN, GARFIELD?
DEFINE "AGAIN"
©1989 PAWS, INC. All Rights Reserved.
JIM DAVIS
10-16

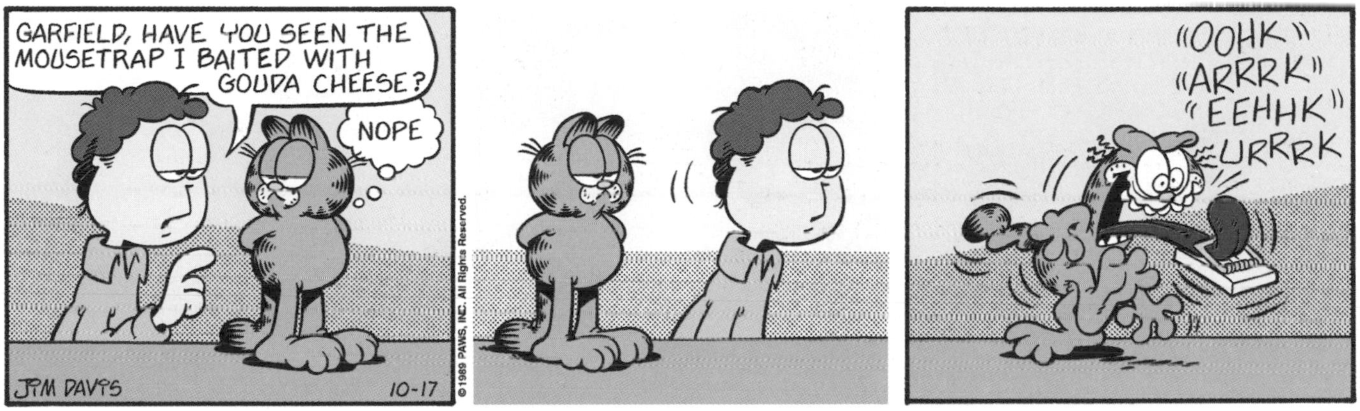
GARFIELD, HAVE YOU SEEN THE MOUSETRAP I BAITED WITH GOUDA CHEESE?
NOPE
«OOHK»
«ARRRK»
«EEHHK»
URRRK
©1989 PAWS, INC. All Rights Reserved.
JIM DAVIS
10-17

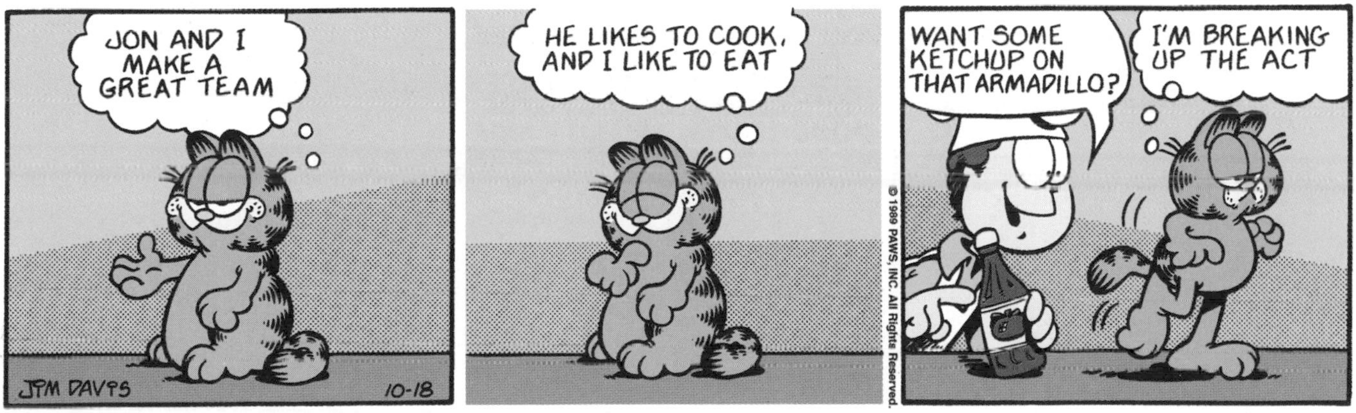
JON AND I MAKE A GREAT TEAM
HE LIKES TO COOK, AND I LIKE TO EAT
WANT SOME KETCHUP ON THAT ARMADILLO?
I'M BREAKING UP THE ACT
©1989 PAWS, INC. All Rights Reserved.
JIM DAVIS
10-18

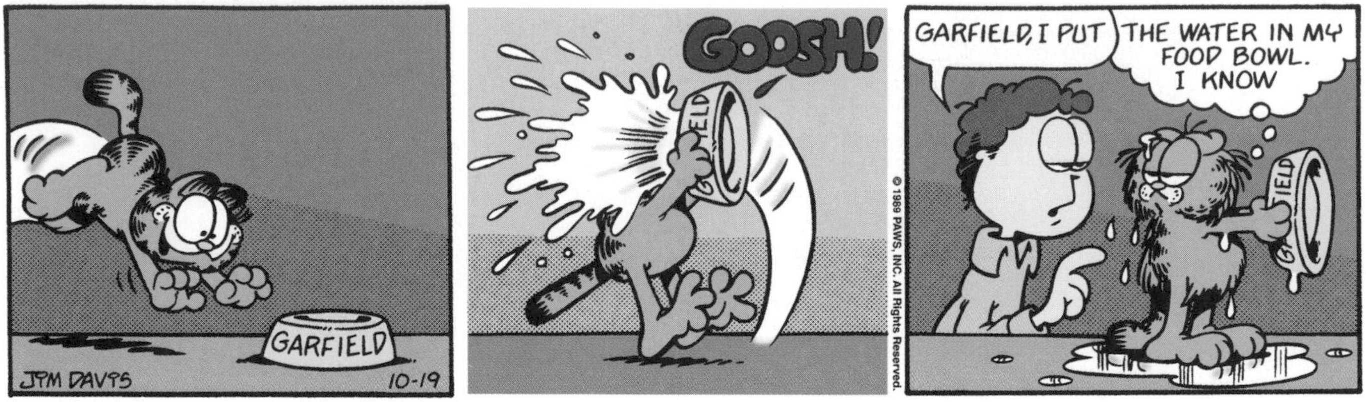
GARFIELD
JIM DAVIS
10-19
GOOSH!
GARFIELD, I PUT
THE WATER IN MY FOOD BOWL. I KNOW
© 1989 PAWS, INC. All Rights Reserved.

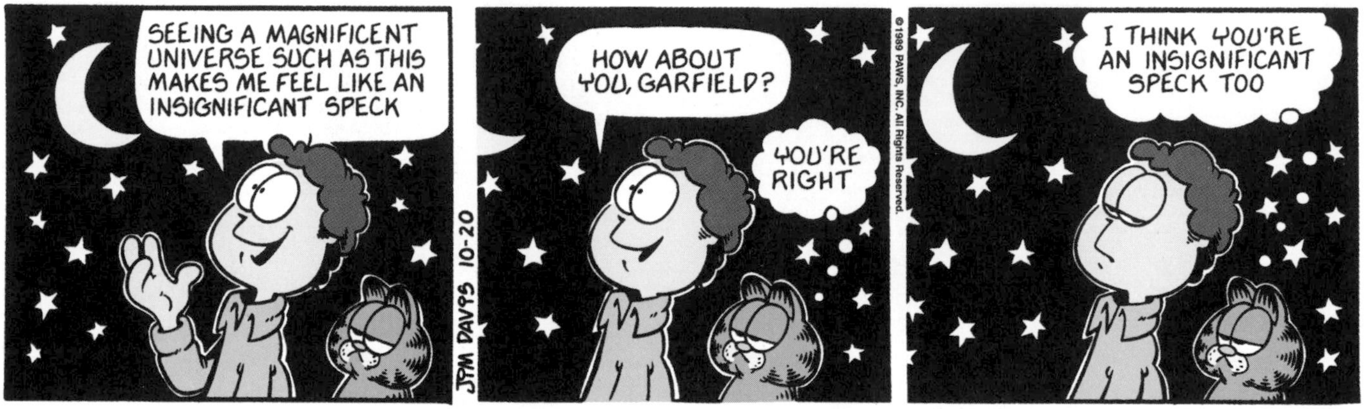
SEEING A MAGNIFICENT UNIVERSE SUCH AS THIS MAKES ME FEEL LIKE AN INSIGNIFICANT SPECK
JIM DAVIS 10-20
HOW ABOUT YOU, GARFIELD?
YOU'RE RIGHT
© 1989 PAWS, INC. All Rights Reserved.
I THINK YOU'RE AN INSIGNIFICANT SPECK TOO

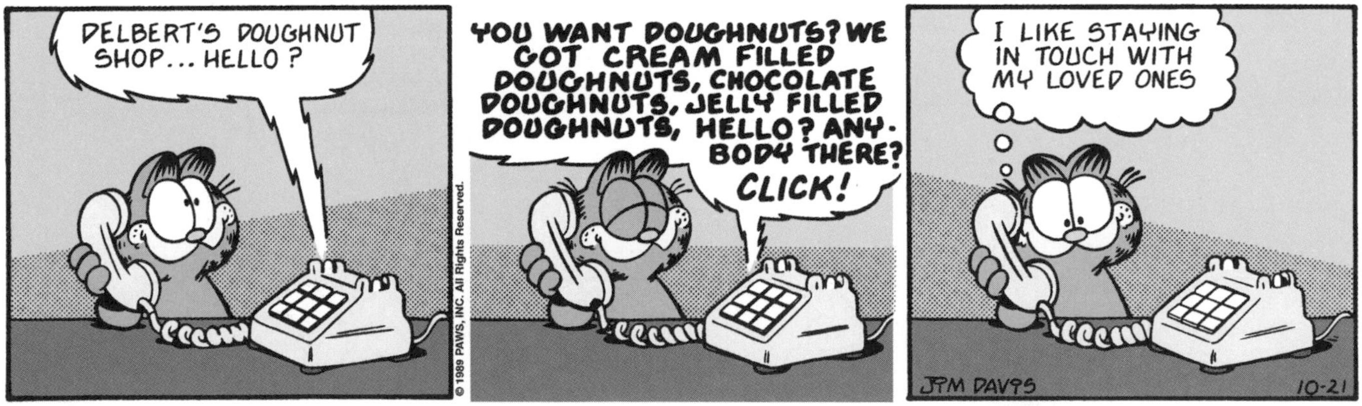
DELBERT'S DOUGHNUT SHOP... HELLO?
© 1989 PAWS, INC. All Rights Reserved.
YOU WANT DOUGHNUTS? WE GOT CREAM FILLED DOUGHNUTS, CHOCOLATE DOUGHNUTS, JELLY FILLED DOUGHNUTS, HELLO? ANY-BODY THERE?
CLICK!
I LIKE STAYING IN TOUCH WITH MY LOVED ONES
JIM DAVIS
10-21

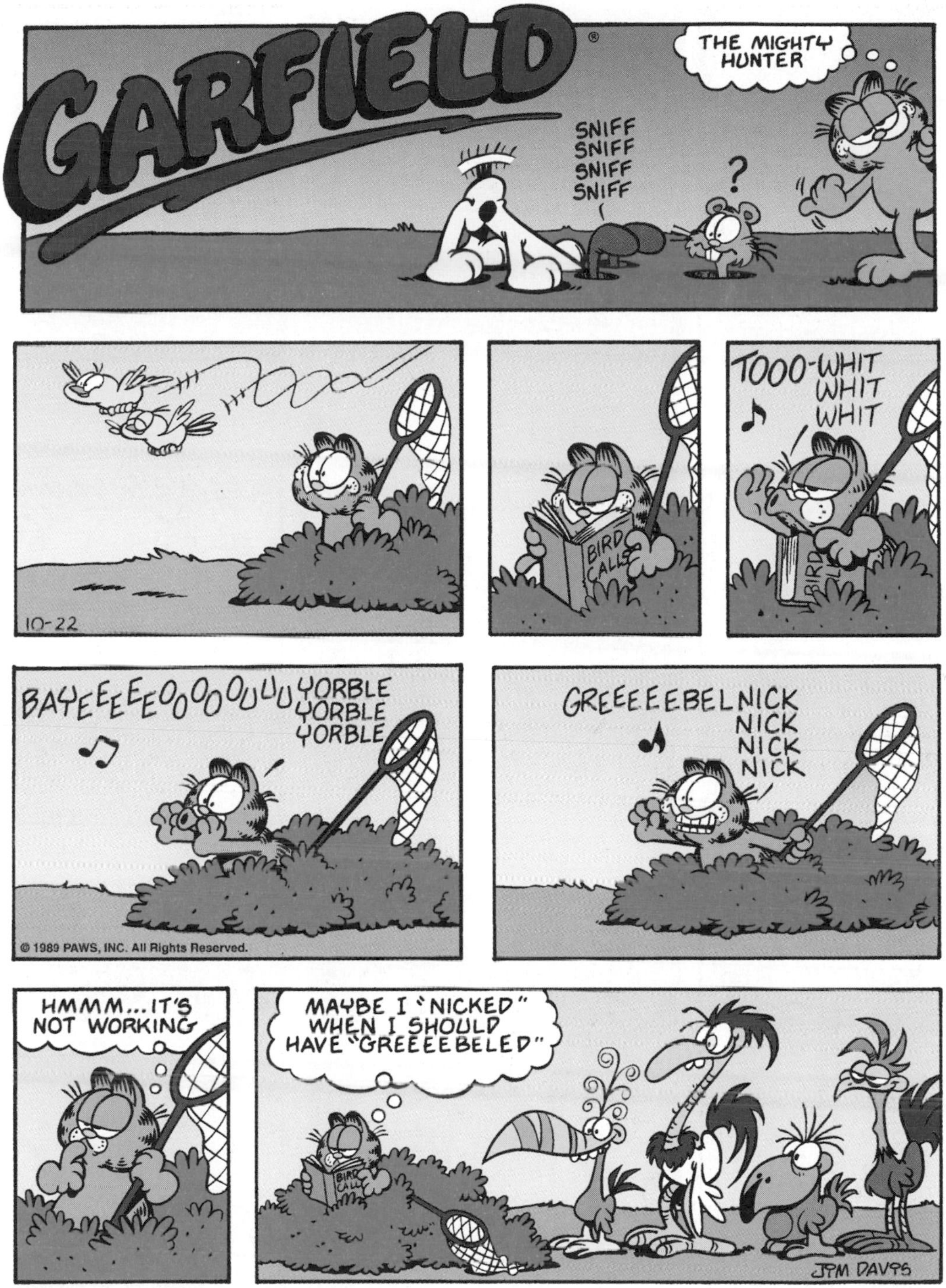
GARFIELD
THE MIGHTY HUNTER
SNIFF SNIFF SNIFF SNIFF
?
10-22
BIRD CALLS
TOOO-WHIT WHIT WHIT
BAYEEEEEOOOOOUUUYORBLE YORBLE YORBLE
© 1989 PAWS, INC. All Rights Reserved.
GREEEEEBELNICK NICK NICK NICK
HMMM... IT'S NOT WORKING
MAYBE I "NICKED" WHEN I SHOULD HAVE "GREEEEBELED"
BIRD CALLS
JIM DAVIS

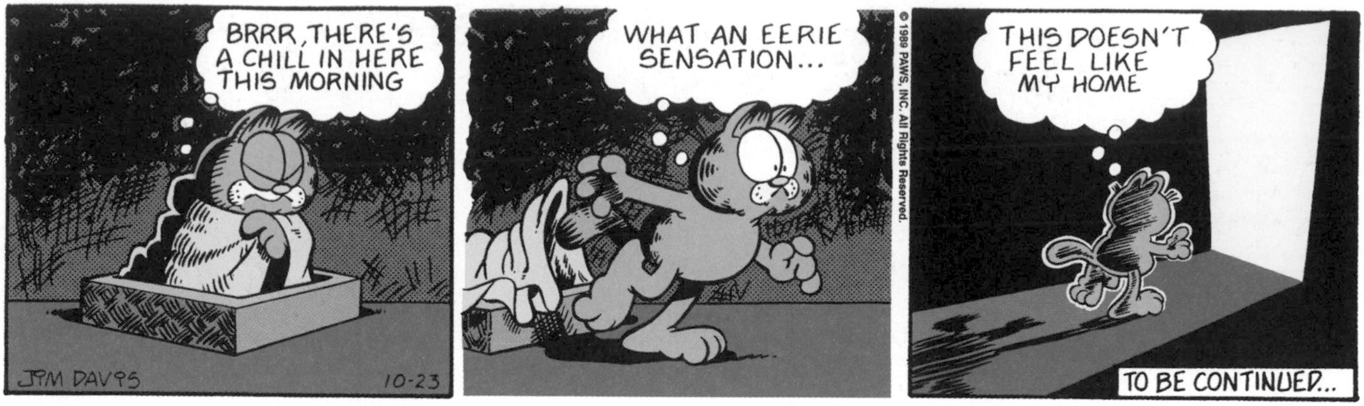
BRRR, THERE'S A CHILL IN HERE THIS MORNING
JIM DAVIS
10-23
WHAT AN EERIE SENSATION...
© 1989 PAWS, INC. All Rights Reserved.
THIS DOESN'T FEEL LIKE MY HOME
TO BE CONTINUED...

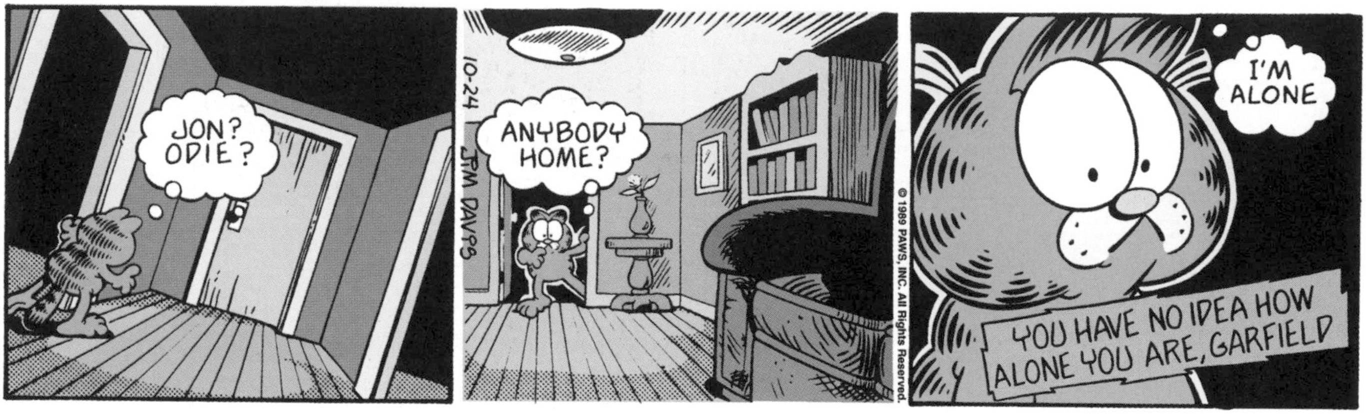
JON? ODIE?
10-24
JIM DAVIS
ANYBODY HOME?
© 1989 PAWS, INC. All Rights Reserved.
I'M ALONE
YOU HAVE NO IDEA HOW ALONE YOU ARE, GARFIELD

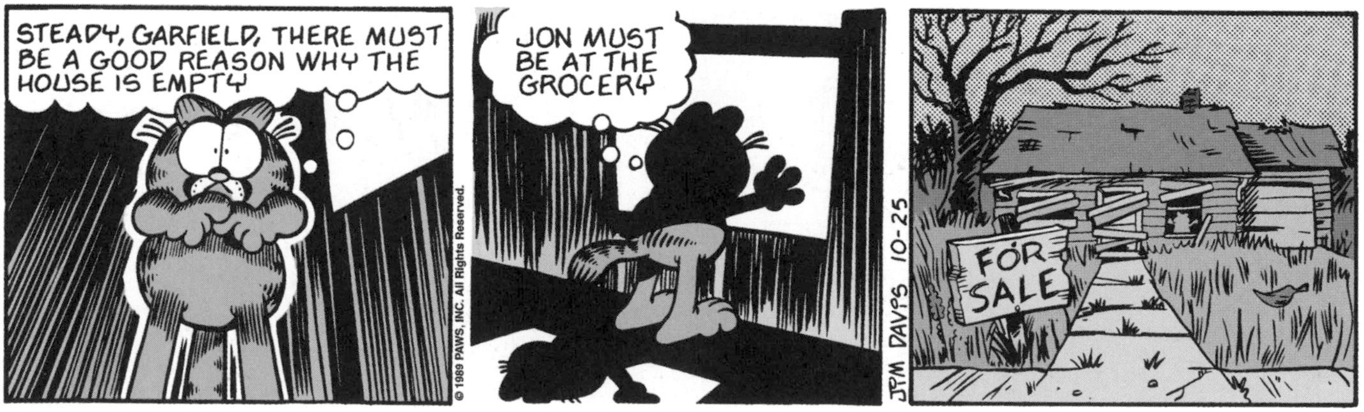
STEADY, GARFIELD, THERE MUST BE A GOOD REASON WHY THE HOUSE IS EMPTY
© 1989 PAWS, INC. All Rights Reserved.
JON MUST BE AT THE GROCERY
JIM DAVIS 10-25
FOR SALE

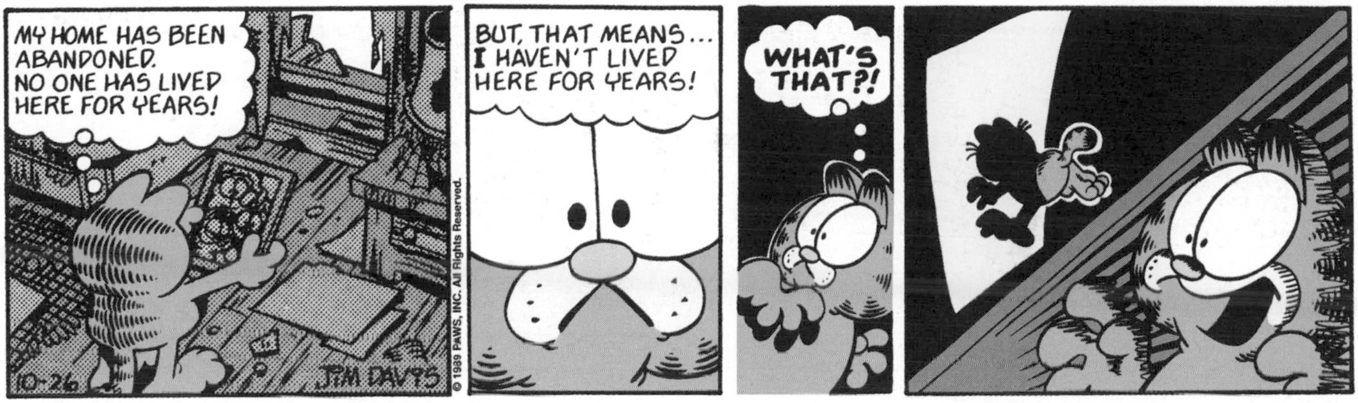
MY HOME HAS BEEN ABANDONED. NO ONE HAS LIVED HERE FOR YEARS!
10-26
JIM DAVIS
© 1989 PAWS, INC. All Rights Reserved.
BUT, THAT MEANS... I HAVEN'T LIVED HERE FOR YEARS!
WHAT'S THAT?!

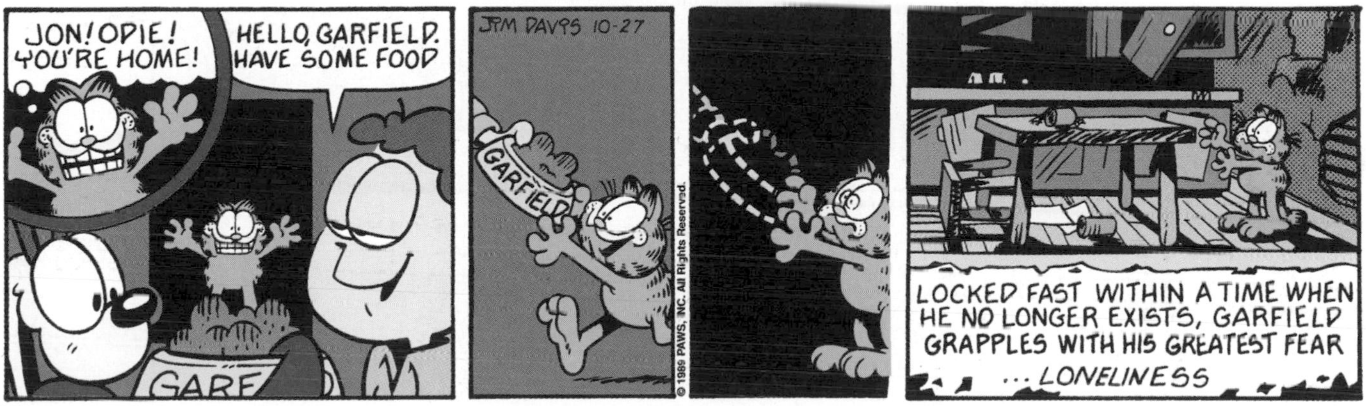
JON! ODIE! YOU'RE HOME!
HELLO, GARFIELD. HAVE SOME FOOD
GARF
JIM DAVIS 10-27
GARFIELD
© 1989 PAWS, INC. All Rights Reserved.
LOCKED FAST WITHIN A TIME WHEN HE NO LONGER EXISTS, GARFIELD GRAPPLES WITH HIS GREATEST FEAR
...LONELINESS

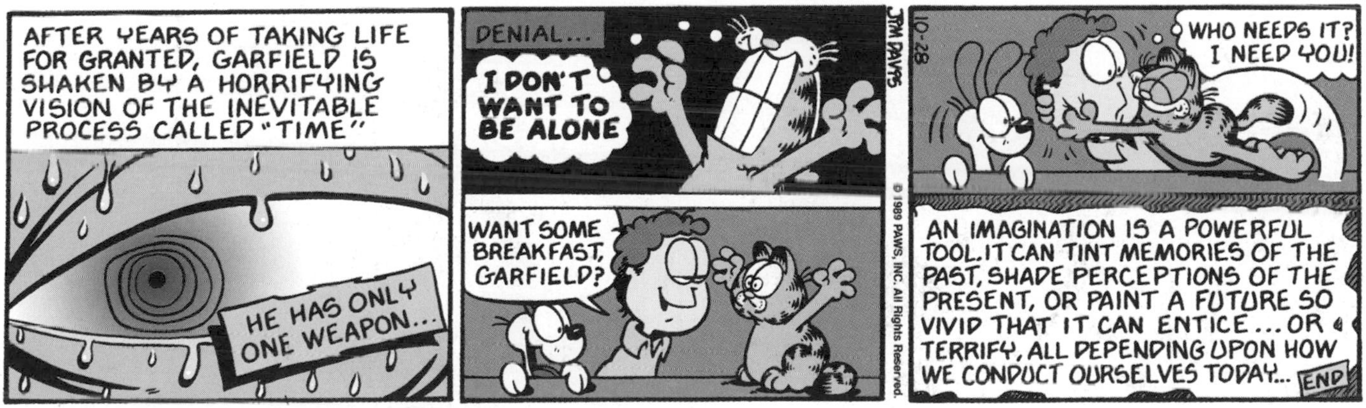
AFTER YEARS OF TAKING LIFE FOR GRANTED, GARFIELD IS SHAKEN BY A HORRIFYING VISION OF THE INEVITABLE PROCESS CALLED "TIME"
HE HAS ONLY ONE WEAPON...
DENIAL...
I DON'T WANT TO BE ALONE
WANT SOME BREAKFAST, GARFIELD?
JIM DAVIS 10-28
© 1989 PAWS, INC. All Rights Reserved.
WHO NEEDS IT? I NEED YOU!
AN IMAGINATION IS A POWERFUL TOOL. IT CAN TINT MEMORIES OF THE PAST, SHADE PERCEPTIONS OF THE PRESENT, OR PAINT A FUTURE SO VIVID THAT IT CAN ENTICE... OR TERRIFY, ALL DEPENDING UPON HOW WE CONDUCT OURSELVES TODAY...
END

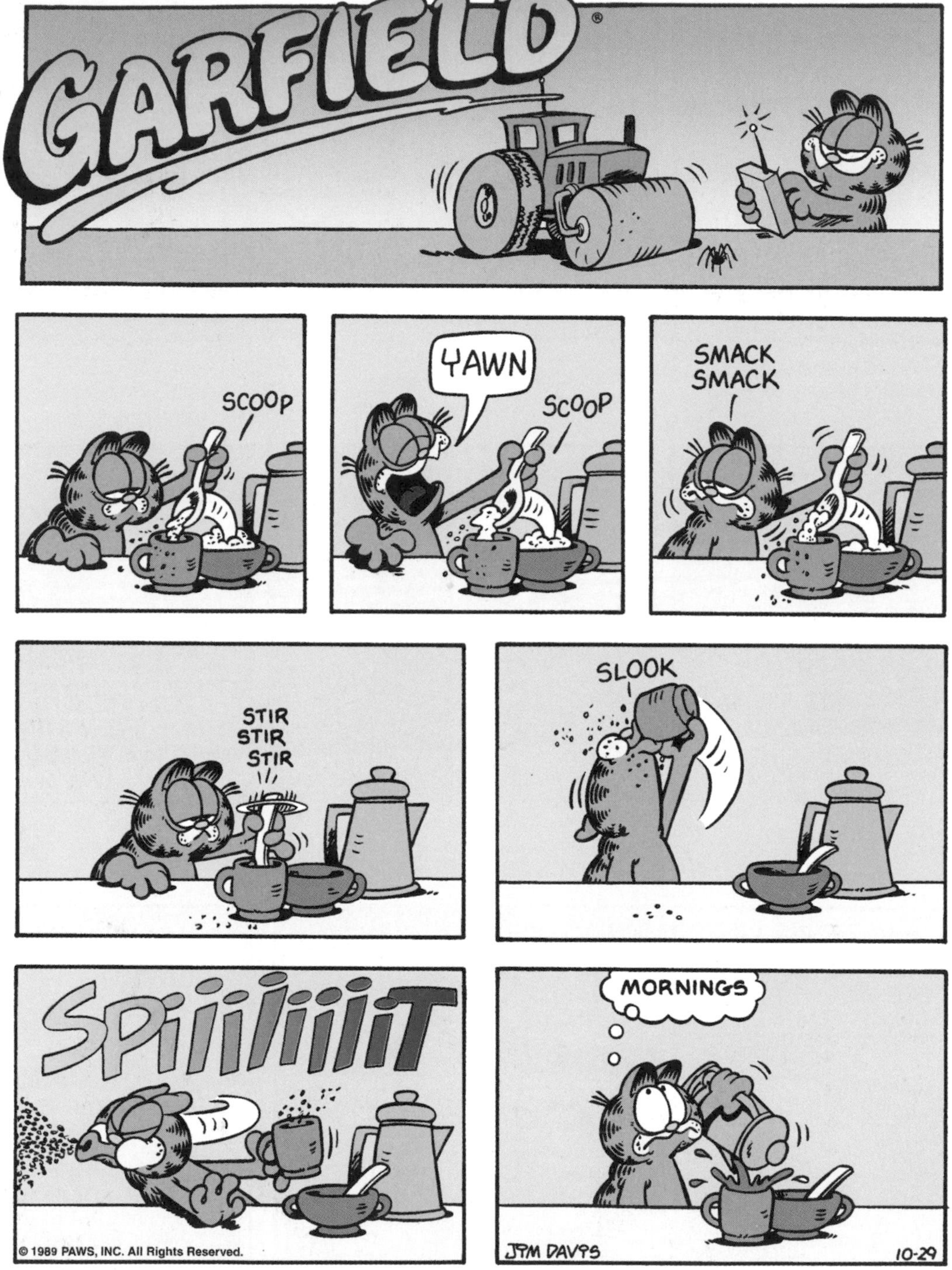
GARFIELD®
SCOOP
YAWN
SCOOP
SMACK SMACK
STIR STIR STIR
SLOOK
SPIIIIIIIIT
MORNINGS
JPM DAVPS
10-29

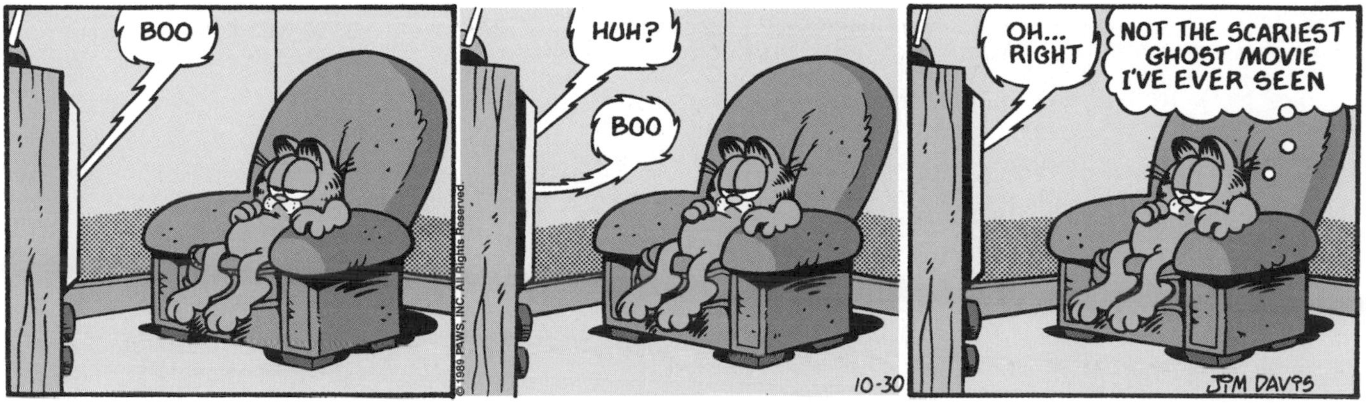
BOO
© 1989 PAWS, INC. All Rights Reserved.
HUH?
BOO
10-30
OH... RIGHT
NOT THE SCARIEST GHOST MOVIE I'VE EVER SEEN
JIM DAVIS

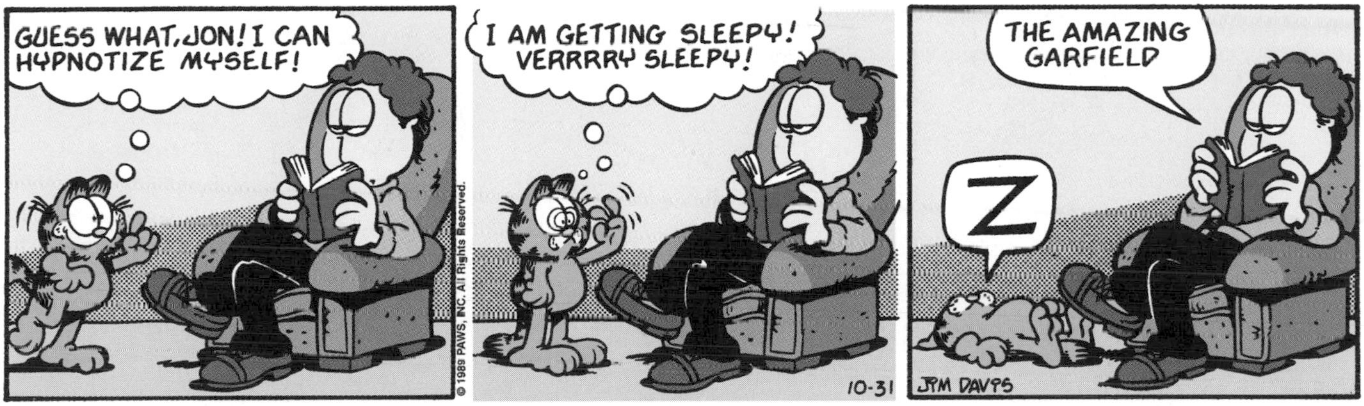
GUESS WHAT, JON! I CAN HYPNOTIZE MYSELF!
© 1989 PAWS, INC. All Rights Reserved.
I AM GETTING SLEEPY! VERRRRY SLEEPY!
10-31
THE AMAZING GARFIELD
Z
JIM DAVIS

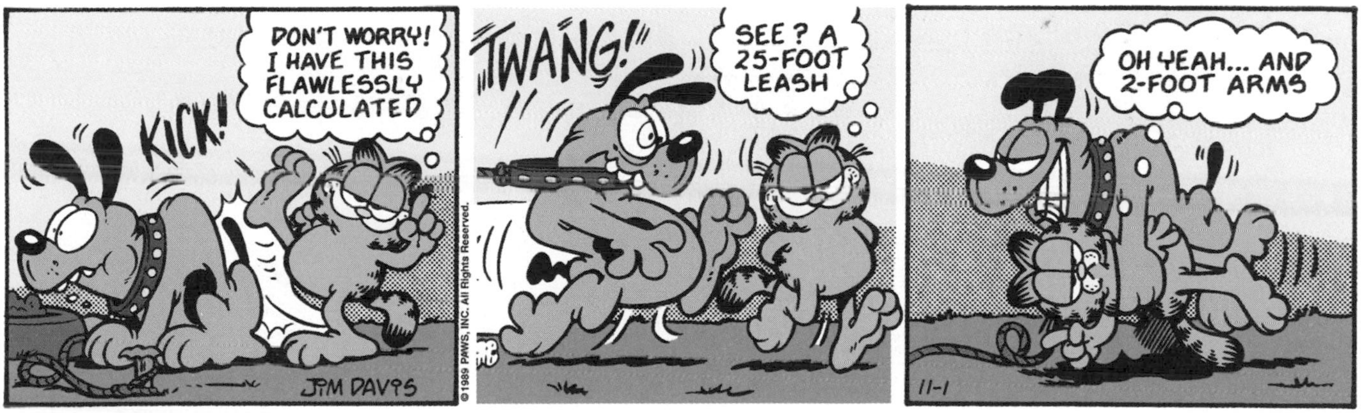
KICK!
DON'T WORRY! I HAVE THIS FLAWLESSLY CALCULATED
JIM DAVIS
© 1989 PAWS, INC. All Rights Reserved.
TWANG!
SEE? A 25-FOOT LEASH
OH YEAH... AND 2-FOOT ARMS
11-1

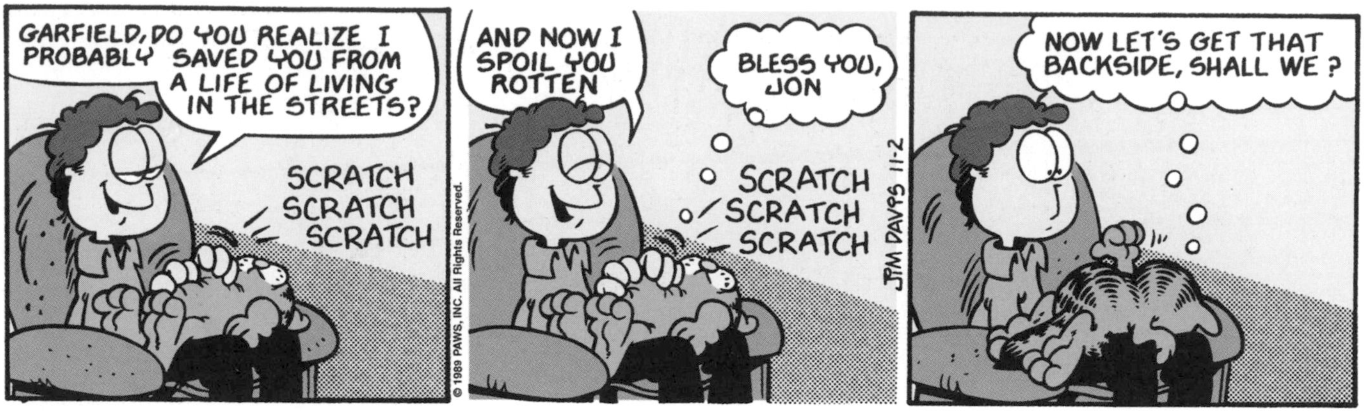
GARFIELD, DO YOU REALIZE I PROBABLY SAVED YOU FROM A LIFE OF LIVING IN THE STREETS?
SCRATCH SCRATCH SCRATCH
© 1989 PAWS, INC. All Rights Reserved.
AND NOW I SPOIL YOU ROTTEN
BLESS YOU, JON
SCRATCH SCRATCH SCRATCH
JIM DAVIS 11-2
NOW LET'S GET THAT BACKSIDE, SHALL WE ?

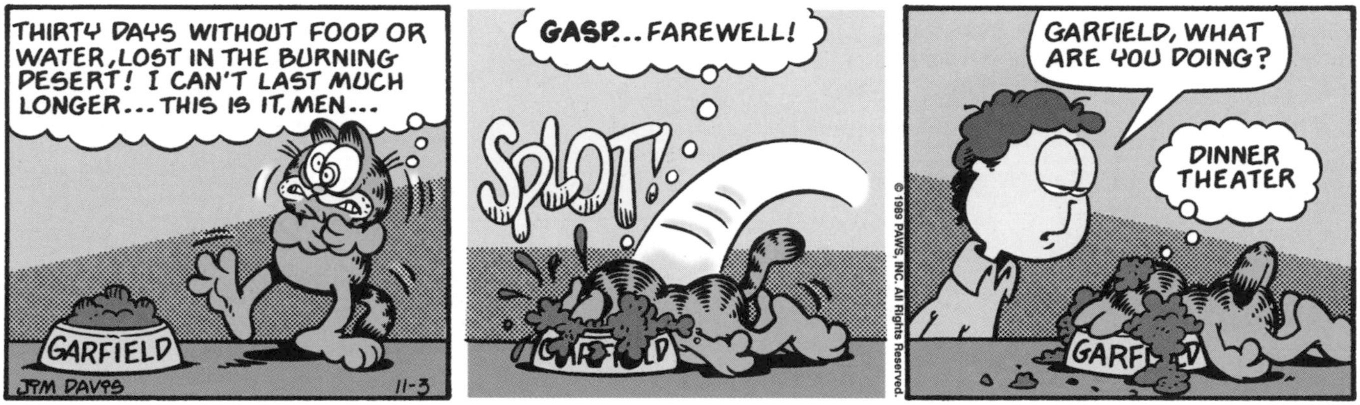
THIRTY DAYS WITHOUT FOOD OR WATER, LOST IN THE BURNING DESERT! I CAN'T LAST MUCH LONGER... THIS IS IT, MEN...
GARFIELD
JIM DAVIS 11-3
GASP... FAREWELL!
SPLOT!
© 1989 PAWS, INC. All Rights Reserved.
GARFIELD, WHAT ARE YOU DOING?
DINNER THEATER

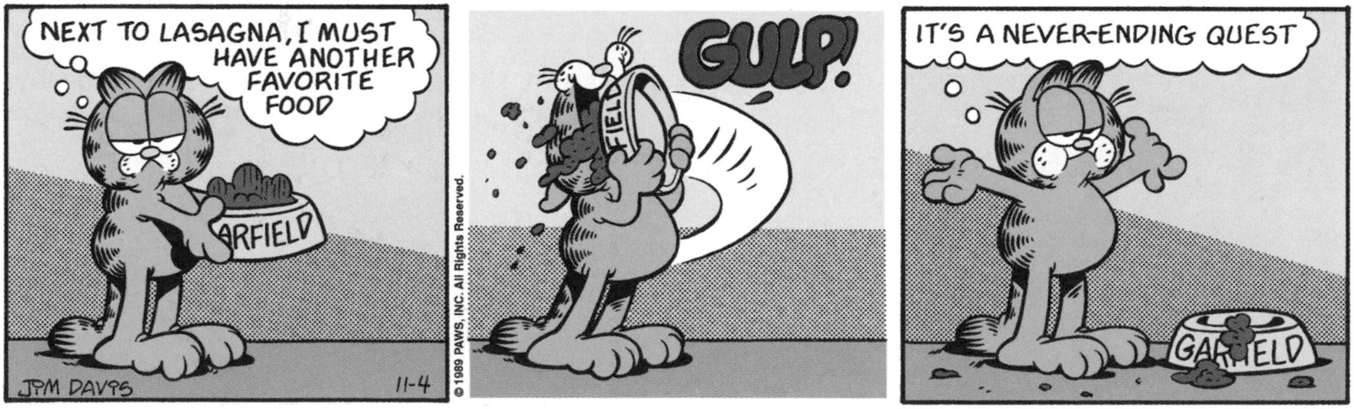
NEXT TO LASAGNA, I MUST HAVE ANOTHER FAVORITE FOOD
ARFIELD
JIM DAVIS 11-4
© 1989 PAWS, INC. All Rights Reserved.
GULP!
IT'S A NEVER-ENDING QUEST

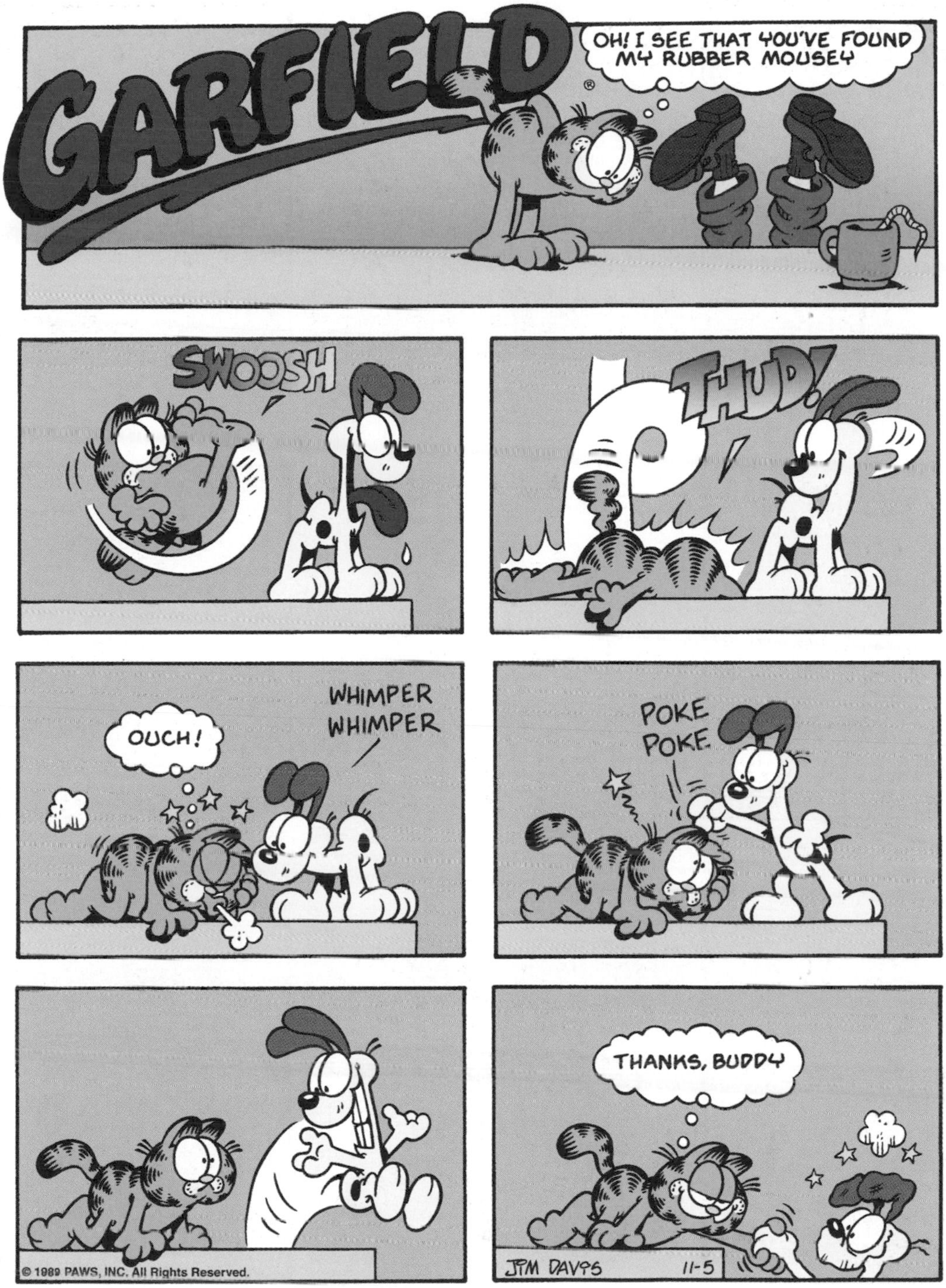
GARFIELD
OH! I SEE THAT YOU'VE FOUND MY RUBBER MOUSEY
SWOOSH
THUD!
OUCH!
WHIMPER WHIMPER
POKE POKE
THANKS, BUDDY
© 1989 PAWS, INC. All Rights Reserved.
JIM DAVIS 11-5

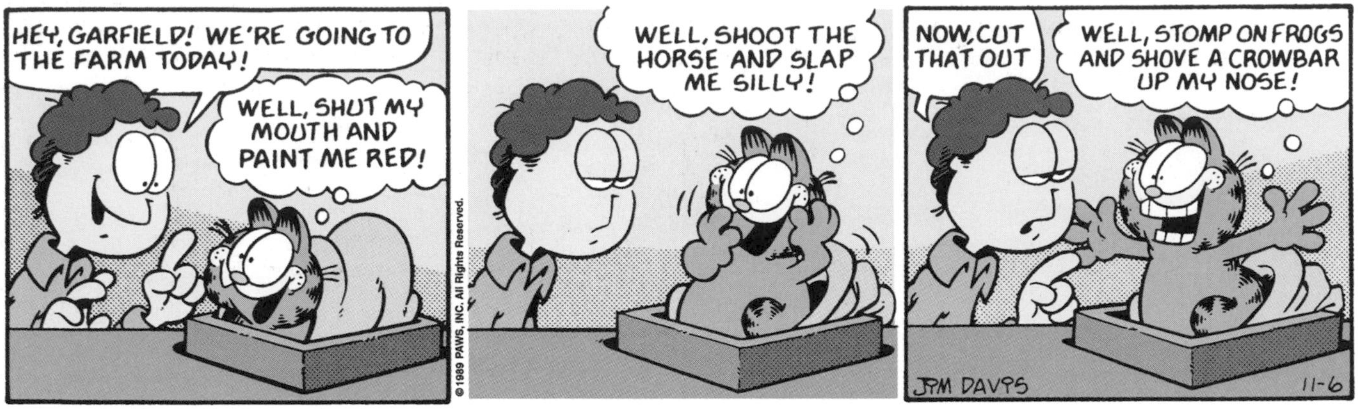
HEY, GARFIELD! WE'RE GOING TO THE FARM TODAY!
WELL, SHUT MY MOUTH AND PAINT ME RED!
© 1989 PAWS, INC. All Rights Reserved.
WELL, SHOOT THE HORSE AND SLAP ME SILLY!
NOW, CUT THAT OUT
WELL, STOMP ON FROGS AND SHOVE A CROWBAR UP MY NOSE!
JIM DAVIS
11-6

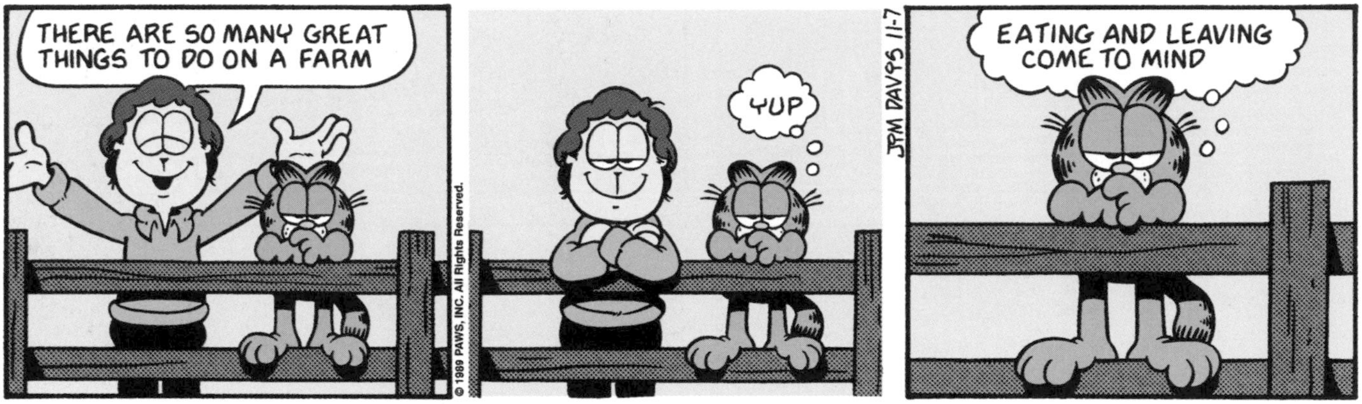
THERE ARE SO MANY GREAT THINGS TO DO ON A FARM
© 1989 PAWS, INC. All Rights Reserved.
YUP
JIM DAVIS 11-7
EATING AND LEAVING COME TO MIND

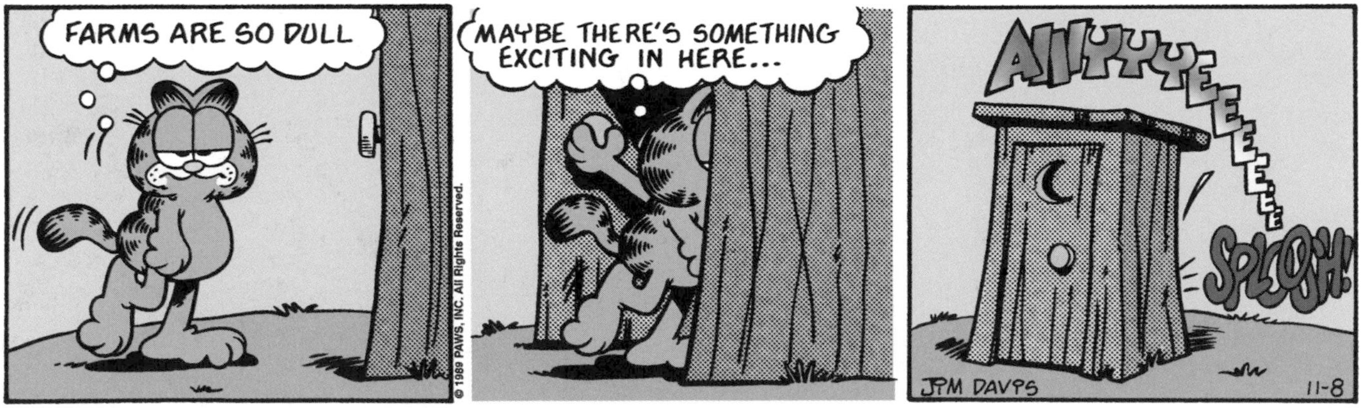
FARMS ARE SO DULL
© 1989 PAWS, INC. All Rights Reserved.
MAYBE THERE'S SOMETHING EXCITING IN HERE...
AIIYYYEEEEEEE
SPLOOSH!
JIM DAVIS
11-8

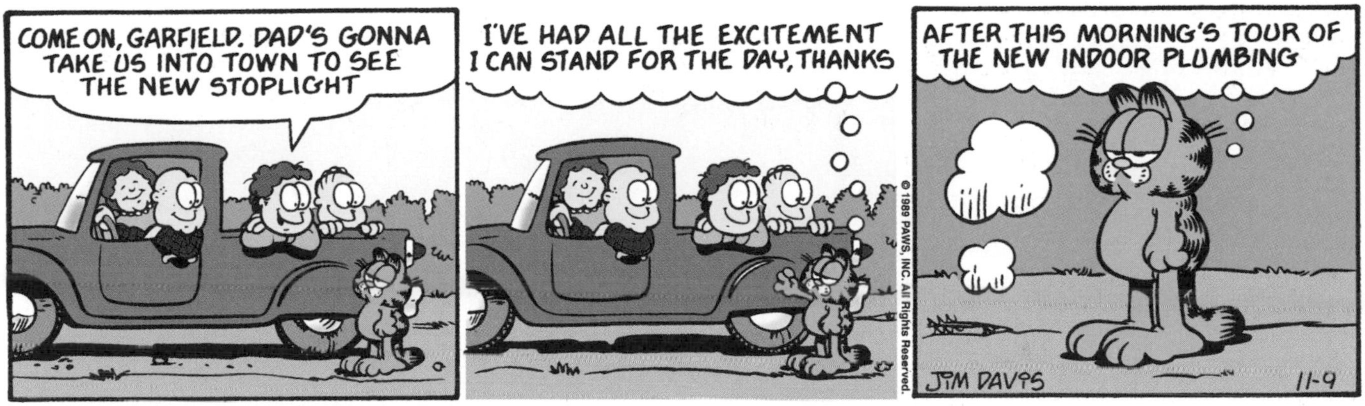
COME ON, GARFIELD. DAD'S GONNA TAKE US INTO TOWN TO SEE THE NEW STOPLIGHT
I'VE HAD ALL THE EXCITEMENT I CAN STAND FOR THE DAY, THANKS
AFTER THIS MORNING'S TOUR OF THE NEW INDOOR PLUMBING
© 1989 PAWS, INC. All Rights Reserved.
JIM DAVIS 11-9

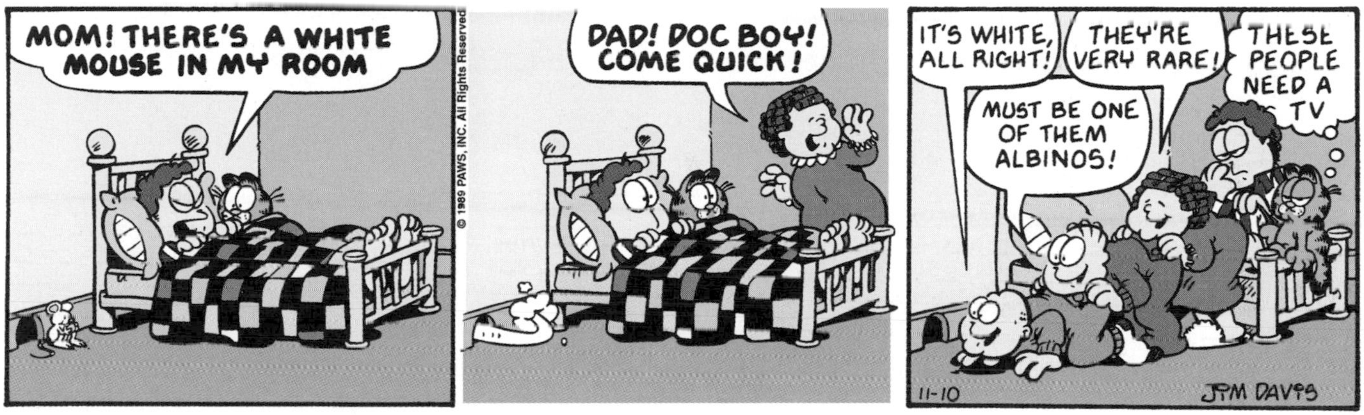
MOM! THERE'S A WHITE MOUSE IN MY ROOM
© 1989 PAWS, INC. All Rights Reserved
DAD! DOC BOY! COME QUICK!
IT'S WHITE, ALL RIGHT!
THEY'RE VERY RARE!
MUST BE ONE OF THEM ALBINOS!
THESE PEOPLE NEED A TV
11-10 JIM DAVIS

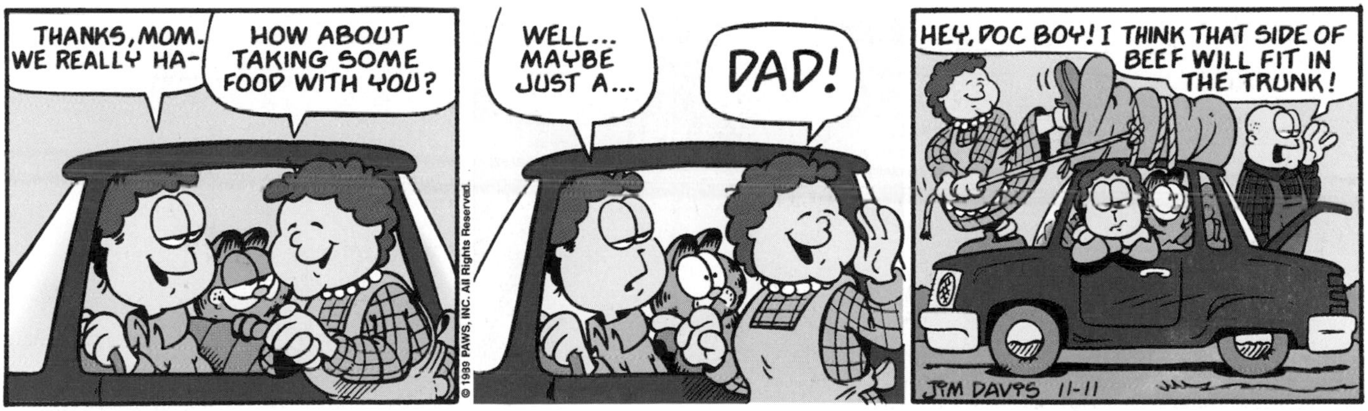
THANKS, MOM. WE REALLY HA-
HOW ABOUT TAKING SOME FOOD WITH YOU?
© 1989 PAWS, INC. All Rights Reserved.
WELL... MAYBE JUST A...
DAD!
HEY, DOC BOY! I THINK THAT SIDE OF BEEF WILL FIT IN THE TRUNK!
JIM DAVIS 11-11

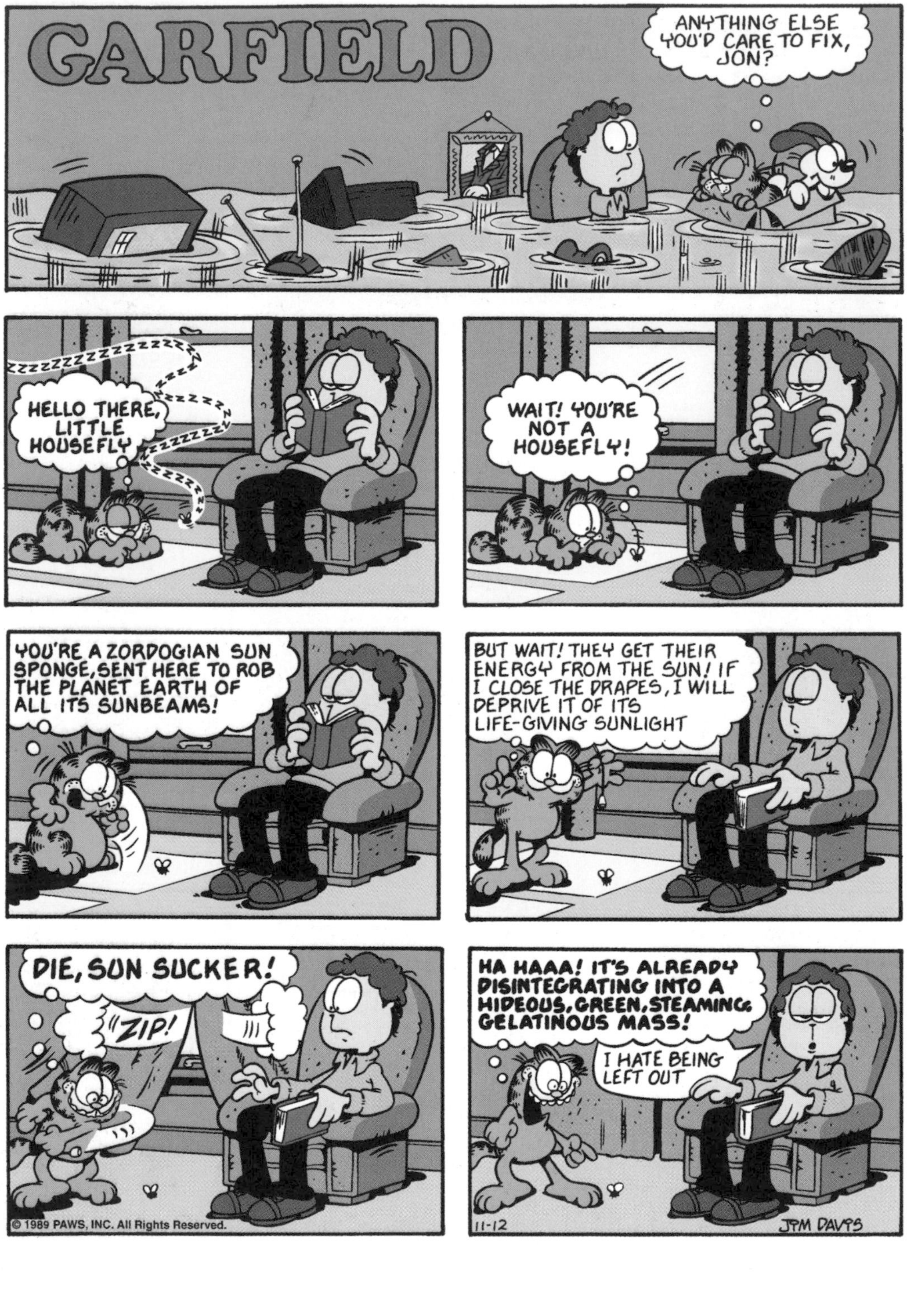
GARFIELD
ANYTHING ELSE YOU'D CARE TO FIX, JON?
HELLO THERE, LITTLE HOUSEFLY
WAIT! YOU'RE NOT A HOUSEFLY!
YOU'RE A ZORDOGIAN SUN SPONGE, SENT HERE TO ROB THE PLANET EARTH OF ALL ITS SUNBEAMS!
BUT WAIT! THEY GET THEIR ENERGY FROM THE SUN! IF I CLOSE THE DRAPES, I WILL DEPRIVE IT OF ITS LIFE-GIVING SUNLIGHT
DIE, SUN SUCKER!
ZIP!
HA HAAA! IT'S ALREADY DISINTEGRATING INTO A HIDEOUS, GREEN, STEAMING, GELATINOUS MASS!
I HATE BEING LEFT OUT
© 1989 PAWS, INC. All Rights Reserved.
11-12
JIM DAVIS

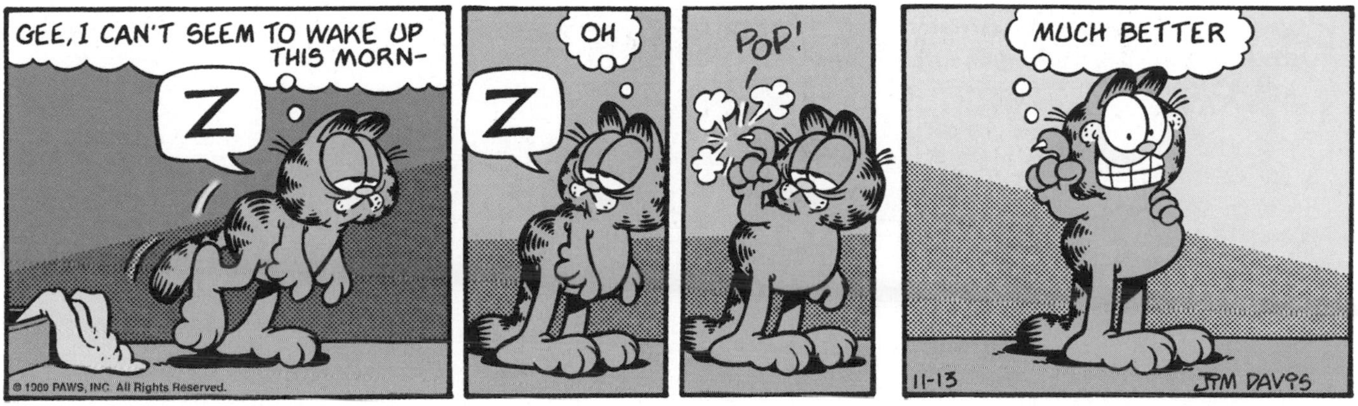
GEE, I CAN'T SEEM TO WAKE UP THIS MORN-
Z
© 1989 PAWS, INC. All Rights Reserved.
OH
Z
POP!
MUCH BETTER
11-13
JIM DAVIS

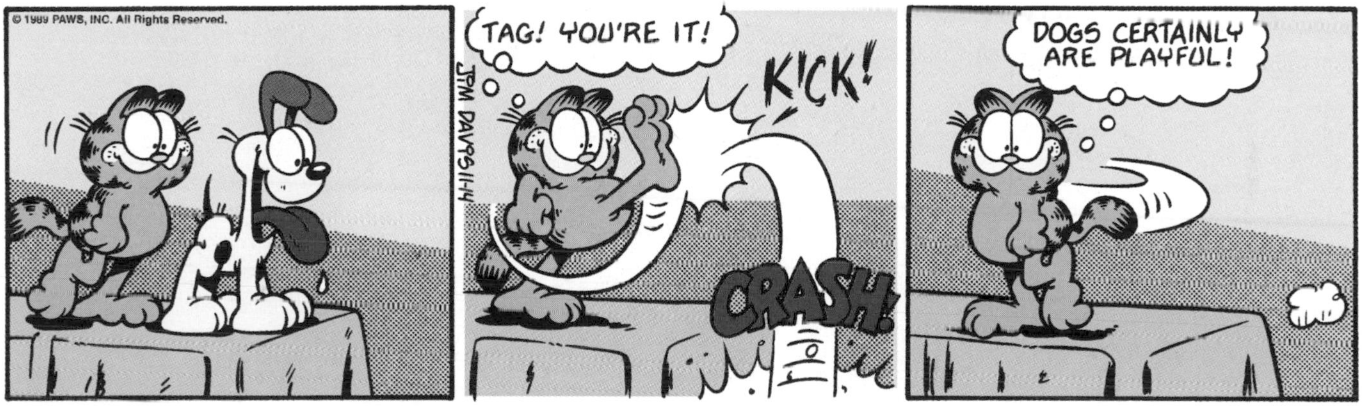
© 1989 PAWS, INC. All Rights Reserved.
TAG! YOU'RE IT!
JIM DAVIS 11-14
KICK!
CRASH!
DOGS CERTAINLY ARE PLAYFUL!

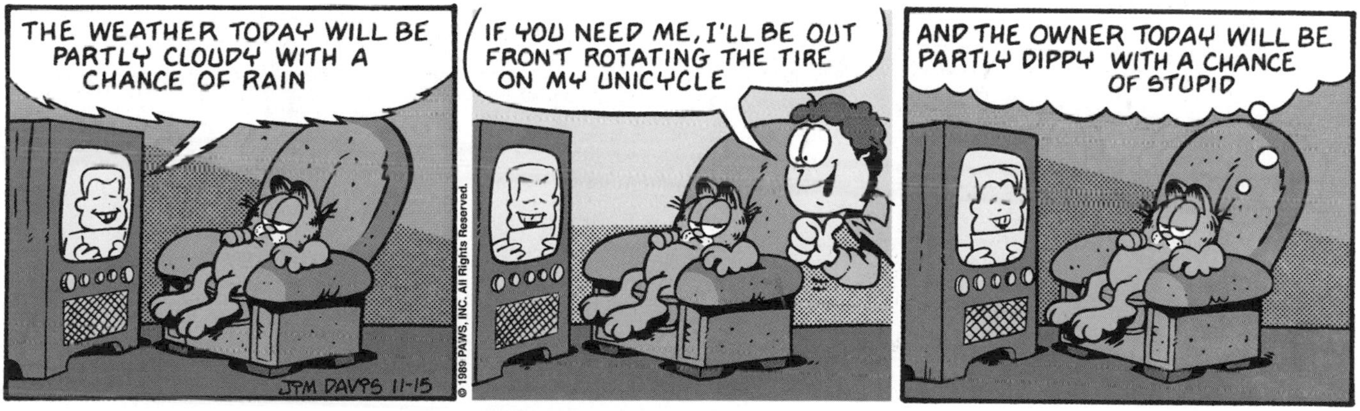
THE WEATHER TODAY WILL BE PARTLY CLOUDY WITH A CHANCE OF RAIN
JIM DAVIS 11-15
© 1989 PAWS, INC. All Rights Reserved.
IF YOU NEED ME, I'LL BE OUT FRONT ROTATING THE TIRE ON MY UNICYCLE
AND THE OWNER TODAY WILL BE PARTLY DIPPY WITH A CHANCE OF STUPID

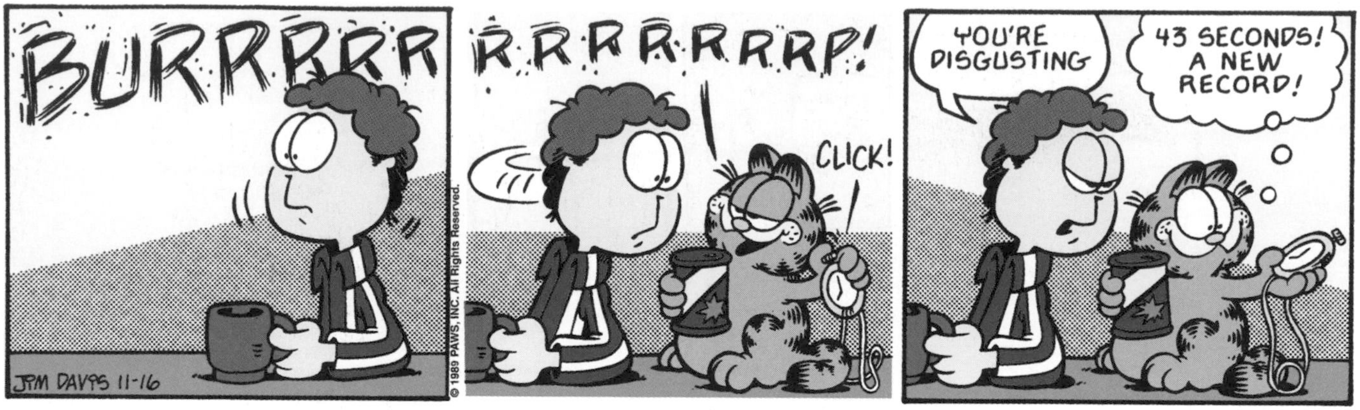
BURRRRRR RRRRRRRRP!
JIM DAVIS 11-16
© 1989 PAWS, INC. All Rights Reserved.
CLICK!
YOU'RE DISGUSTING
43 SECONDS! A NEW RECORD!

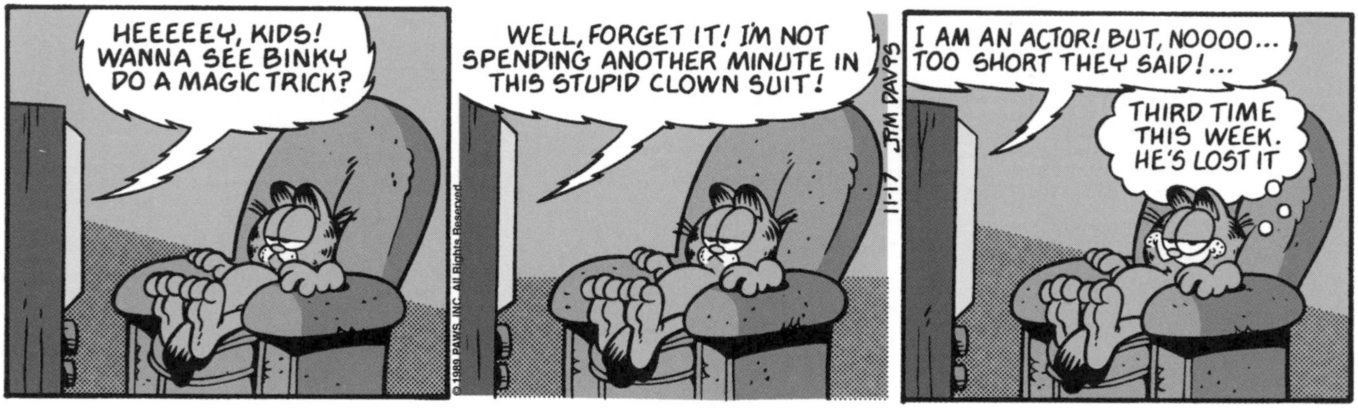
HEEEEEY, KIDS! WANNA SEE BINKY DO A MAGIC TRICK?
© 1989 PAWS, INC. All Rights Reserved.
WELL, FORGET IT! I'M NOT SPENDING ANOTHER MINUTE IN THIS STUPID CLOWN SUIT!
JIM DAVIS 11-17
I AM AN ACTOR! BUT, NOOOO... TOO SHORT THEY SAID!...
THIRD TIME THIS WEEK. HE'S LOST IT

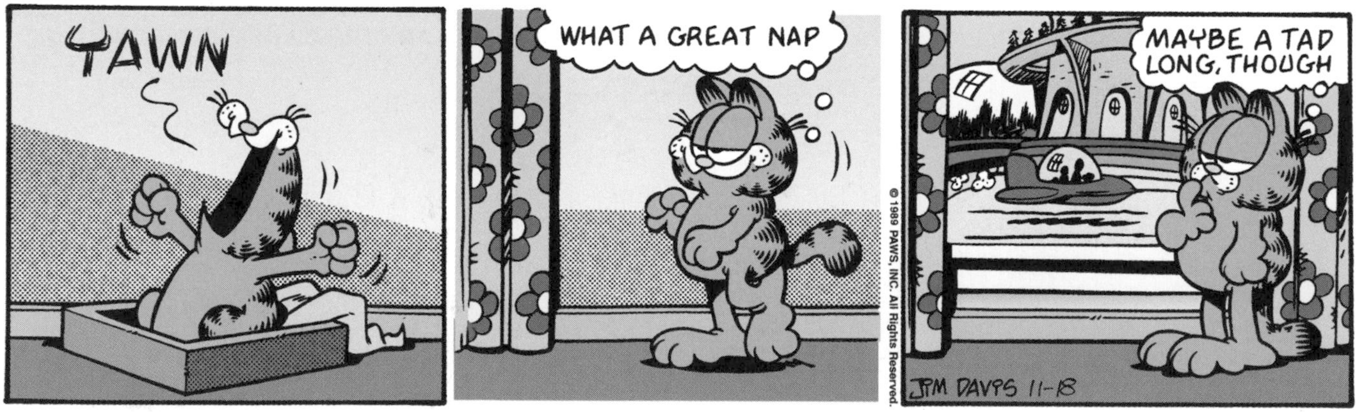
YAWN
WHAT A GREAT NAP
© 1989 PAWS, INC. All Rights Reserved.
MAYBE A TAD LONG, THOUGH
JIM DAVIS 11-18

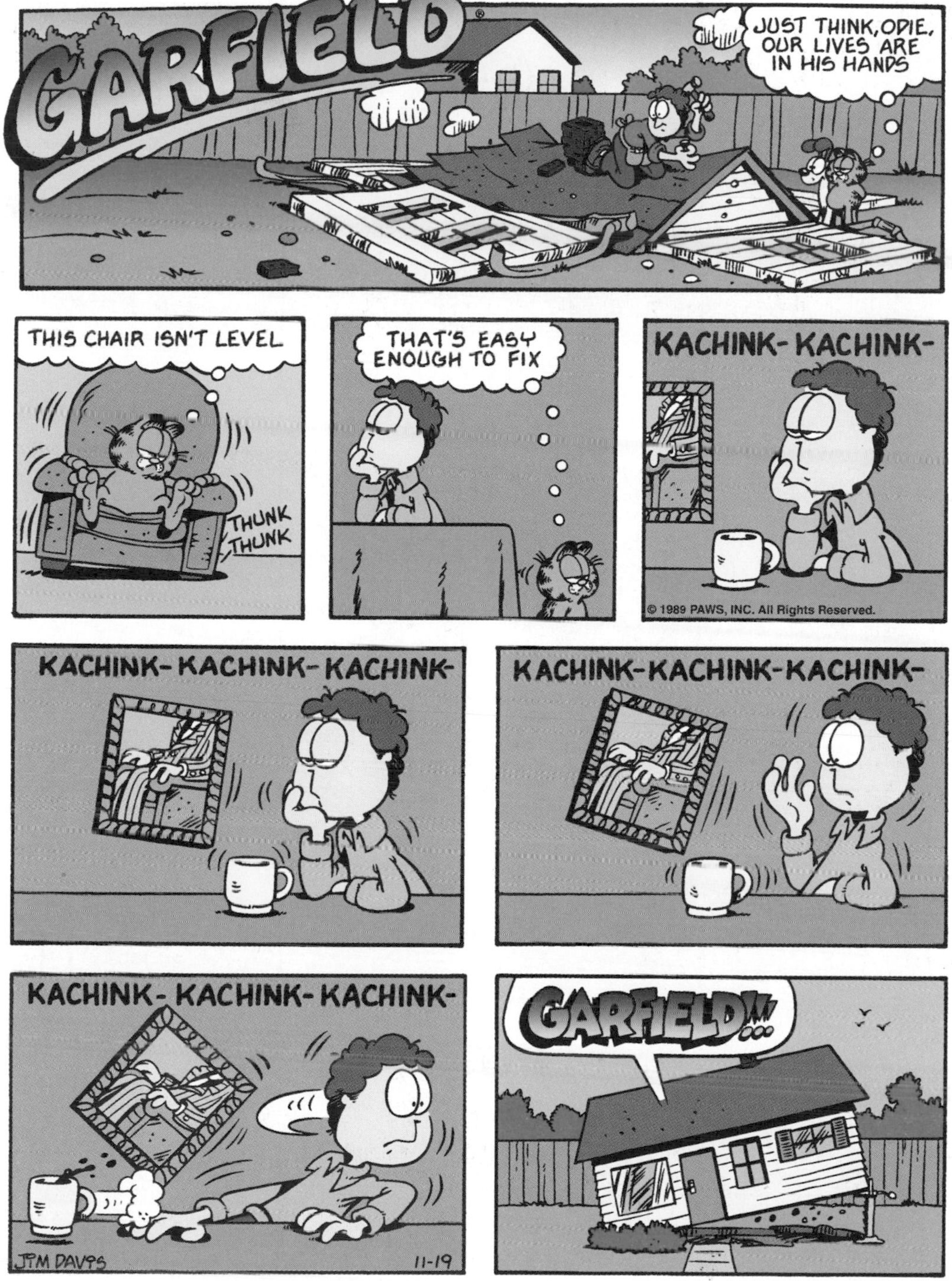
GARFIELD®
JUST THINK, ODIE, OUR LIVES ARE IN HIS HANDS
THIS CHAIR ISN'T LEVEL
THUNK THUNK
THAT'S EASY ENOUGH TO FIX
KACHINK- KACHINK-
© 1989 PAWS, INC. All Rights Reserved.
KACHINK- KACHINK- KACHINK-
KACHINK- KACHINK- KACHINK-
KACHINK- KACHINK- KACHINK-
JIM DAVIS
11-19
GARFIELD!!!

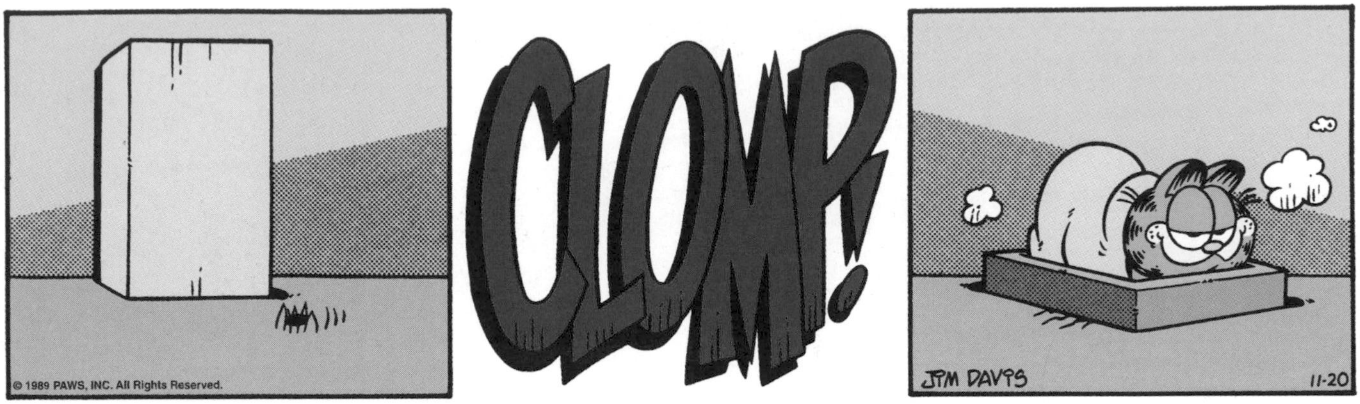
© 1989 PAWS, INC. All Rights Reserved.
CLOMP!
JIM DAVIS
11-20

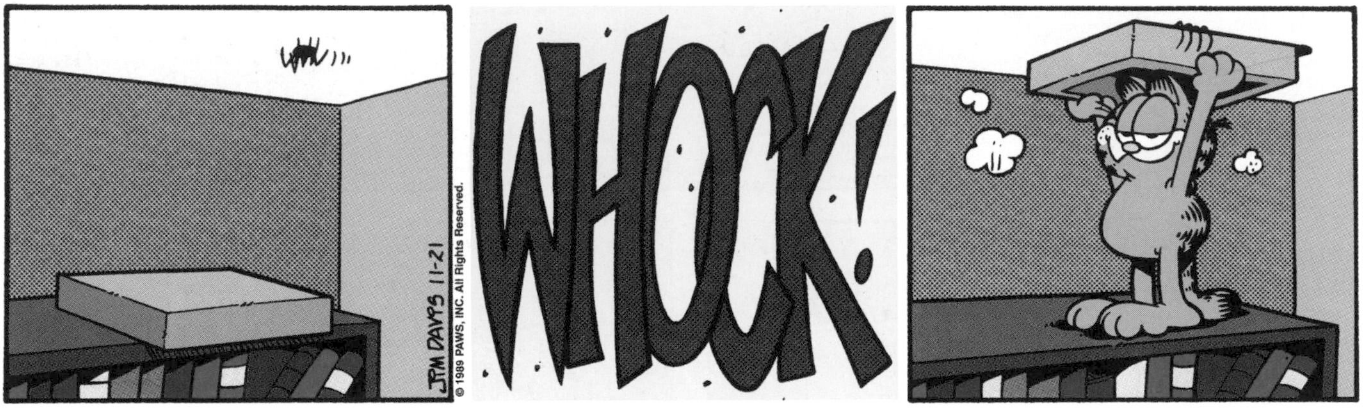
JIM DAVIS 11-21
© 1989 PAWS, INC. All Rights Reserved.
WHOCK!

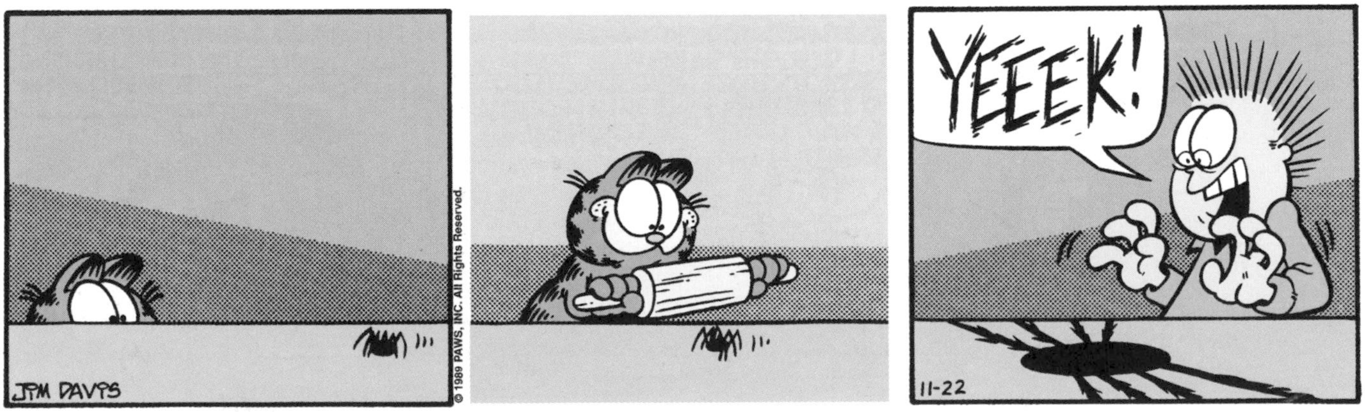
JIM DAVIS
© 1989 PAWS, INC. All Rights Reserved.
YEEEK!
11-22

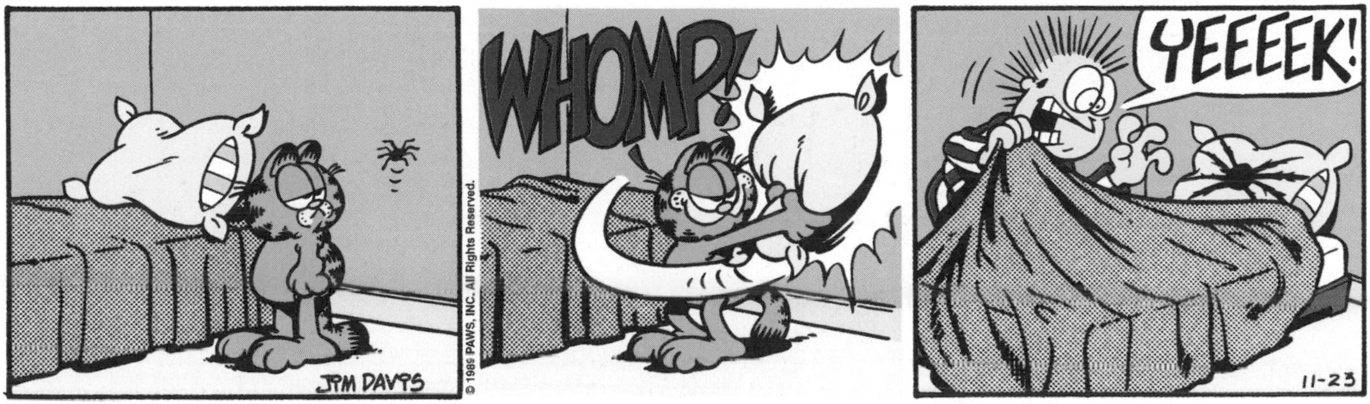
JIM DAVIS
WHOMP!
© 1989 PAWS, INC. All Rights Reserved.
YEEEEK!
11-23

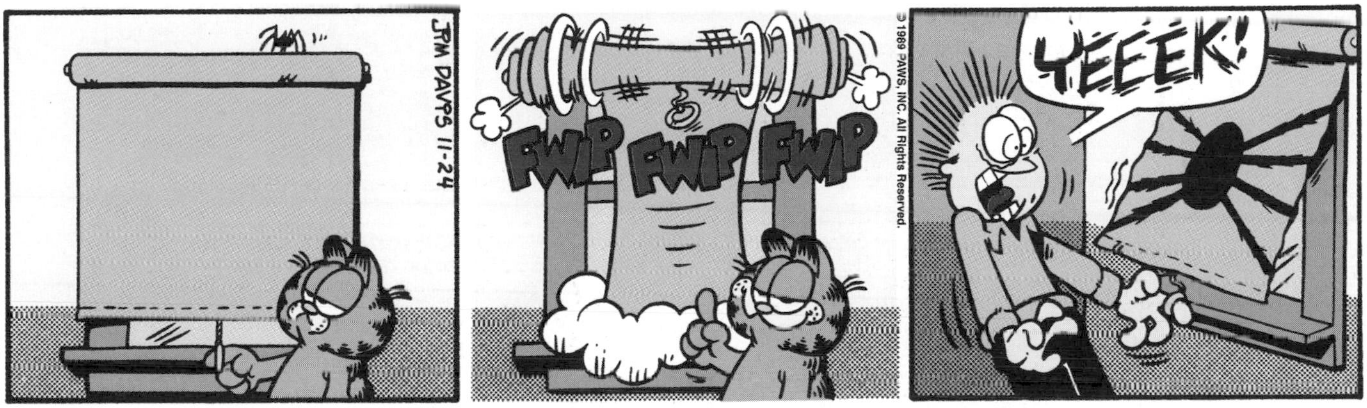
JIM DAVIS 11-24
FWIP FWIP FWIP
© 1989 PAWS, INC. All Rights Reserved.
YEEEK!

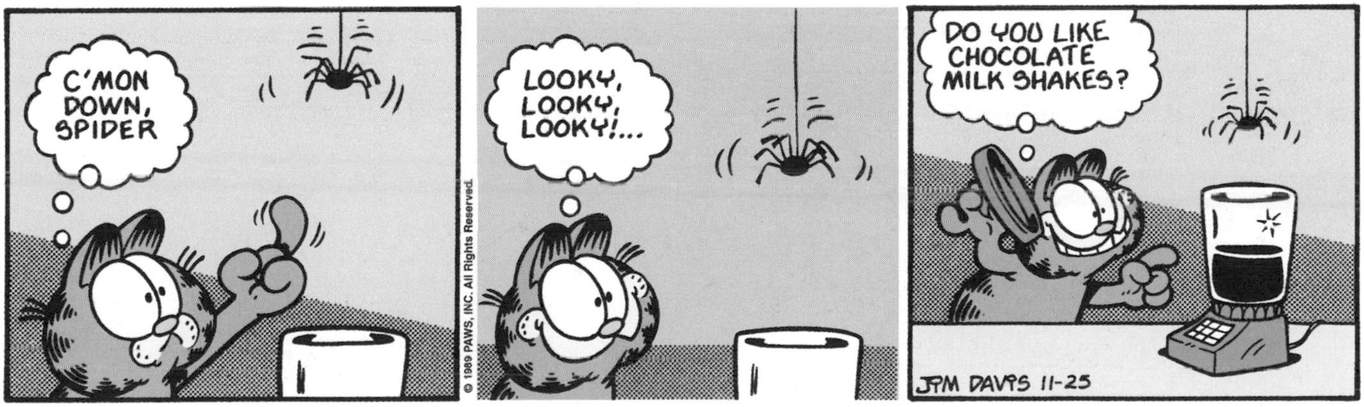
C'MON DOWN, SPIDER
© 1989 PAWS, INC. All Rights Reserved.
LOOKY, LOOKY, LOOKY!...
DO YOU LIKE CHOCOLATE MILK SHAKES?
JIM DAVIS 11-25

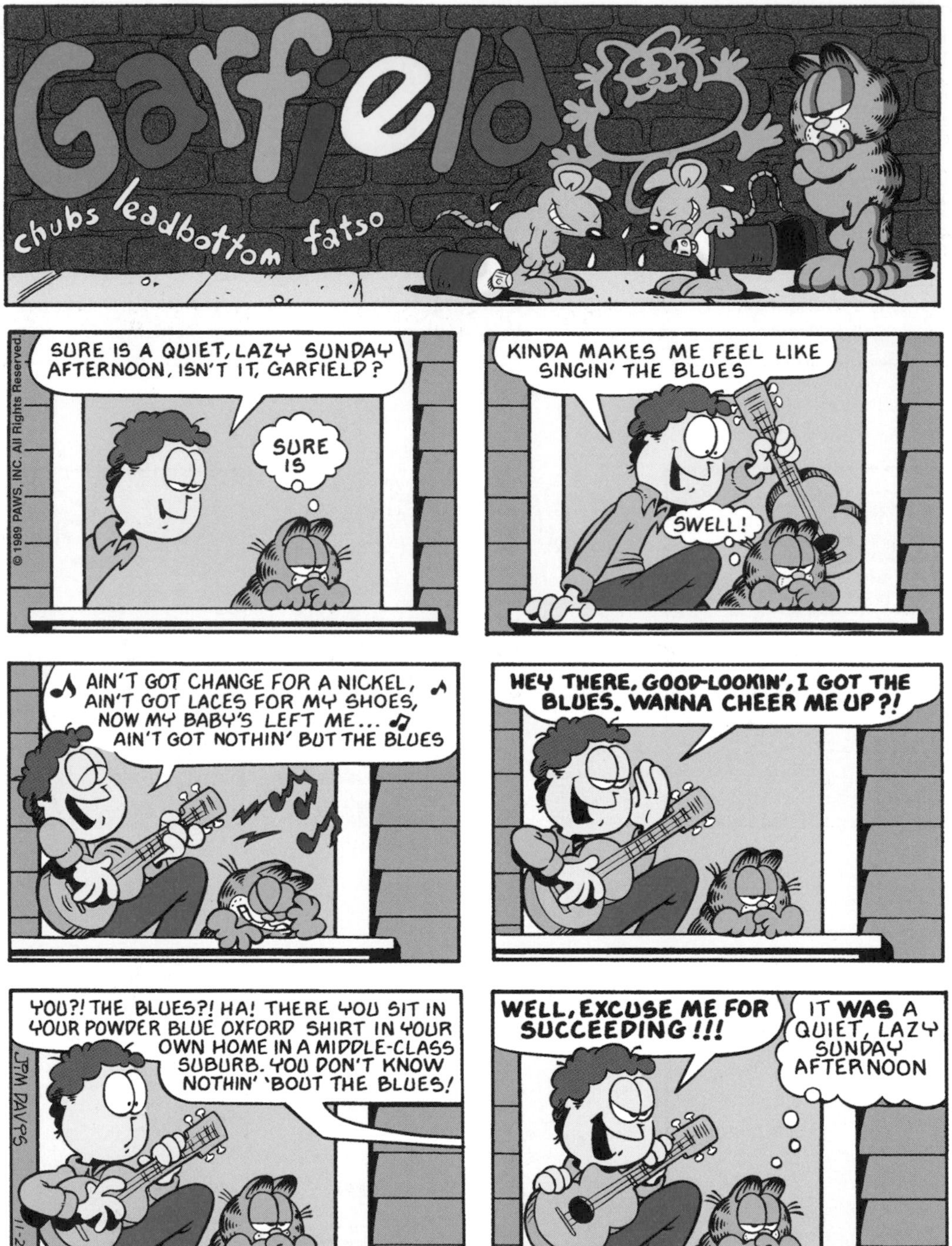
Garfield
chubs leadbottom fatso
© 1989 PAWS, INC. All Rights Reserved.
SURE IS A QUIET, LAZY SUNDAY AFTERNOON, ISN'T IT, GARFIELD?
SURE IS
KINDA MAKES ME FEEL LIKE SINGIN' THE BLUES
SWELL!
AIN'T GOT CHANGE FOR A NICKEL, AIN'T GOT LACES FOR MY SHOES, NOW MY BABY'S LEFT ME... AIN'T GOT NOTHIN' BUT THE BLUES
HEY THERE, GOOD-LOOKIN', I GOT THE BLUES. WANNA CHEER ME UP?!
YOU?! THE BLUES?! HA! THERE YOU SIT IN YOUR POWDER BLUE OXFORD SHIRT IN YOUR OWN HOME IN A MIDDLE-CLASS SUBURB. YOU DON'T KNOW NOTHIN' 'BOUT THE BLUES!
JIM DAVIS
11-26
WELL, EXCUSE ME FOR SUCCEEDING!!!
IT WAS A QUIET, LAZY SUNDAY AFTERNOON

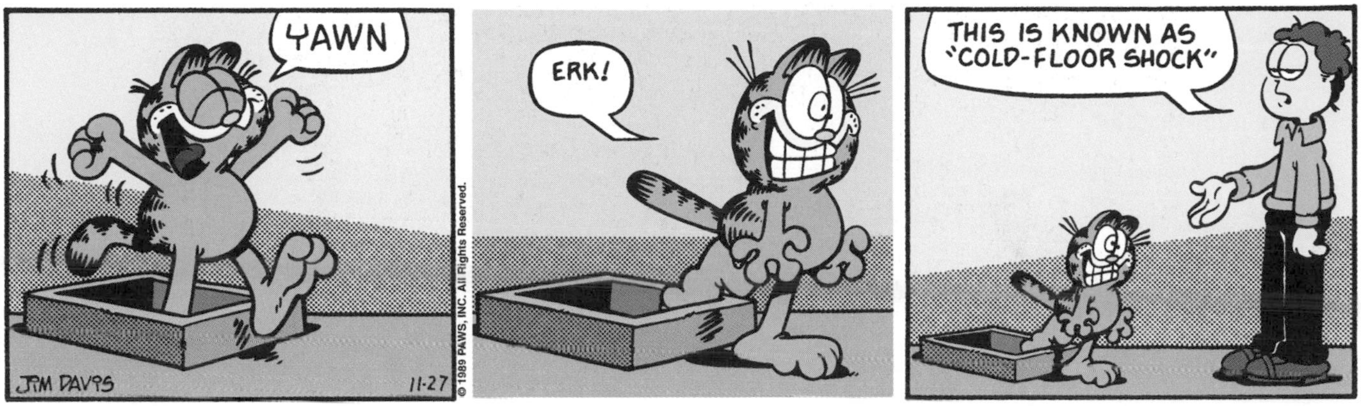
YAWN
ERK!
THIS IS KNOWN AS "COLD-FLOOR SHOCK"
JIM DAVIS 11-27
© 1989 PAWS, INC. All Rights Reserved.

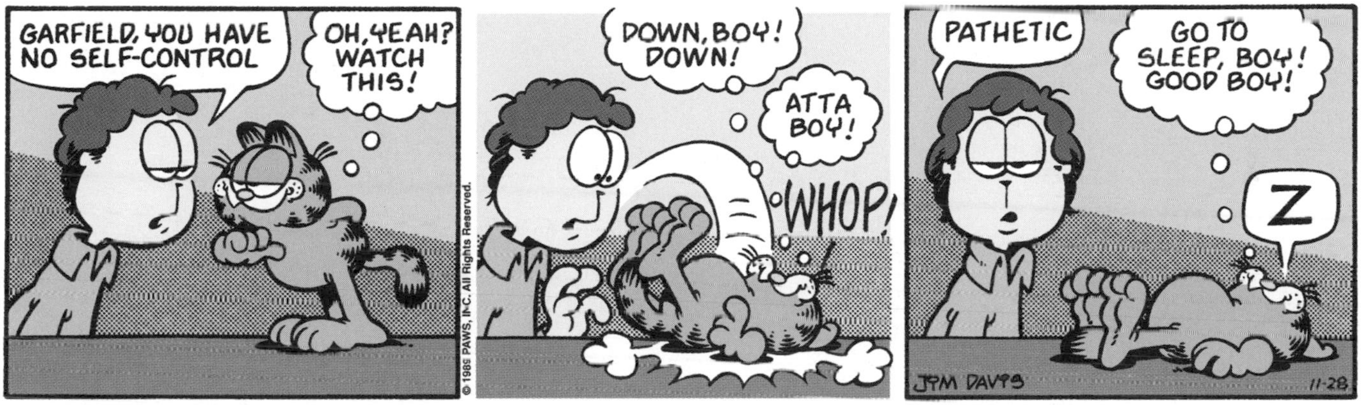
GARFIELD, YOU HAVE NO SELF-CONTROL
OH, YEAH? WATCH THIS!
DOWN, BOY! DOWN!
ATTA BOY!
WHOP!
PATHETIC
GO TO SLEEP, BOY! GOOD BOY!
Z
JIM DAVIS 11-28
© 1989 PAWS, INC. All Rights Reserved.

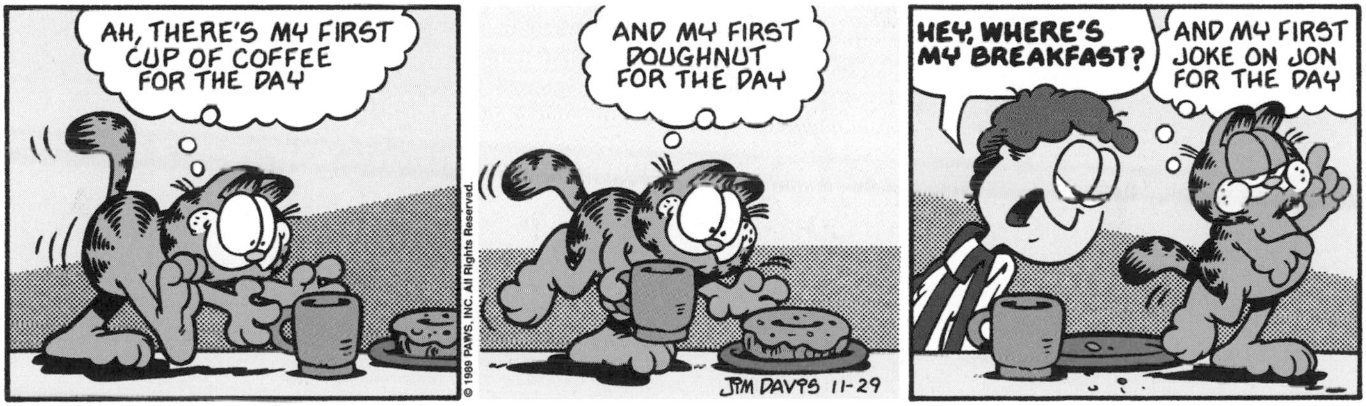
AH, THERE'S MY FIRST CUP OF COFFEE FOR THE DAY
AND MY FIRST DOUGHNUT FOR THE DAY
HEY, WHERE'S MY BREAKFAST?
AND MY FIRST JOKE ON JON FOR THE DAY
JIM DAVIS 11-29
© 1989 PAWS, INC. All Rights Reserved.

MY, YOU'RE LOOKING PLEASANT TODAY!
JPM DAVPS
11-30
I'M MAKING A CONSCIOUS EFFORT
I TIED MY EARS BEHIND MY HEAD

I HAVE THE LAST OF THE ICE CREAM, GARFIELD
FINE
JPM DAVPS
12-1
I'M GOING TO EAT IT, AND YOU'RE NOT
ENJOY
I REPLACED IT WITH LARD

THIS IS A FLEA COLLAR, GARFIELD
AND DO YOU KNOW WHAT WE DO WITH FLEA COLLARS?
NOOOO...GUESS AGAIN
JPM DAVPS
12-2

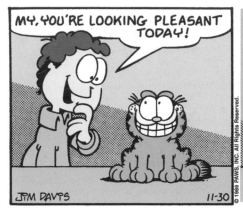

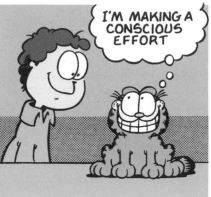

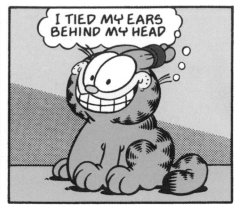

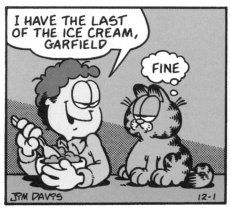

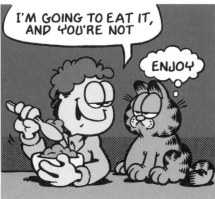

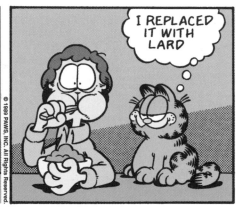

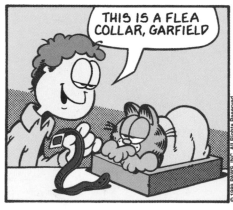

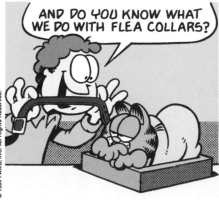

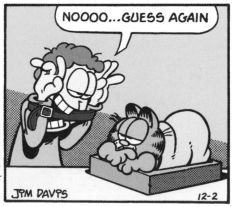

GARFIELD
I COULD HAVE SWORN I LEFT MY SECRET FORMULA HERE SOMEWHERE
JIM DAVIS
12-3
© 1989 PAWS, INC. All Rights Reserved.
CLICK
HEEEY, KIDS!

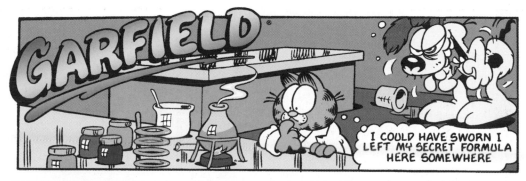

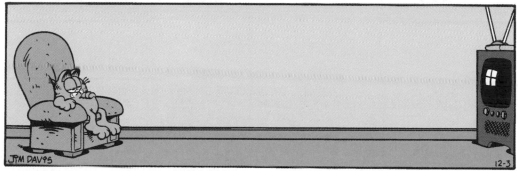

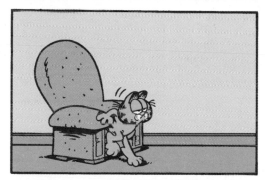

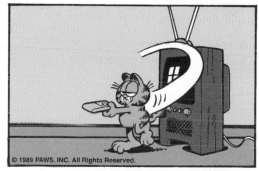

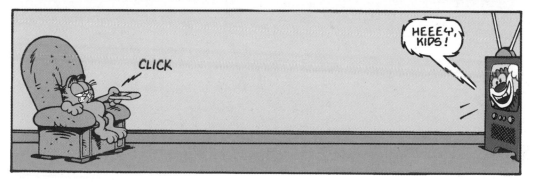

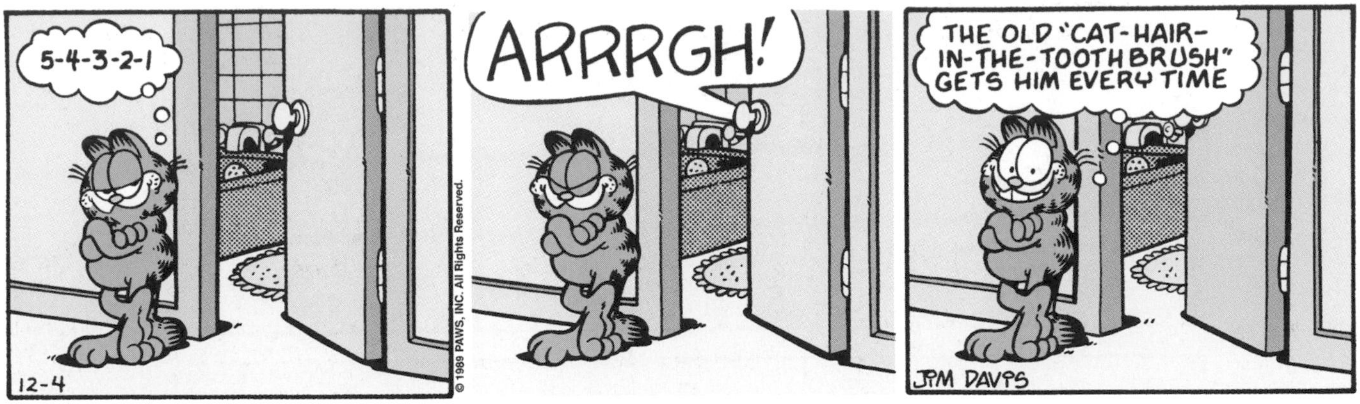
5-4-3-2-1
12-4
© 1989 PAWS, INC. All Rights Reserved.
ARRRGH!
THE OLD "CAT-HAIR-IN-THE-TOOTHBRUSH" GETS HIM EVERY TIME
JIM DAVIS

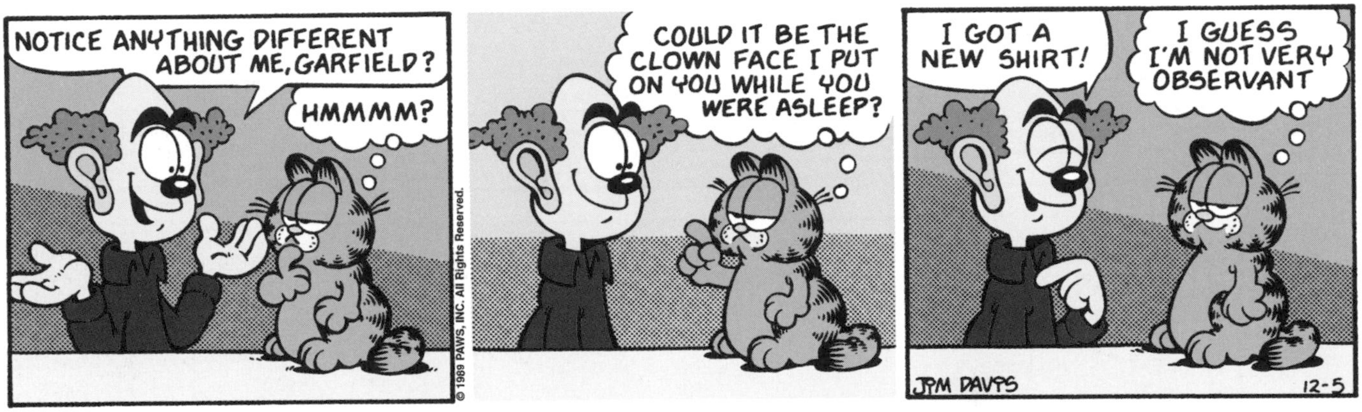
NOTICE ANYTHING DIFFERENT ABOUT ME, GARFIELD?
HMMMM?
© 1989 PAWS, INC. All Rights Reserved.
COULD IT BE THE CLOWN FACE I PUT ON YOU WHILE YOU WERE ASLEEP?
I GOT A NEW SHIRT!
I GUESS I'M NOT VERY OBSERVANT
JIM DAVIS
12-5

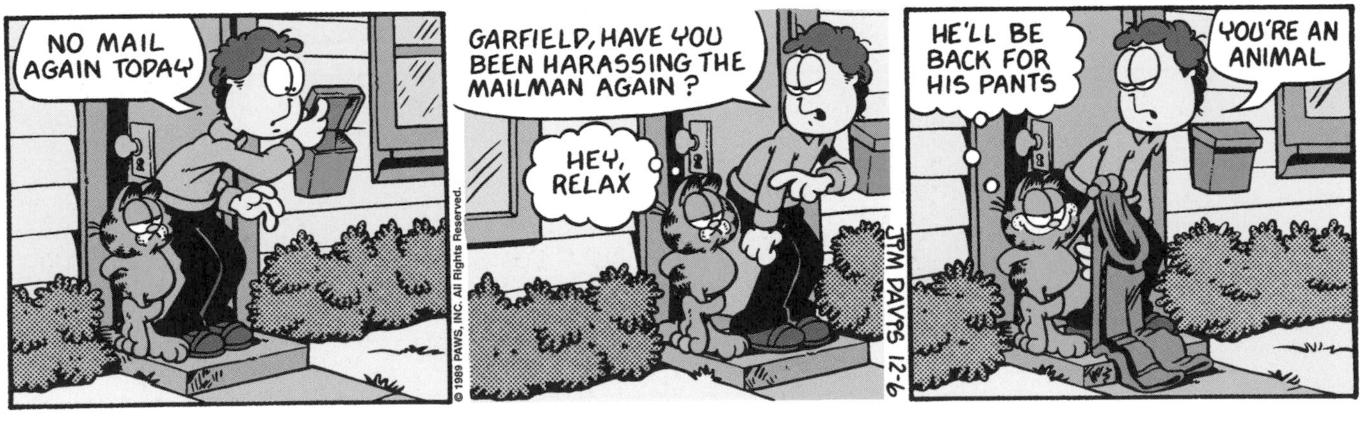
NO MAIL AGAIN TODAY
© 1989 PAWS, INC. All Rights Reserved.
GARFIELD, HAVE YOU BEEN HARASSING THE MAILMAN AGAIN?
HEY, RELAX
JIM DAVIS 12-6
HE'LL BE BACK FOR HIS PANTS
YOU'RE AN ANIMAL

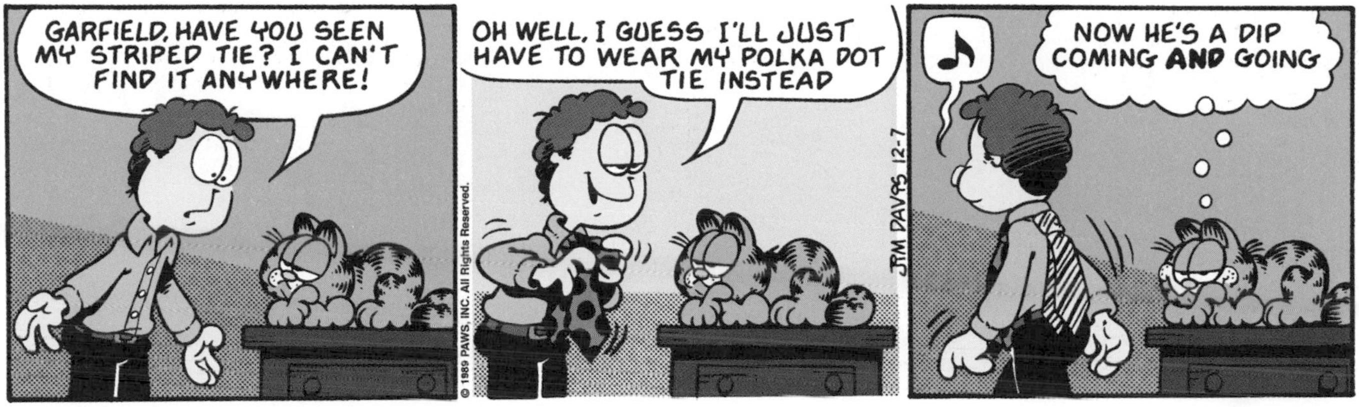
GARFIELD, HAVE YOU SEEN MY STRIPED TIE? I CAN'T FIND IT ANYWHERE!
OH WELL, I GUESS I'LL JUST HAVE TO WEAR MY POLKA DOT TIE INSTEAD
© 1989 PAWS, INC. All Rights Reserved.
JIM DAVIS 12-7
♪
NOW HE'S A DIP COMING **AND** GOING

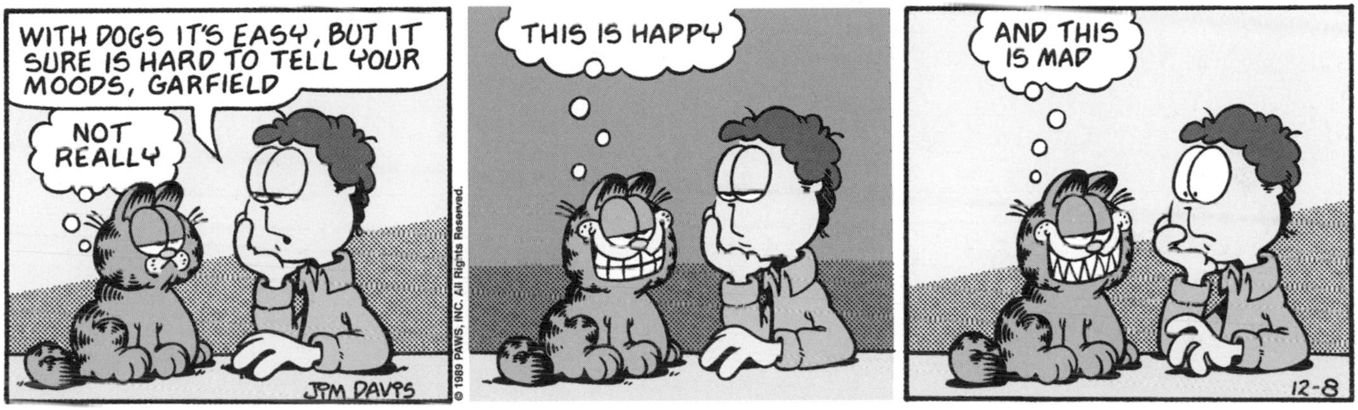
WITH DOGS IT'S EASY, BUT IT SURE IS HARD TO TELL YOUR MOODS, GARFIELD
NOT REALLY
JIM DAVIS
© 1989 PAWS, INC. All Rights Reserved.
THIS IS HAPPY
AND THIS IS MAD
12-8

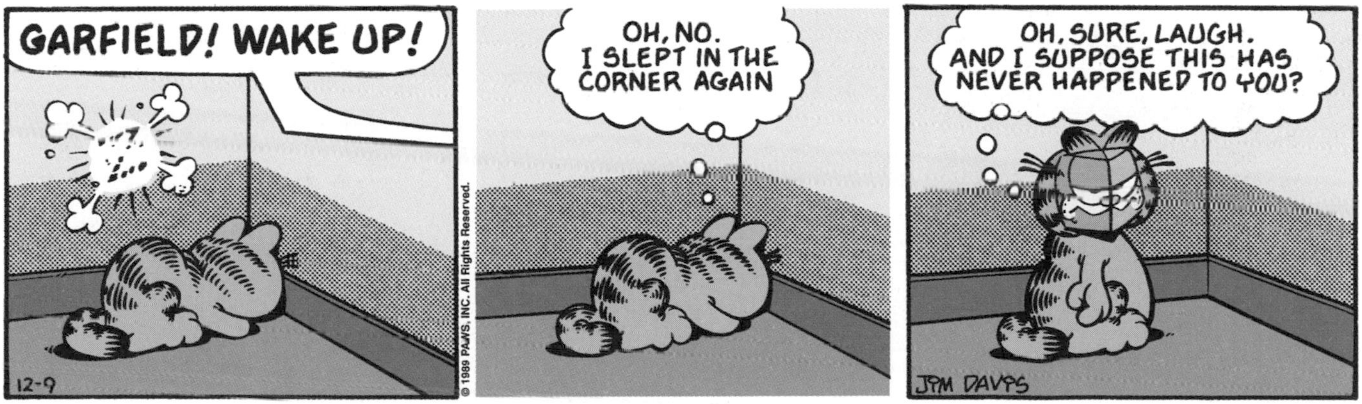
GARFIELD! WAKE UP!
12-9
© 1989 PAWS, INC. All Rights Reserved.
OH, NO. I SLEPT IN THE CORNER AGAIN
OH, SURE, LAUGH. AND I SUPPOSE THIS HAS NEVER HAPPENED TO YOU?
JIM DAVIS

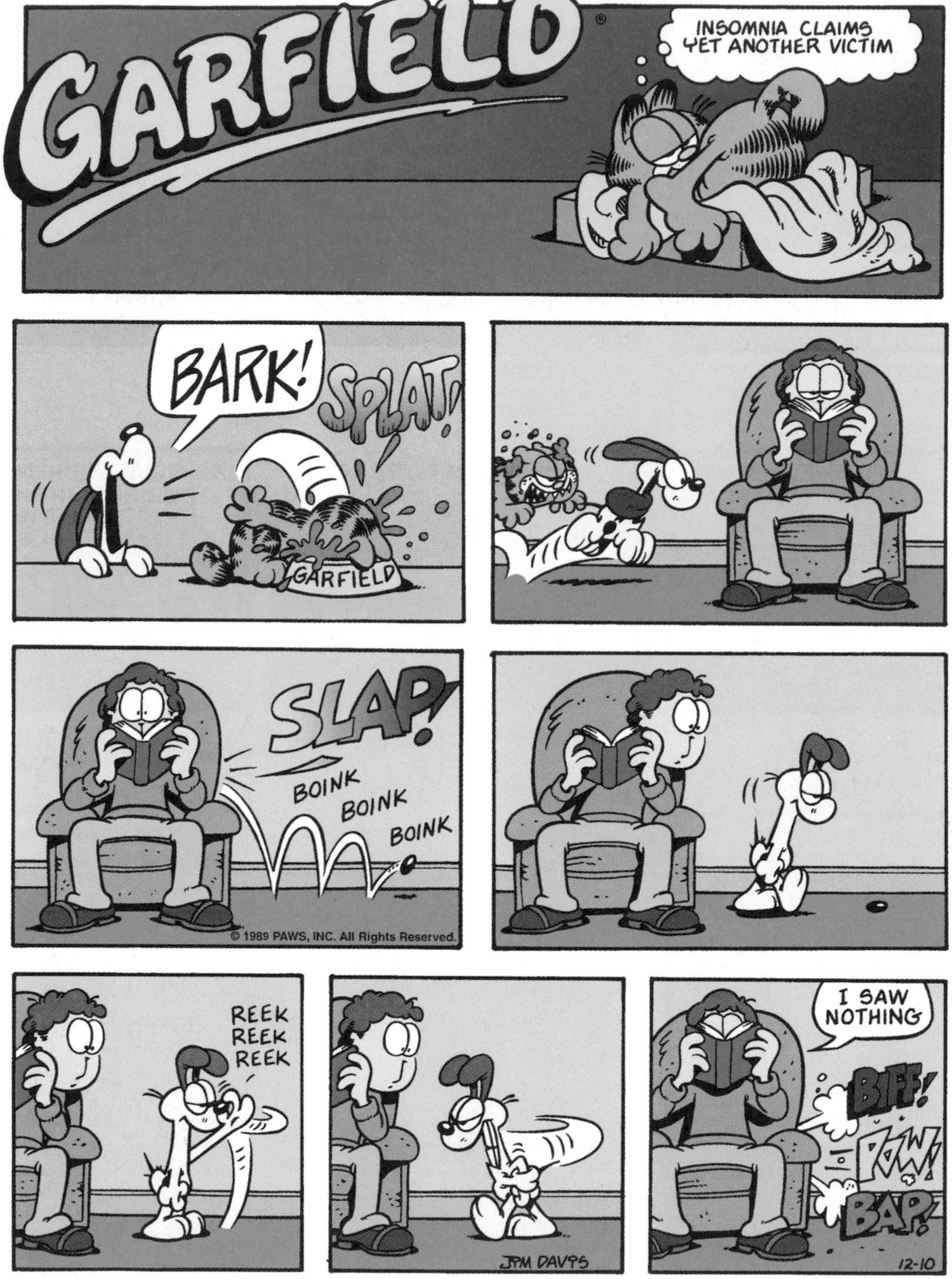
GARFIELD®
INSOMNIA CLAIMS YET ANOTHER VICTIM
BARK!
SPLAT!
GARFIELD
SLAP!
BOINK
BOINK
BOINK
© 1989 PAWS, INC. All Rights Reserved.
REEK
REEK
REEK
JPM DAVPS
I SAW NOTHING
BIFF!
POW!
BAP!
12-10

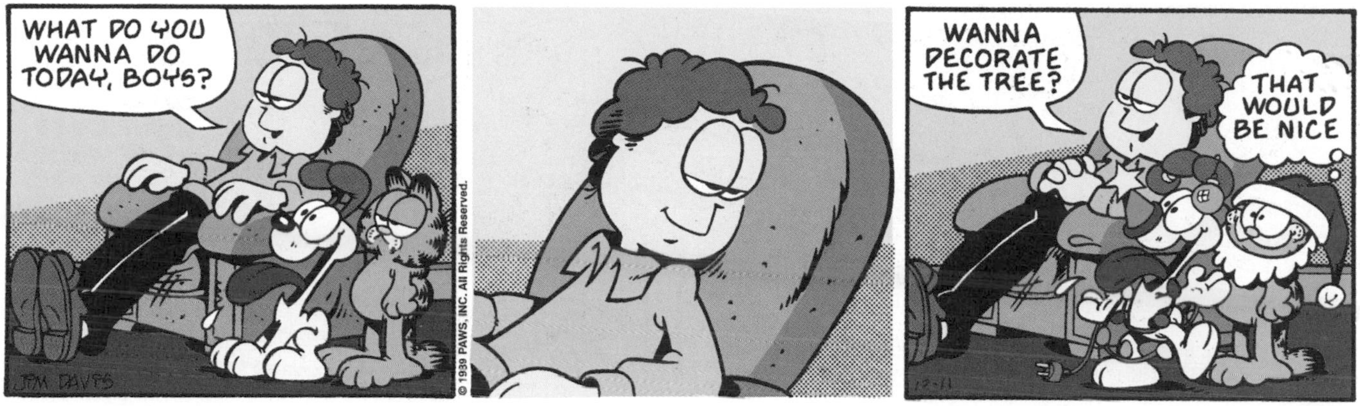
WHAT DO YOU WANNA DO TODAY, BOYS?
© 1939 PAWS, INC. All Rights Reserved.
WANNA DECORATE THE TREE?
THAT WOULD BE NICE

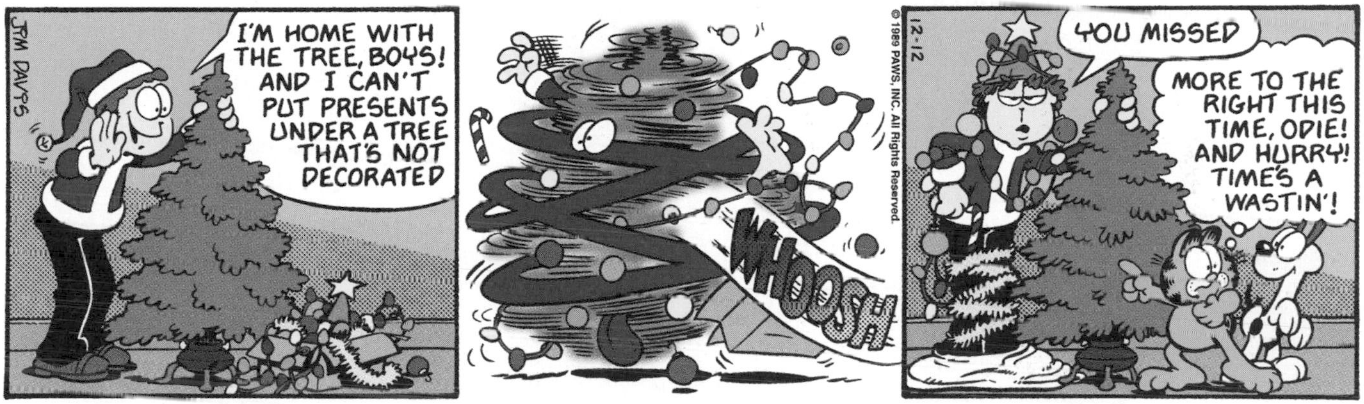
I'M HOME WITH THE TREE, BOYS! AND I CAN'T PUT PRESENTS UNDER A TREE THAT'S NOT DECORATED
WHOOSH
© 1989 PAWS, INC. All Rights Reserved.
YOU MISSED
MORE TO THE RIGHT THIS TIME, ODIE! AND HURRY! TIME'S A WASTIN'!

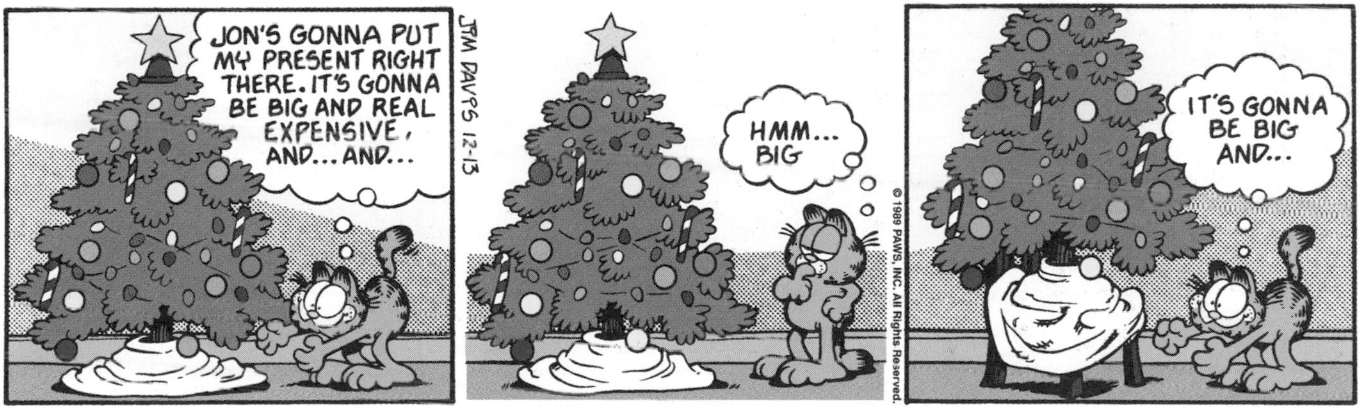
JON'S GONNA PUT MY PRESENT RIGHT THERE. IT'S GONNA BE BIG AND REAL EXPENSIVE, AND... AND...
HMM... BIG
© 1989 PAWS, INC. All Rights Reserved.
IT'S GONNA BE BIG AND...

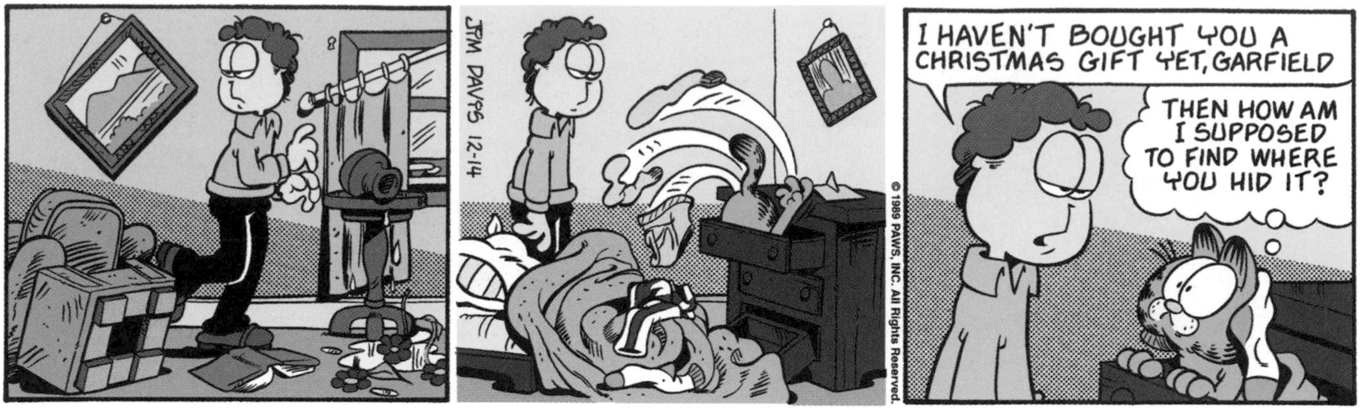
JIM DAVIS 12-14
I HAVEN'T BOUGHT YOU A CHRISTMAS GIFT YET, GARFIELD
THEN HOW AM I SUPPOSED TO FIND WHERE YOU HID IT?
© 1989 PAWS, INC. All Rights Reserved.

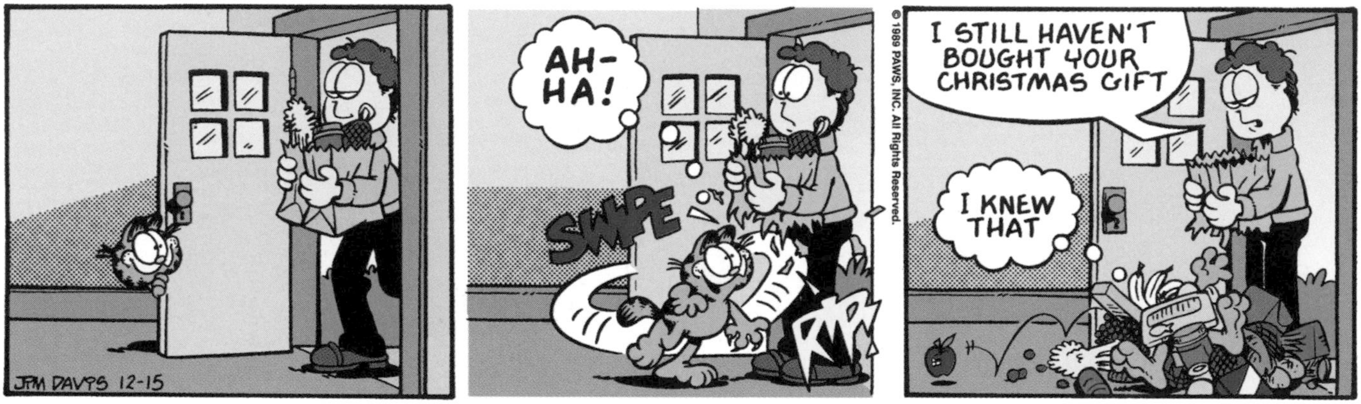
JIM DAVIS 12-15
AH-HA!
SWIPE
RIP
I STILL HAVEN'T BOUGHT YOUR CHRISTMAS GIFT
I KNEW THAT
© 1989 PAWS, INC. All Rights Reserved.

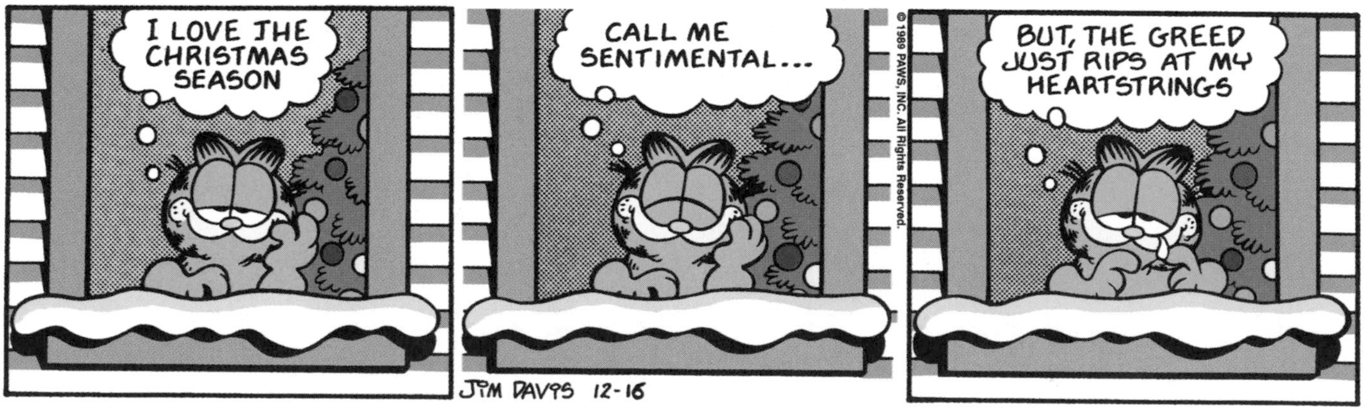
I LOVE THE CHRISTMAS SEASON
CALL ME SENTIMENTAL...
BUT, THE GREED JUST RIPS AT MY HEARTSTRINGS
JIM DAVIS 12-16
© 1989 PAWS, INC. All Rights Reserved.

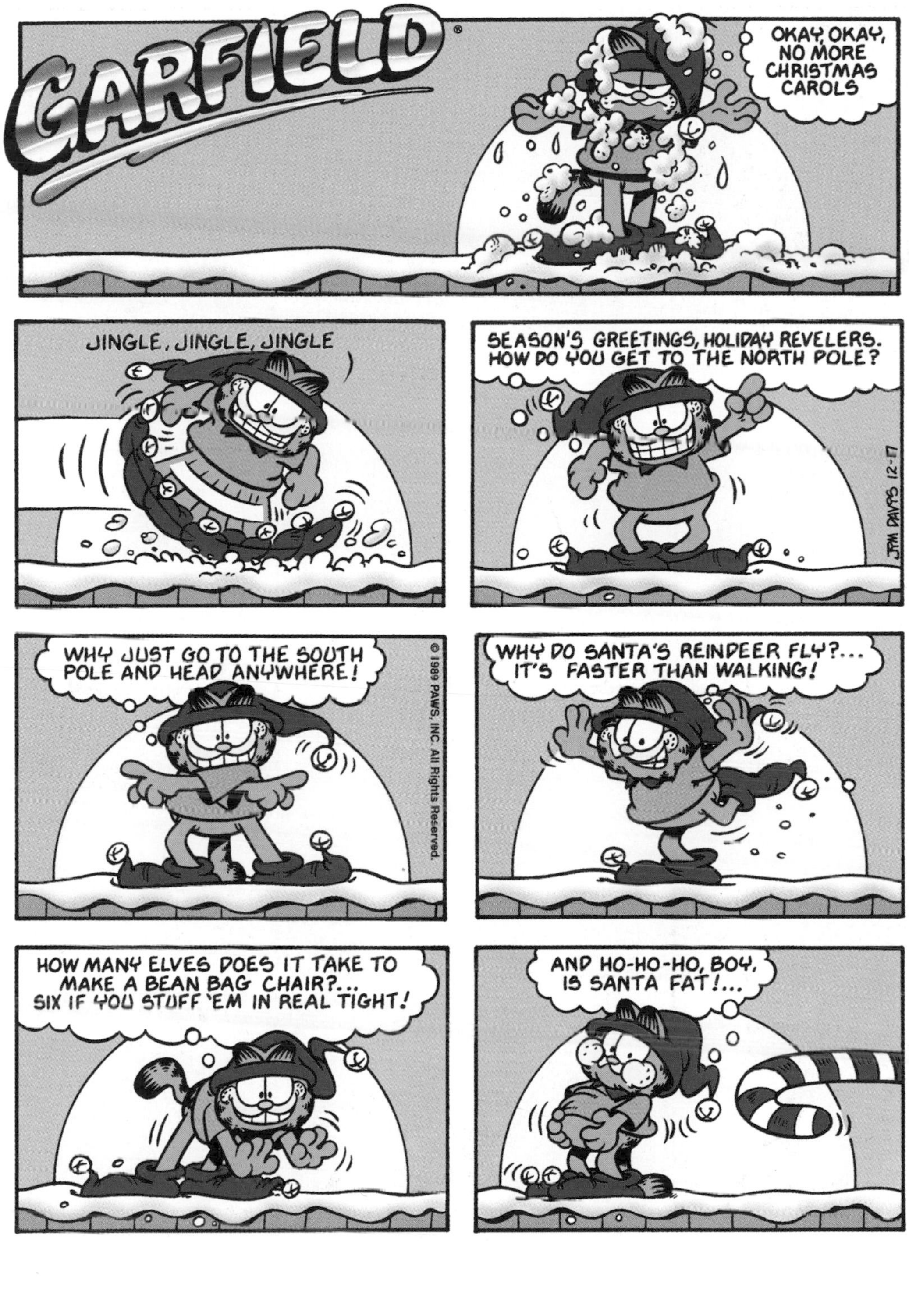
GARFIELD
OKAY, OKAY, NO MORE CHRISTMAS CAROLS
JINGLE, JINGLE, JINGLE
SEASON'S GREETINGS, HOLIDAY REVELERS. HOW DO YOU GET TO THE NORTH POLE?
JIM DAVIS 12-17
WHY JUST GO TO THE SOUTH POLE AND HEAD ANYWHERE!
© 1989 PAWS, INC. All Rights Reserved.
WHY DO SANTA'S REINDEER FLY?... IT'S FASTER THAN WALKING!
HOW MANY ELVES DOES IT TAKE TO MAKE A BEAN BAG CHAIR?... SIX IF YOU STUFF 'EM IN REAL TIGHT!
AND HO-HO-HO, BOY, IS SANTA FAT!...

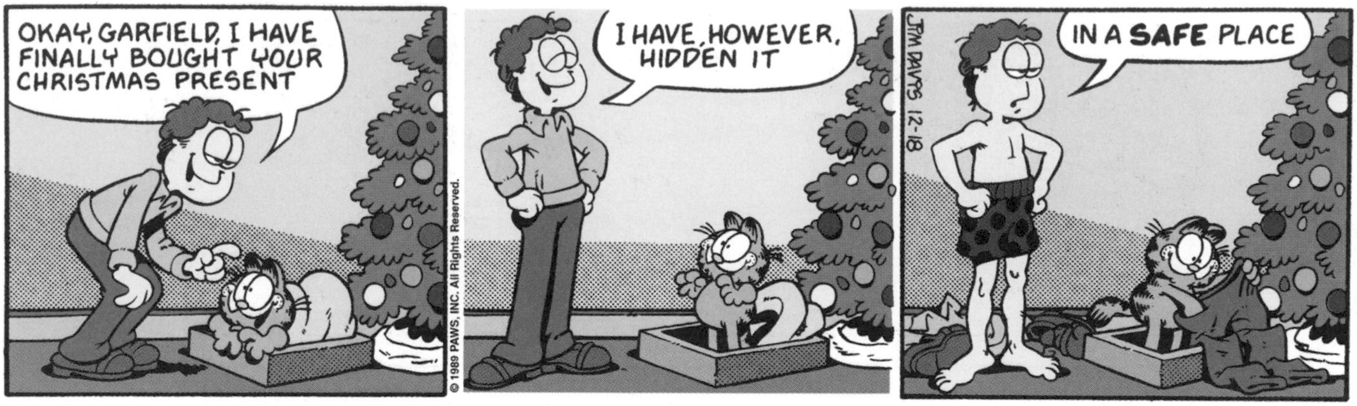
OKAY, GARFIELD, I HAVE FINALLY BOUGHT YOUR CHRISTMAS PRESENT
© 1989 PAWS, INC. All Rights Reserved.
I HAVE, HOWEVER, HIDDEN IT
JIM DAVIS 12-18
IN A **SAFE** PLACE

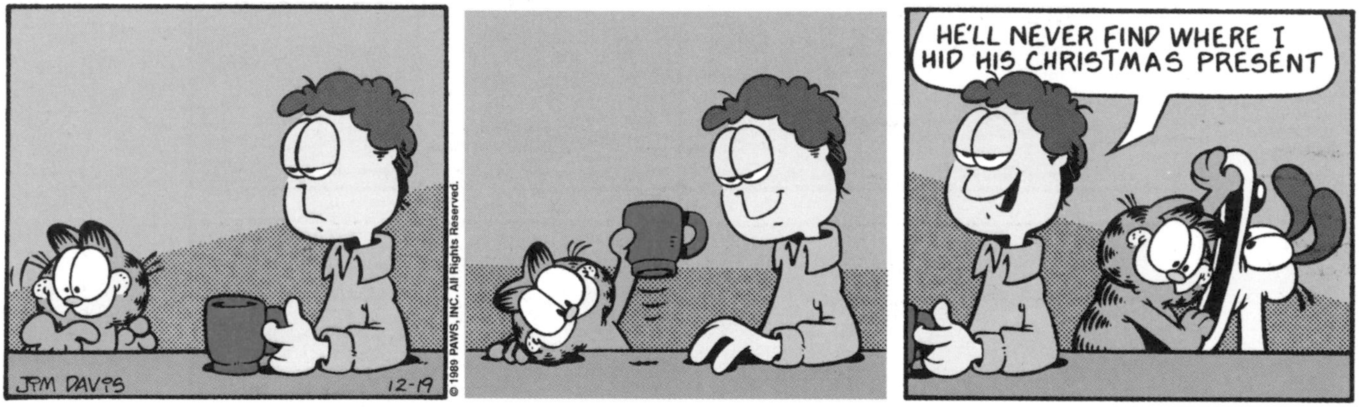
JIM DAVIS
12-19
© 1989 PAWS, INC. All Rights Reserved.
HE'LL NEVER FIND WHERE I HID HIS CHRISTMAS PRESENT

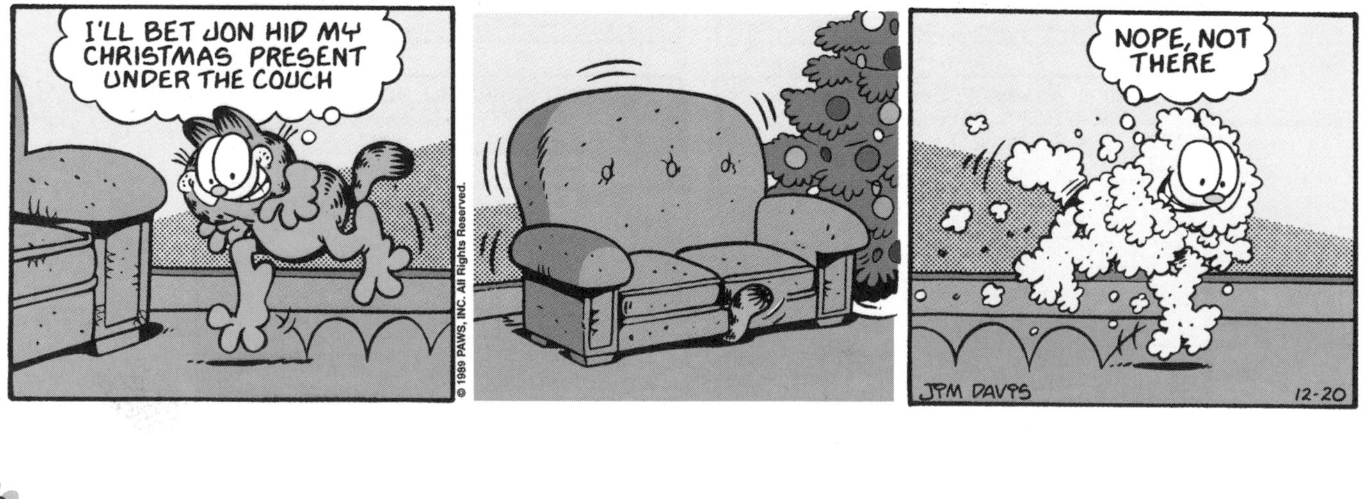
I'LL BET JON HID MY CHRISTMAS PRESENT UNDER THE COUCH
© 1989 PAWS, INC. All Rights Reserved.
NOPE, NOT THERE
JIM DAVIS
12-20

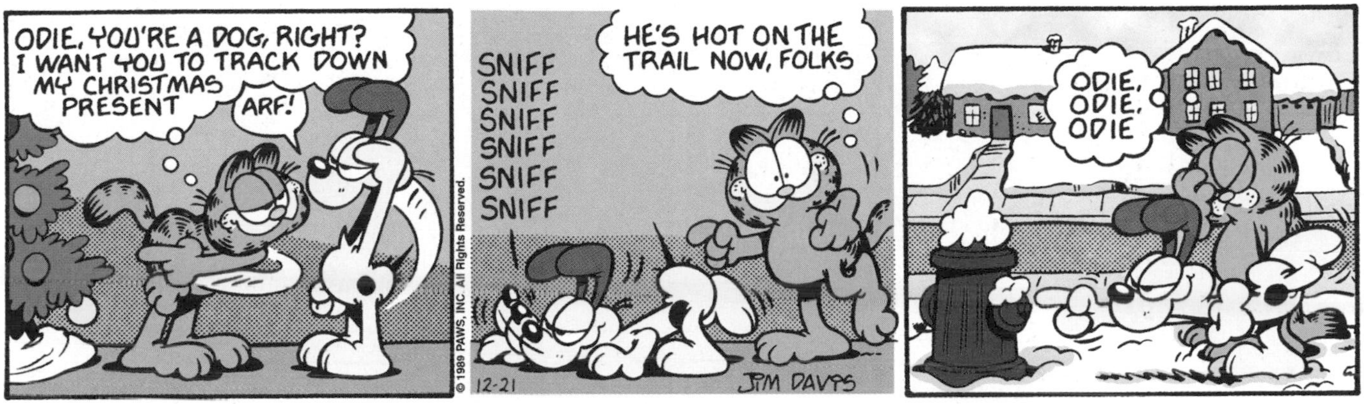
ODIE, YOU'RE A DOG, RIGHT? I WANT YOU TO TRACK DOWN MY CHRISTMAS PRESENT
ARF!
© 1989 PAWS, INC. All Rights Reserved.
12-21
SNIFF SNIFF SNIFF SNIFF SNIFF SNIFF
HE'S HOT ON THE TRAIL NOW, FOLKS
JIM DAVIS
ODIE, ODIE, ODIE

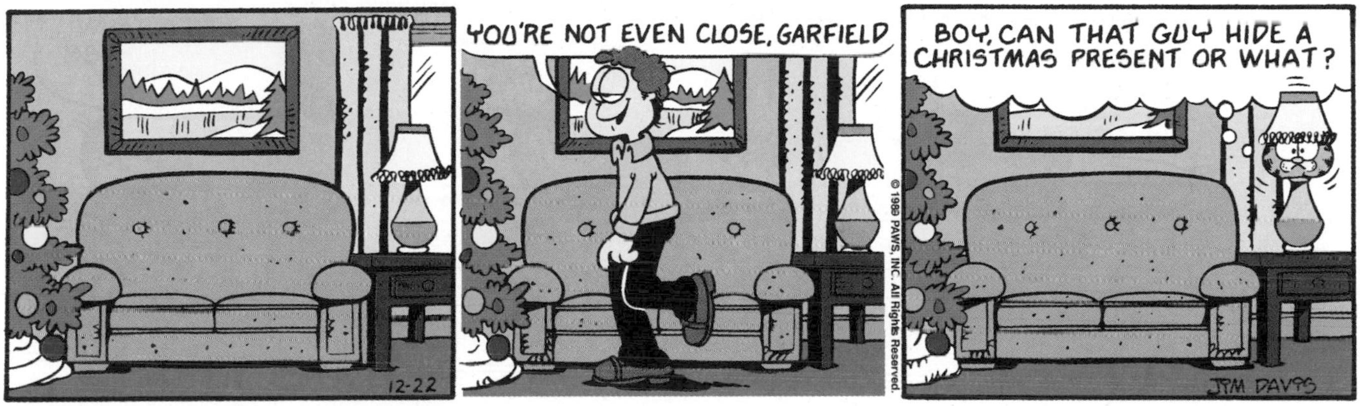
12-22
YOU'RE NOT EVEN CLOSE, GARFIELD
© 1989 PAWS, INC. All Rights Reserved.
BOY, CAN THAT GUY HIDE A CHRISTMAS PRESENT OR WHAT?
JIM DAVIS

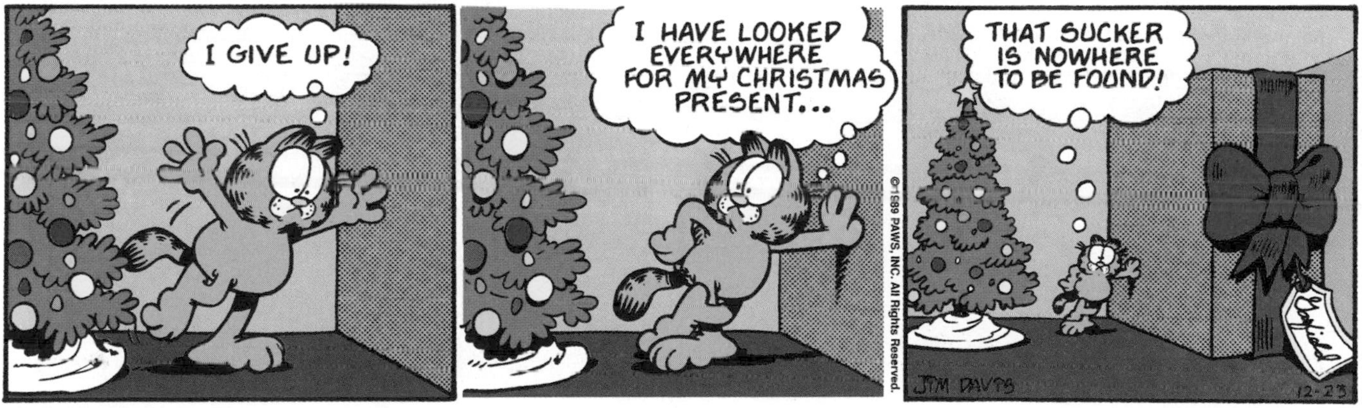
I GIVE UP!
I HAVE LOOKED EVERYWHERE FOR MY CHRISTMAS PRESENT...
© 1989 PAWS, INC. All Rights Reserved.
THAT SUCKER IS NOWHERE TO BE FOUND!
Garfield
JIM DAVIS
12-23

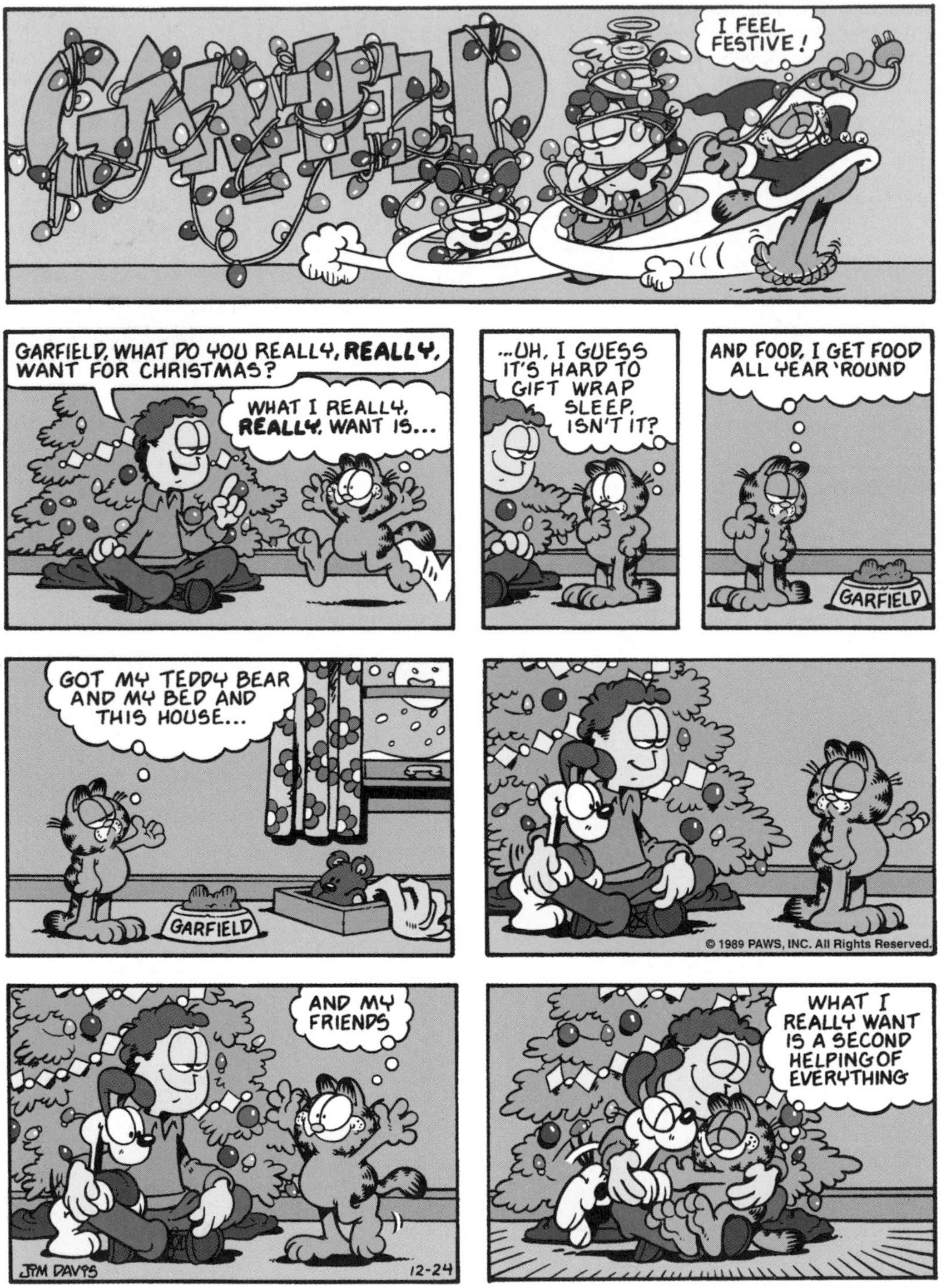
I FEEL FESTIVE!
GARFIELD, WHAT DO YOU REALLY, **REALLY**, WANT FOR CHRISTMAS?
WHAT I REALLY, **REALLY**, WANT IS...
...UH, I GUESS IT'S HARD TO GIFT WRAP SLEEP, ISN'T IT?
AND FOOD, I GET FOOD ALL YEAR 'ROUND
GARFIELD
GOT MY TEDDY BEAR AND MY BED AND THIS HOUSE...
GARFIELD
© 1989 PAWS, INC. All Rights Reserved.
AND MY FRIENDS
JIM DAVIS
12-24
WHAT I REALLY WANT IS A SECOND HELPING OF EVERYTHING

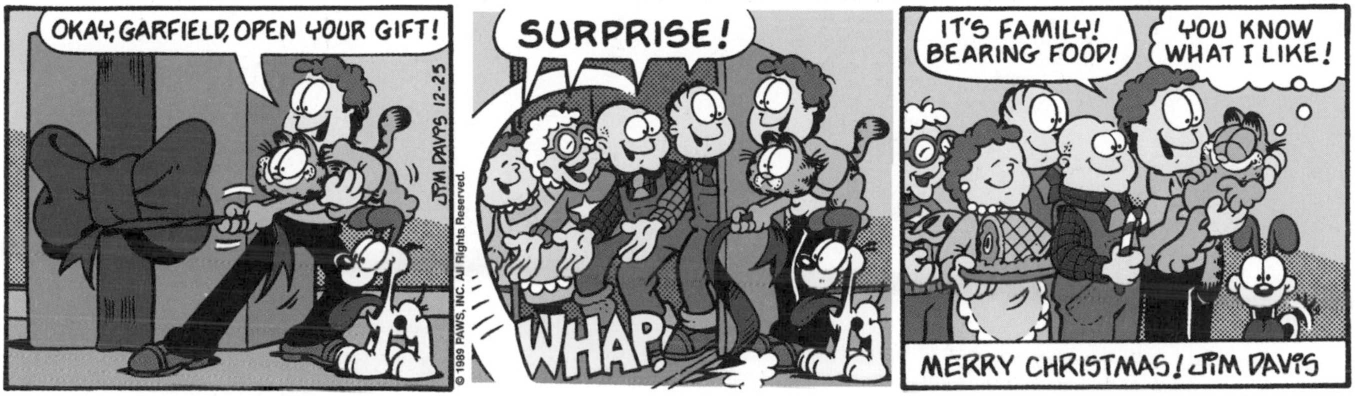
OKAY, GARFIELD, OPEN YOUR GIFT!
JIM DAVIS 12-25
© 1989 PAWS, INC. All Rights Reserved.
SURPRISE!
WHAP!
IT'S FAMILY! BEARING FOOD!
YOU KNOW WHAT I LIKE!
MERRY CHRISTMAS! JIM DAVIS

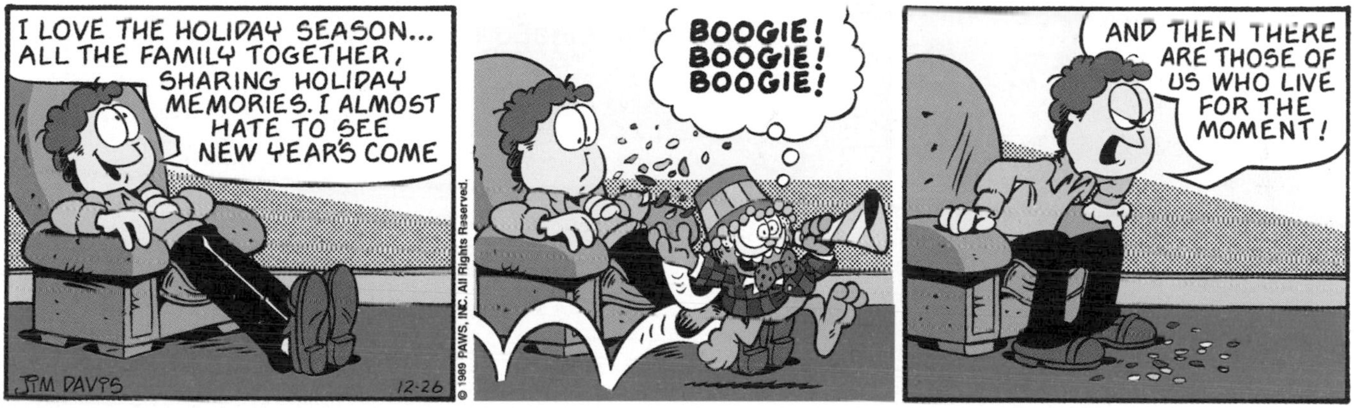
I LOVE THE HOLIDAY SEASON... ALL THE FAMILY TOGETHER, SHARING HOLIDAY MEMORIES. I ALMOST HATE TO SEE NEW YEAR'S COME
JIM DAVIS
12-26
© 1989 PAWS, INC. All Rights Reserved.
BOOGIE! BOOGIE! BOOGIE!
AND THEN THERE ARE THOSE OF US WHO LIVE FOR THE MOMENT!

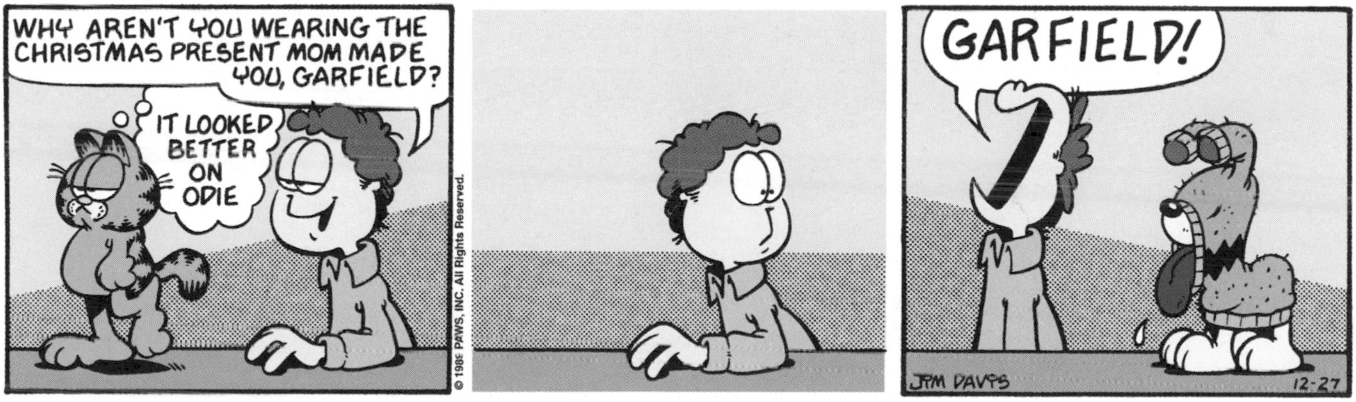
WHY AREN'T YOU WEARING THE CHRISTMAS PRESENT MOM MADE YOU, GARFIELD?
IT LOOKED BETTER ON ODIE
© 1989 PAWS, INC. All Rights Reserved.
GARFIELD!
JIM DAVIS
12-27

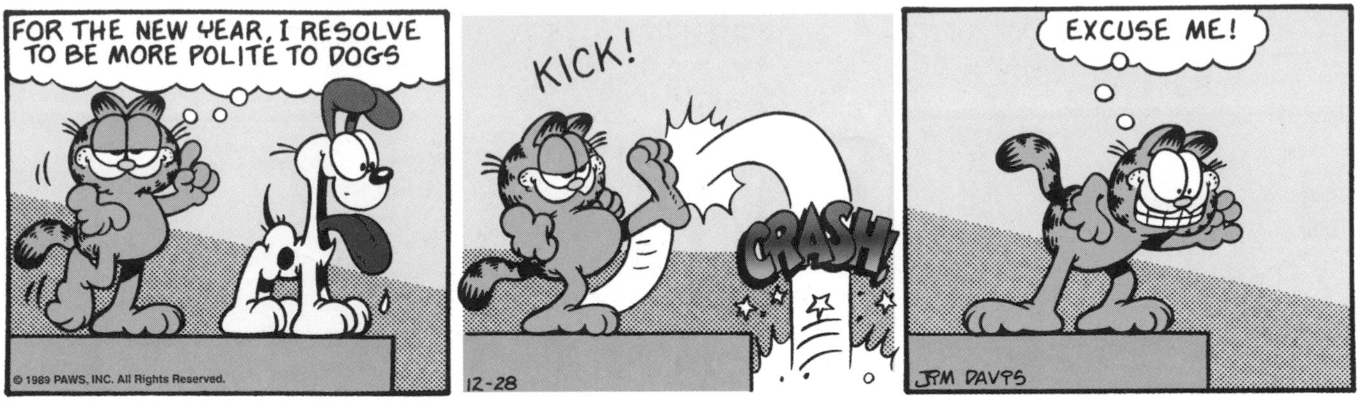
FOR THE NEW YEAR, I RESOLVE TO BE MORE POLITE TO DOGS
© 1989 PAWS, INC. All Rights Reserved.
KICK!
CRASH!
12-28
EXCUSE ME!
JIM DAVIS

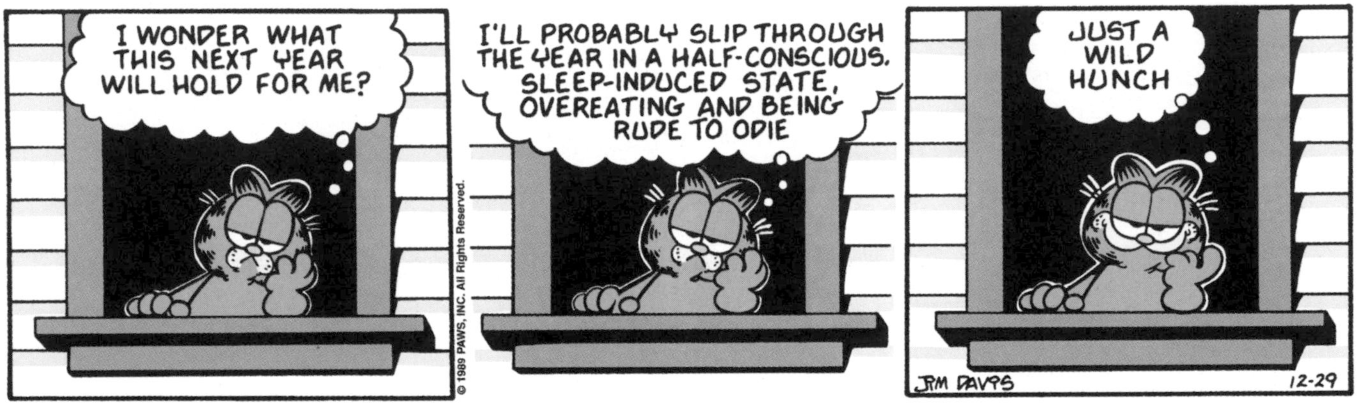
I WONDER WHAT THIS NEXT YEAR WILL HOLD FOR ME?
© 1989 PAWS, INC. All Rights Reserved.
I'LL PROBABLY SLIP THROUGH THE YEAR IN A HALF-CONSCIOUS, SLEEP-INDUCED STATE, OVEREATING AND BEING RUDE TO ODIE
JUST A WILD HUNCH
JIM DAVIS
12-29

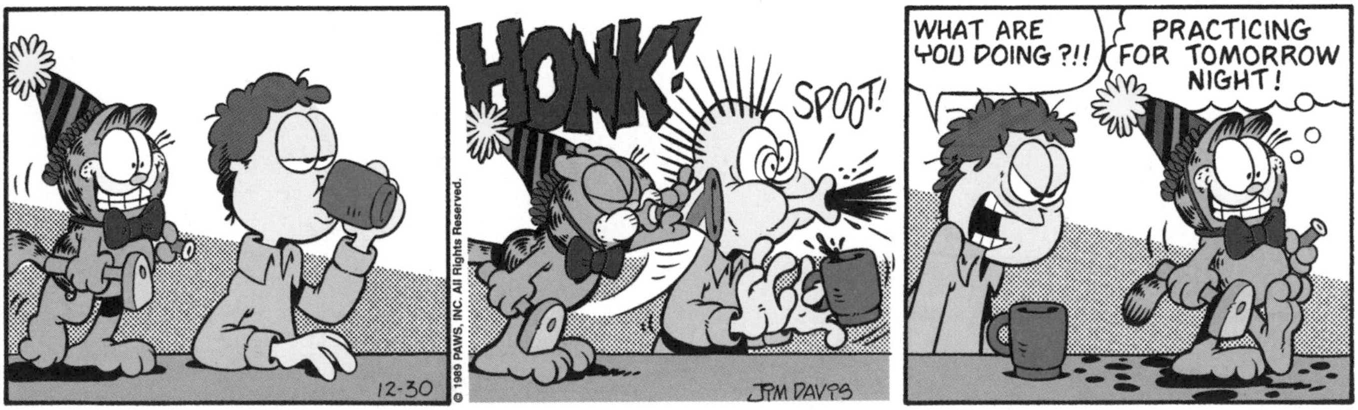
12-30
© 1989 PAWS, INC. All Rights Reserved.
HONK!
SPOOT!
JIM DAVIS
WHAT ARE YOU DOING ?!!
PRACTICING FOR TOMORROW NIGHT!

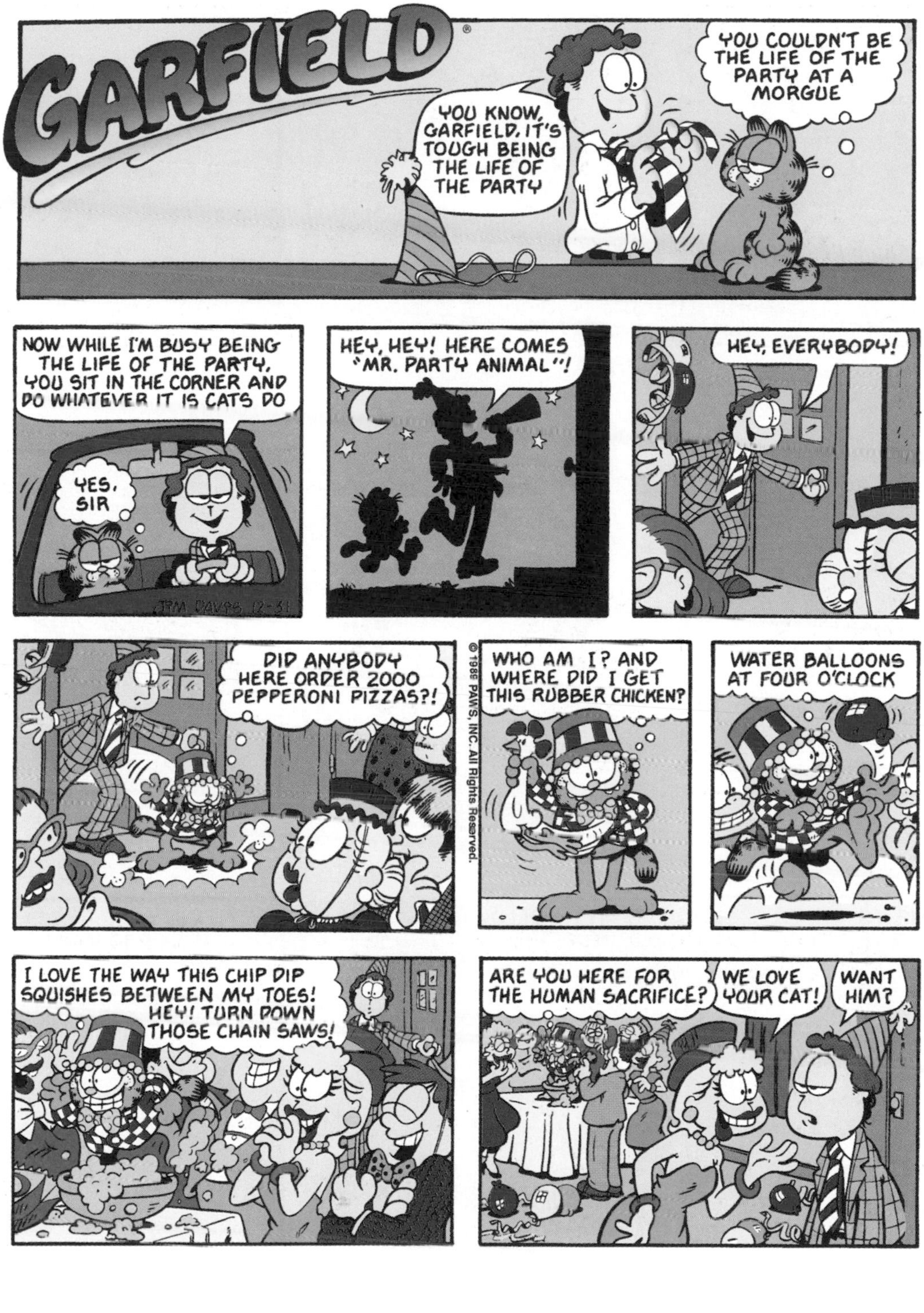
GARFIELD®
YOU KNOW, GARFIELD, IT'S TOUGH BEING THE LIFE OF THE PARTY
YOU COULDN'T BE THE LIFE OF THE PARTY AT A MORGUE
NOW WHILE I'M BUSY BEING THE LIFE OF THE PARTY, YOU SIT IN THE CORNER AND DO WHATEVER IT IS CATS DO
YES, SIR
JIM DAVIS 12-31
HEY, HEY! HERE COMES "MR. PARTY ANIMAL"!
HEY, EVERYBODY!
DID ANYBODY HERE ORDER 2000 PEPPERONI PIZZAS?!
© 1986 PAWS, INC. All Rights Reserved.
WHO AM I? AND WHERE DID I GET THIS RUBBER CHICKEN?
WATER BALLOONS AT FOUR O'CLOCK
I LOVE THE WAY THIS CHIP DIP SQUISHES BETWEEN MY TOES!
HEY! TURN DOWN THOSE CHAIN SAWS!
ARE YOU HERE FOR THE HUMAN SACRIFICE?
WE LOVE YOUR CAT!
WANT HIM?

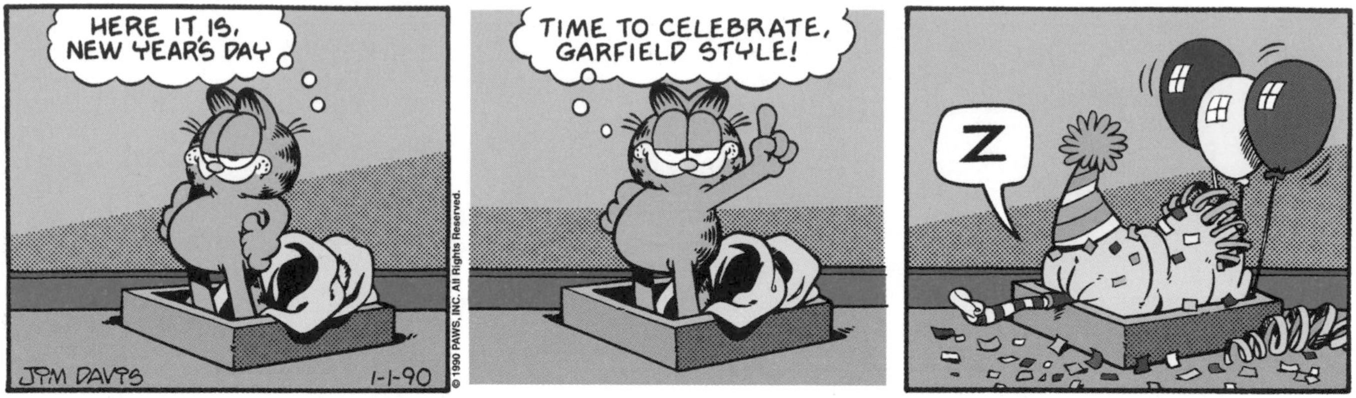
HERE IT IS, NEW YEAR'S DAY
JIM DAVIS
1-1-90
© 1990 PAWS, INC. All Rights Reserved.
TIME TO CELEBRATE, GARFIELD STYLE!
Z

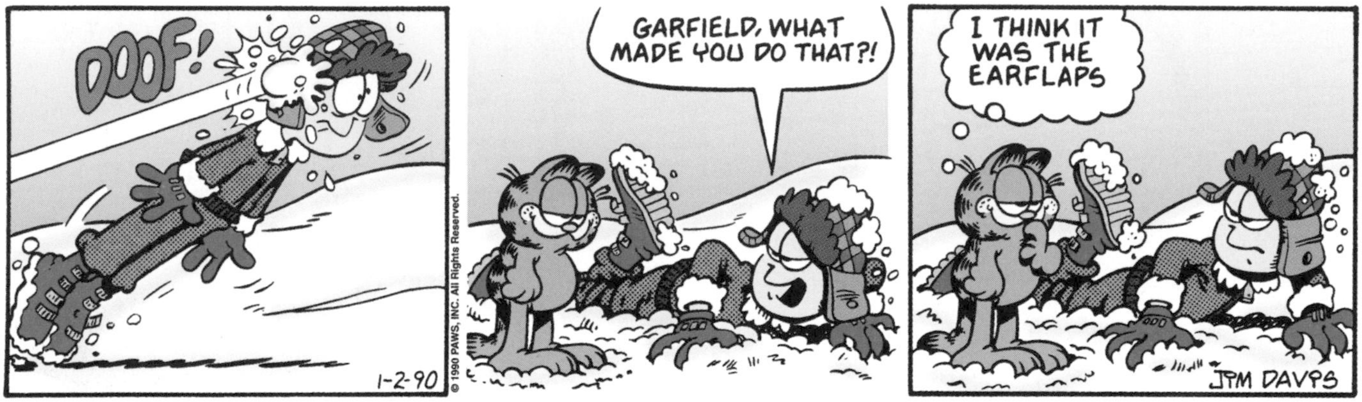
DOOF!
1-2-90
© 1990 PAWS, INC. All Rights Reserved.
GARFIELD, WHAT MADE YOU DO THAT?!
I THINK IT WAS THE EARFLAPS
JIM DAVIS

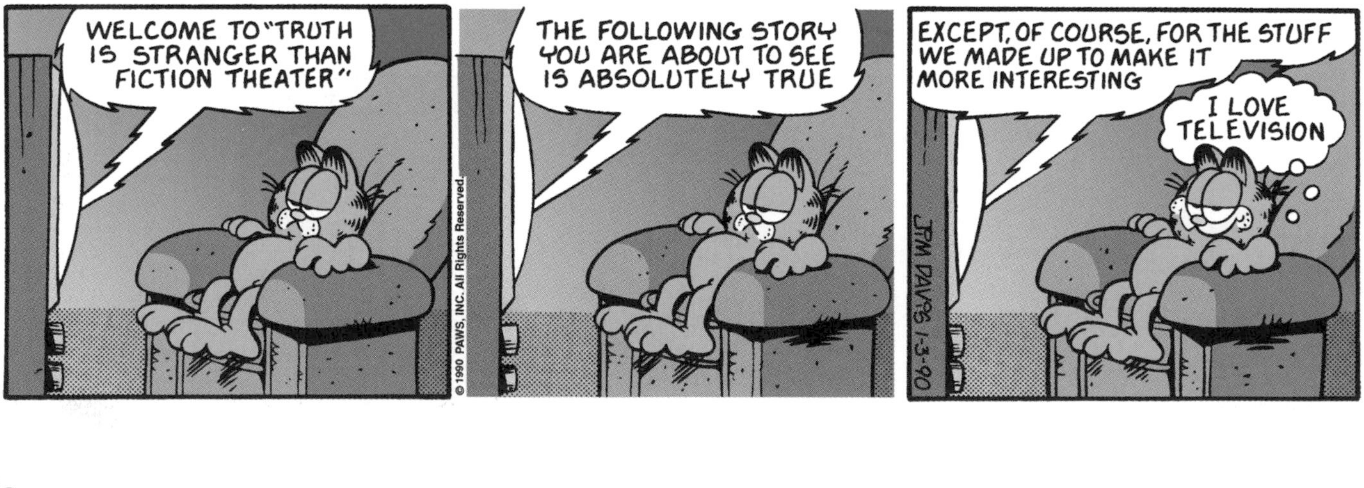
WELCOME TO "TRUTH IS STRANGER THAN FICTION THEATER"
© 1990 PAWS, INC. All Rights Reserved.
THE FOLLOWING STORY YOU ARE ABOUT TO SEE IS ABSOLUTELY TRUE
EXCEPT, OF COURSE, FOR THE STUFF WE MADE UP TO MAKE IT MORE INTERESTING
I LOVE TELEVISION
JIM DAVIS 1-3-90

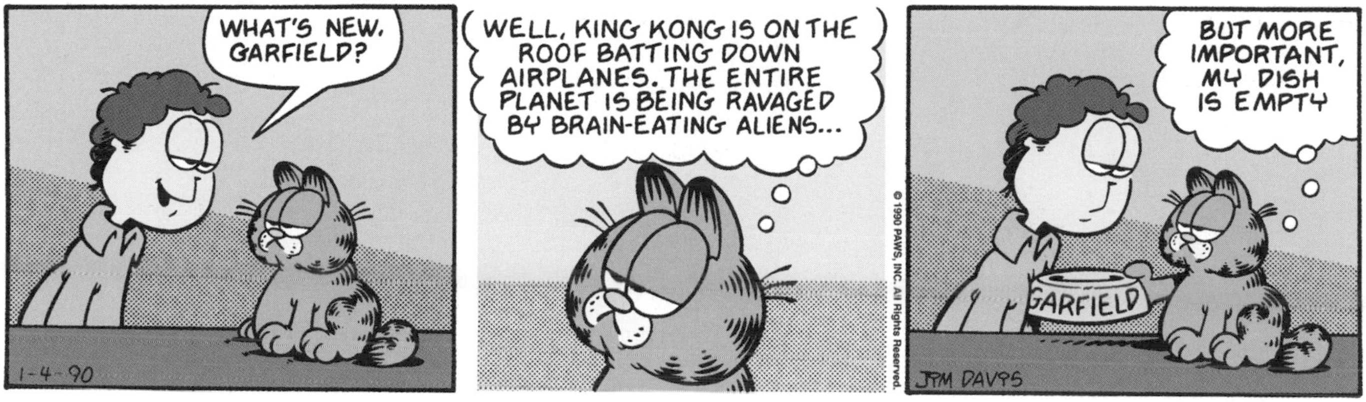
WHAT'S NEW, GARFIELD?
1-4-90
WELL, KING KONG IS ON THE ROOF BATTING DOWN AIRPLANES. THE ENTIRE PLANET IS BEING RAVAGED BY BRAIN-EATING ALIENS...
© 1990 PAWS, INC. All Rights Reserved.
BUT MORE IMPORTANT, MY DISH IS EMPTY
GARFIELD
JIM DAVIS

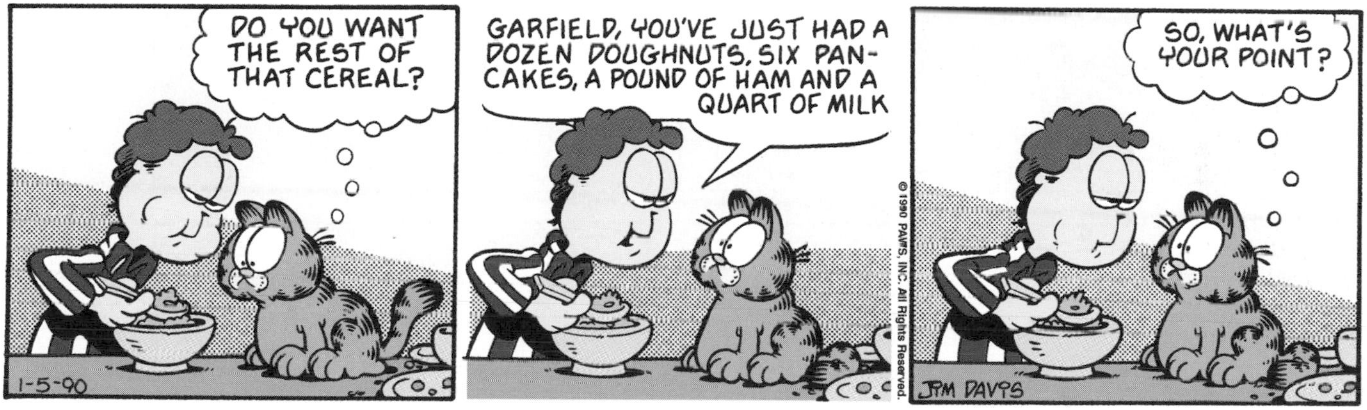
DO YOU WANT THE REST OF THAT CEREAL?
1-5-90
GARFIELD, YOU'VE JUST HAD A DOZEN DOUGHNUTS, SIX PANCAKES, A POUND OF HAM AND A QUART OF MILK
© 1990 PAWS, INC. All Rights Reserved.
SO, WHAT'S YOUR POINT?
JIM DAVIS

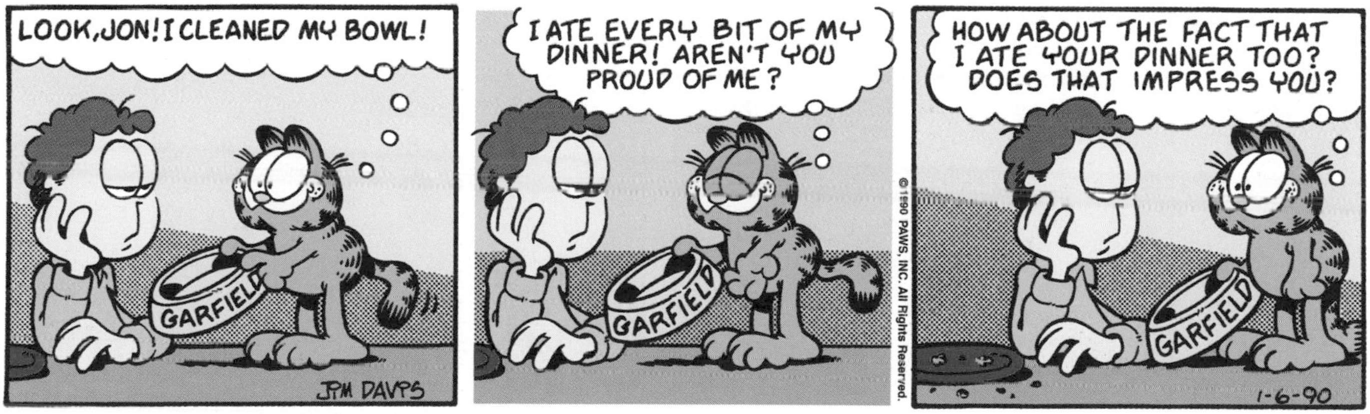
LOOK, JON! I CLEANED MY BOWL!
GARFIELD
JIM DAVIS
I ATE EVERY BIT OF MY DINNER! AREN'T YOU PROUD OF ME?
GARFIELD
© 1990 PAWS, INC. All Rights Reserved.
HOW ABOUT THE FACT THAT I ATE YOUR DINNER TOO? DOES THAT IMPRESS YOU?
GARFIELD
1-6-90

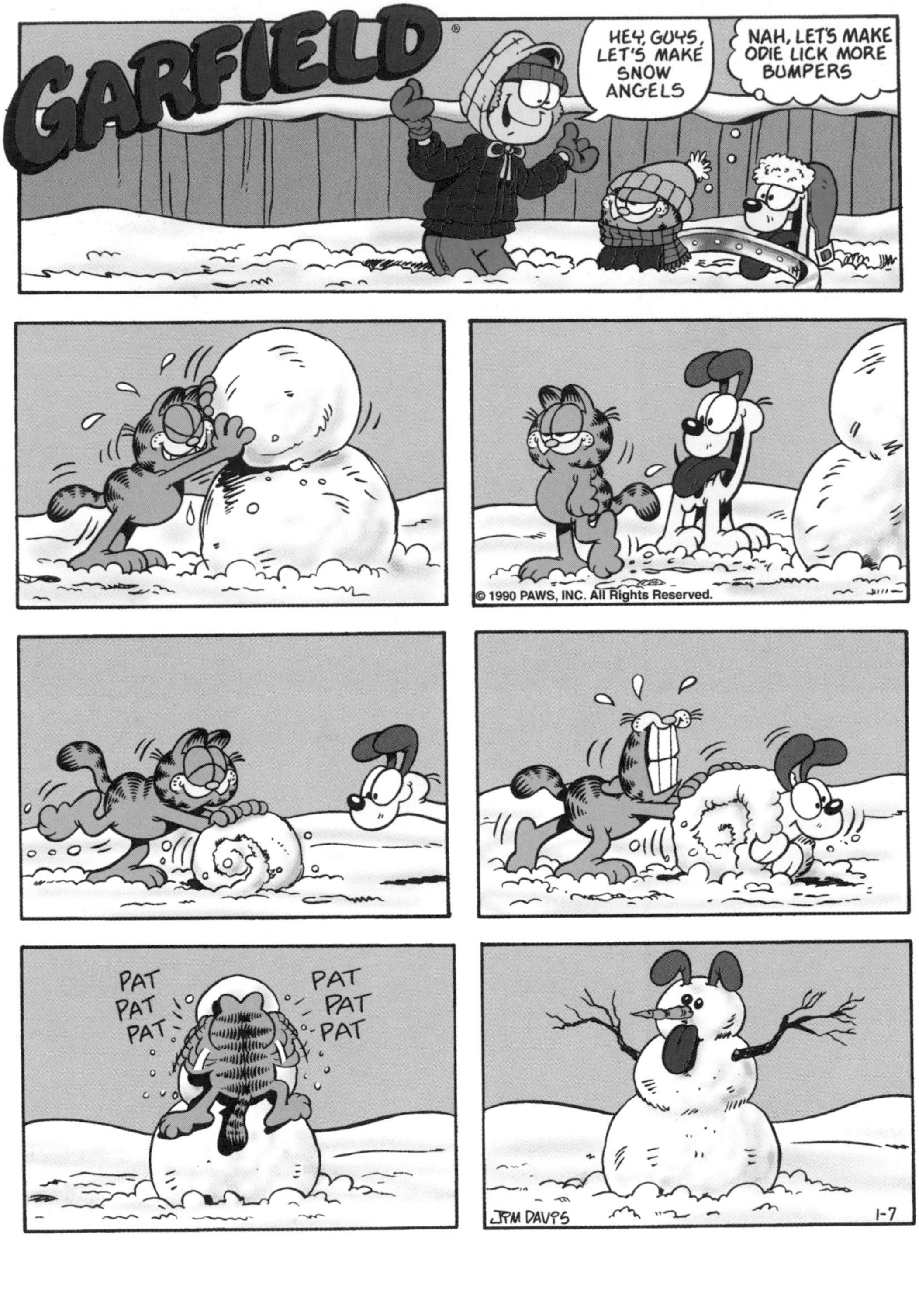
GARFIELD®
HEY, GUYS, LET'S MAKE SNOW ANGELS
NAH, LET'S MAKE ODIE LICK MORE BUMPERS
© 1990 PAWS, INC. All Rights Reserved.
PAT PAT PAT
PAT PAT PAT
JPM DAVIS
1-7

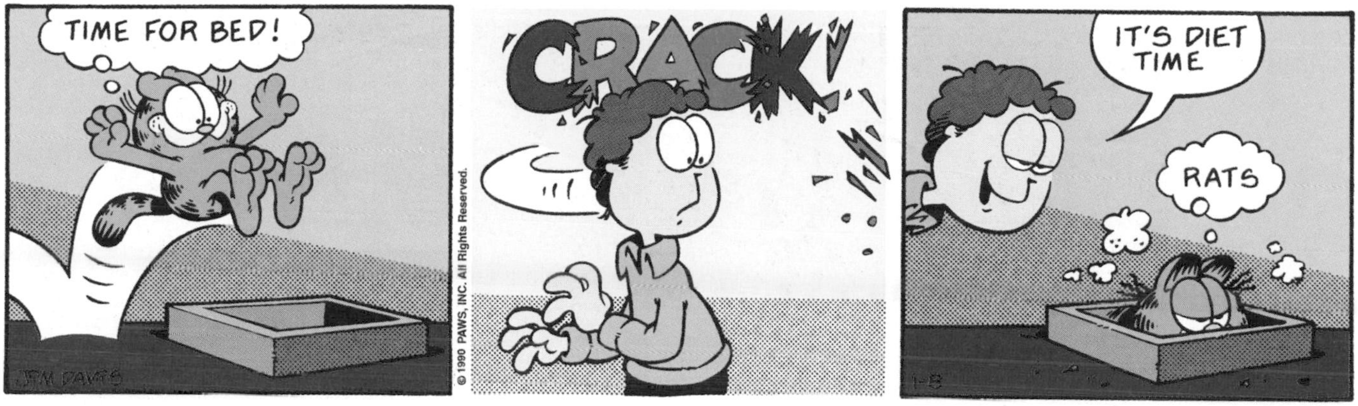
TIME FOR BED!
JIM DAVIS
CRACK!
© 1990 PAWS, INC. All Rights Reserved.
IT'S DIET TIME
RATS
1-8

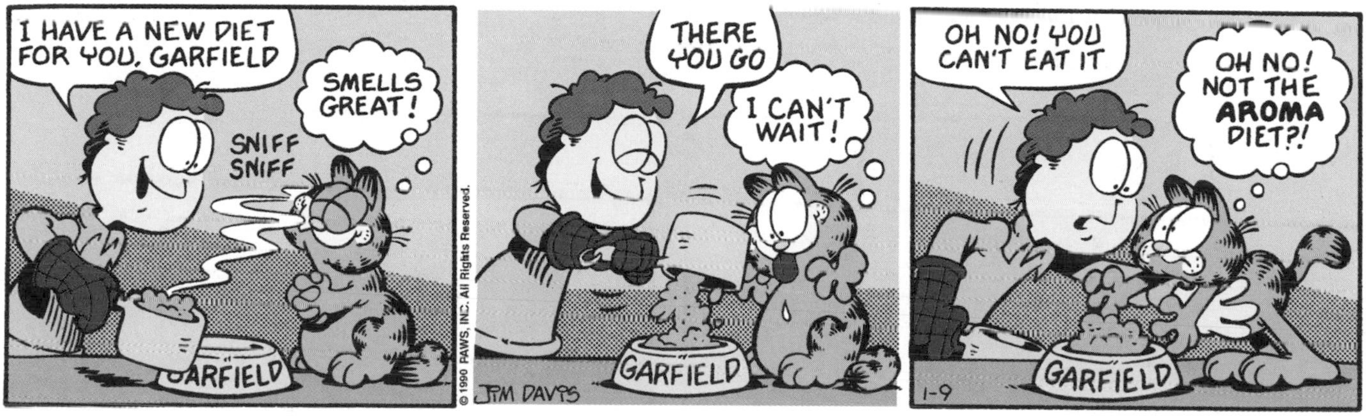
I HAVE A NEW DIET FOR YOU, GARFIELD
SNIFF SNIFF
SMELLS GREAT!
GARFIELD
© 1990 PAWS, INC. All Rights Reserved.
THERE YOU GO
I CAN'T WAIT!
GARFIELD
JIM DAVIS
OH NO! YOU CAN'T EAT IT
OH NO! NOT THE **AROMA** DIET?!
GARFIELD
1-9

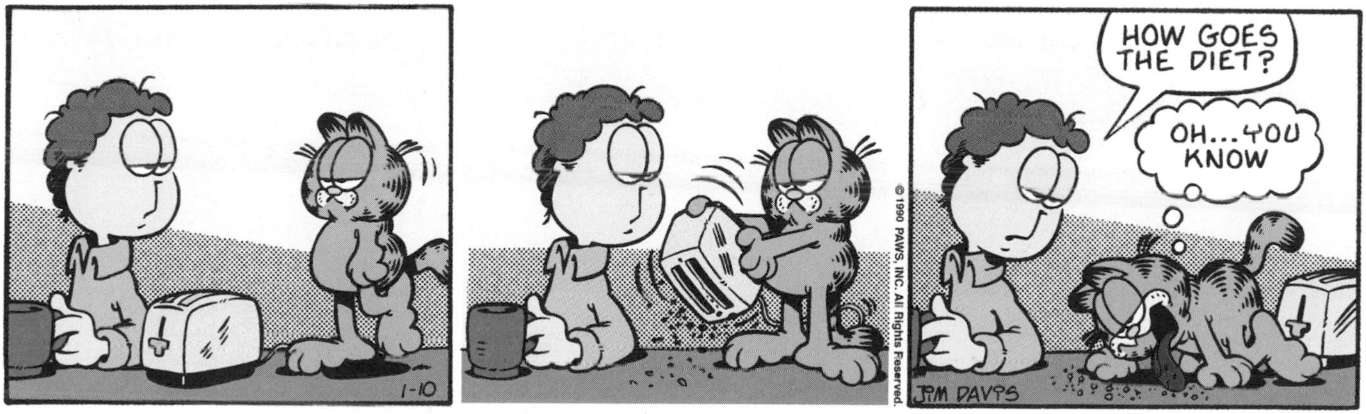
1-10
© 1990 PAWS, INC. All Rights Reserved.
HOW GOES THE DIET?
OH...YOU KNOW
JIM DAVIS

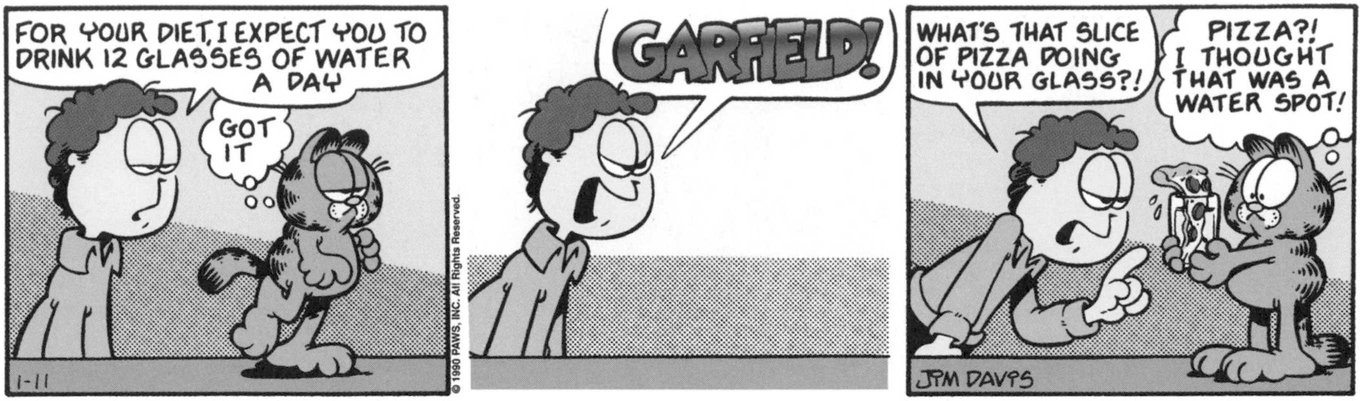
FOR YOUR DIET, I EXPECT YOU TO DRINK 12 GLASSES OF WATER A DAY
GOT IT
GARFIELD!
WHAT'S THAT SLICE OF PIZZA DOING IN YOUR GLASS?!
PIZZA?! I THOUGHT THAT WAS A WATER SPOT!
1-11
JIM DAVIS
© 1990 PAWS, INC. All Rights Reserved.

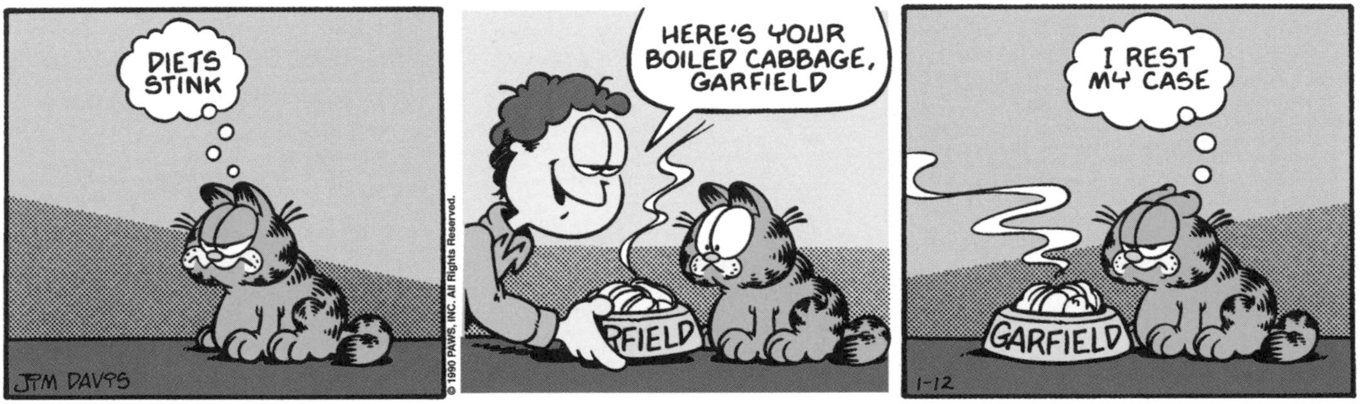
DIETS STINK
JIM DAVIS
HERE'S YOUR BOILED CABBAGE, GARFIELD
RFIELD
I REST MY CASE
GARFIELD
1-12
© 1990 PAWS, INC. All Rights Reserved.

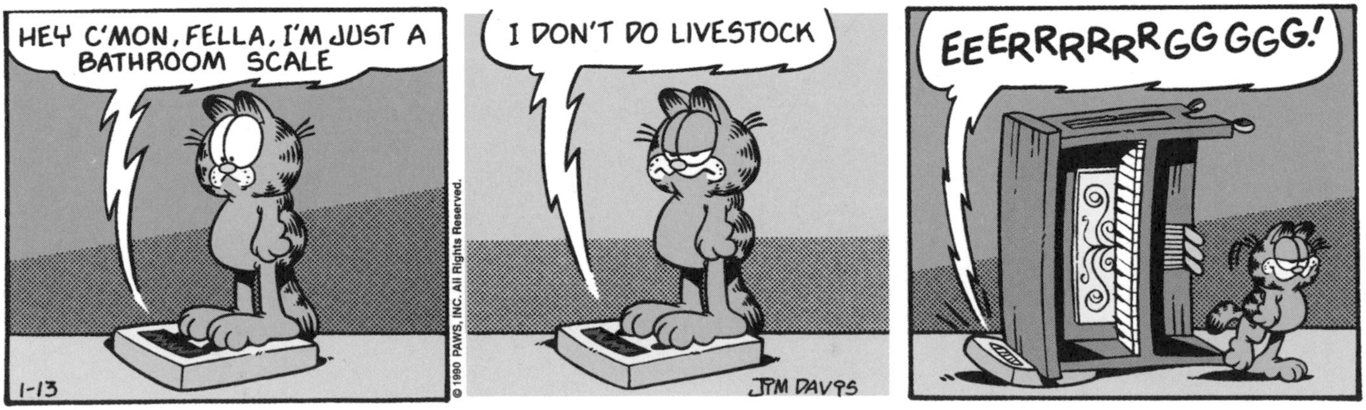
HEY C'MON, FELLA, I'M JUST A BATHROOM SCALE
1-13
I DON'T DO LIVESTOCK
JIM DAVIS
EEERRRRRRGGGGG!
© 1990 PAWS, INC. All Rights Reserved.

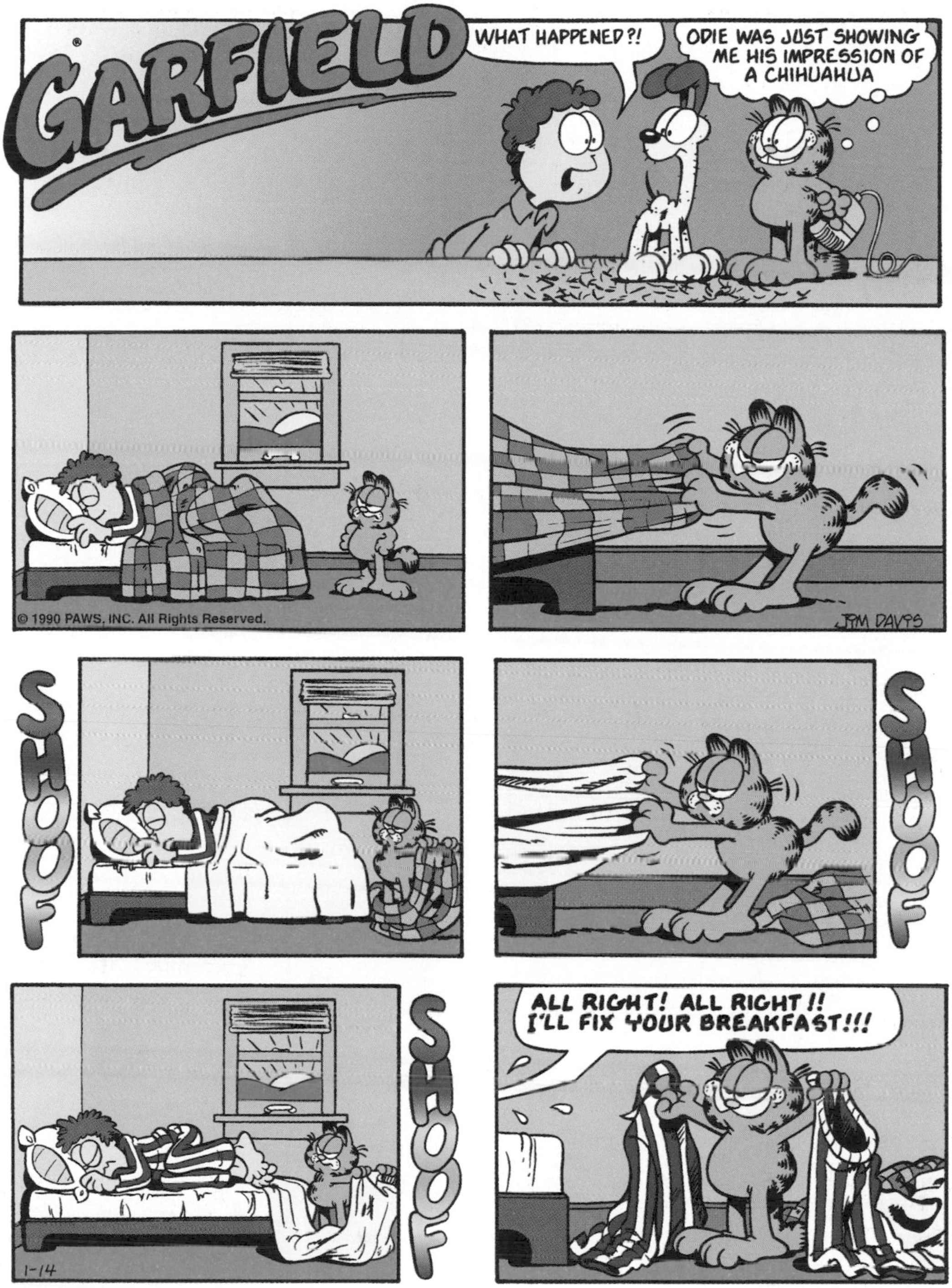
GARFIELD
WHAT HAPPENED?!
ODIE WAS JUST SHOWING ME HIS IMPRESSION OF A CHIHUAHUA
© 1990 PAWS, INC. All Rights Reserved.
JIM DAVIS
SHOOF
SHOOF
SHOOF
1-14
ALL RIGHT! ALL RIGHT!! I'LL FIX YOUR BREAKFAST!!!

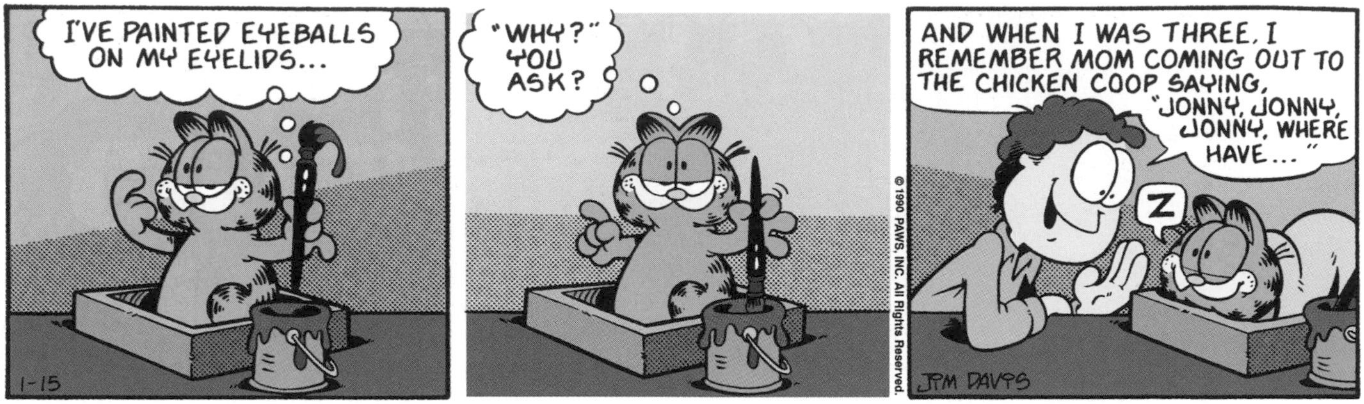
I'VE PAINTED EYEBALLS ON MY EYELIDS...
1-15
"WHY?" YOU ASK?
© 1990 PAWS, INC. All Rights Reserved.
AND WHEN I WAS THREE, I REMEMBER MOM COMING OUT TO THE CHICKEN COOP SAYING, "JONNY, JONNY, JONNY, WHERE HAVE..."
Z
JIM DAVIS

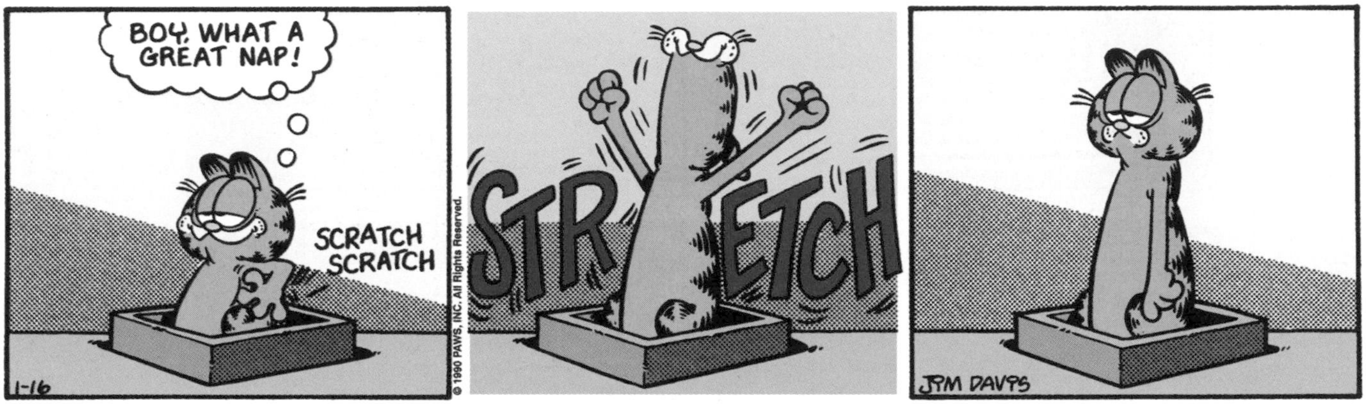
BOY, WHAT A GREAT NAP!
SCRATCH SCRATCH
1-16
© 1990 PAWS, INC. All Rights Reserved.
STRETCH
JIM DAVIS

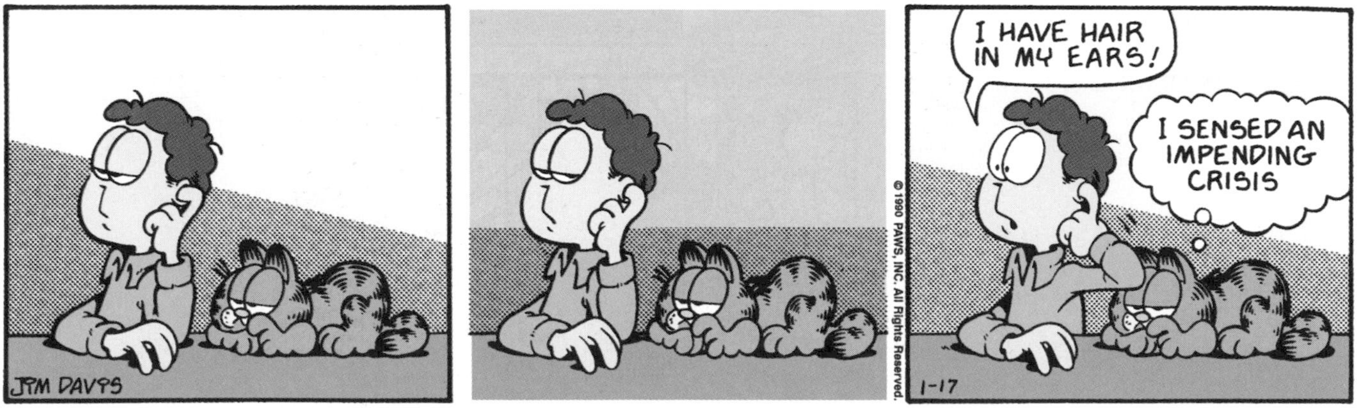
JIM DAVIS
© 1990 PAWS, INC. All Rights Reserved.
I HAVE HAIR IN MY EARS!
I SENSED AN IMPENDING CRISIS
1-17

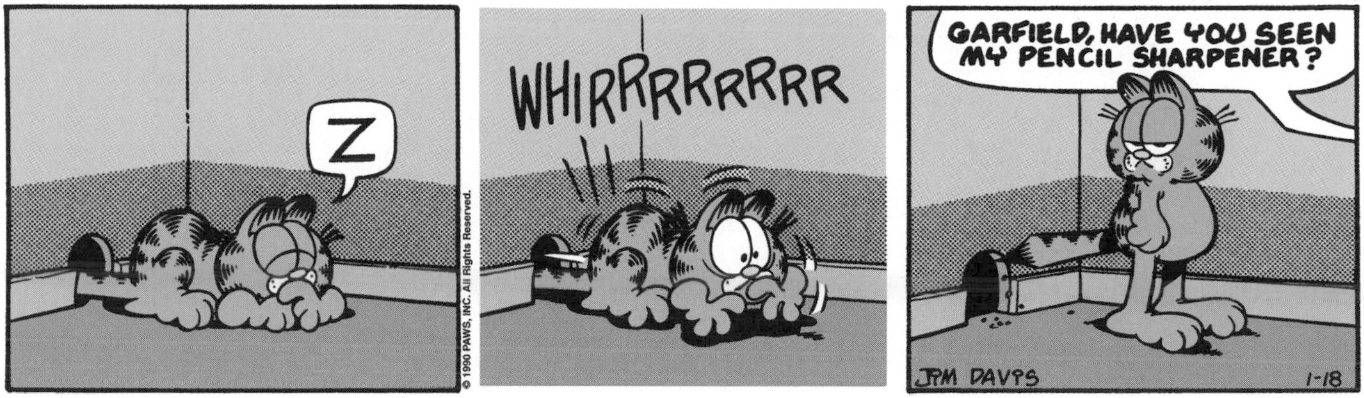
Z
© 1990 PAWS, INC. All Rights Reserved.
WHIRRRRRRRR
GARFIELD, HAVE YOU SEEN MY PENCIL SHARPENER?
JPM DAVPS
1-18

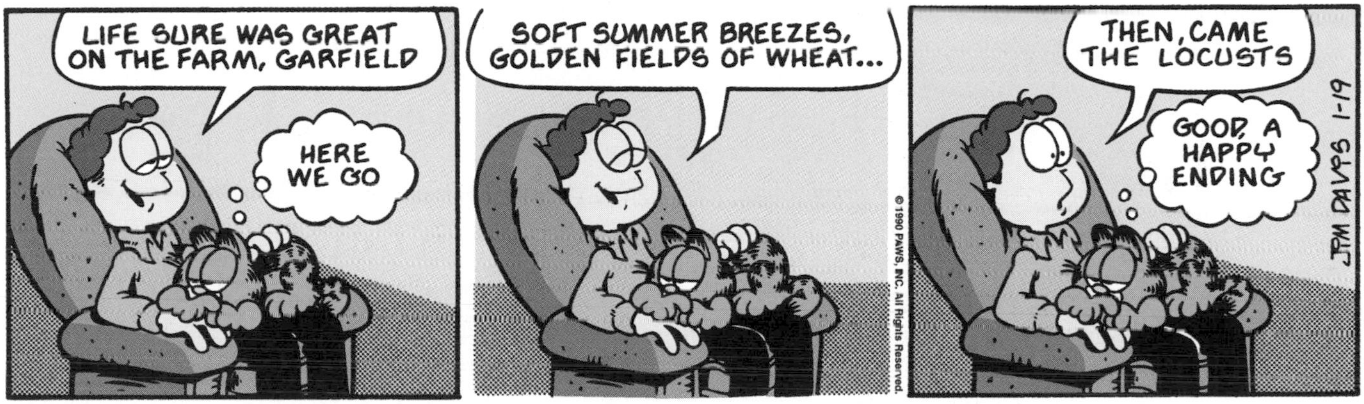
LIFE SURE WAS GREAT ON THE FARM, GARFIELD
HERE WE GO
SOFT SUMMER BREEZES, GOLDEN FIELDS OF WHEAT...
© 1990 PAWS, INC. All Rights Reserved.
THEN, CAME THE LOCUSTS
GOOD, A HAPPY ENDING
JPM DAVPS 1-19

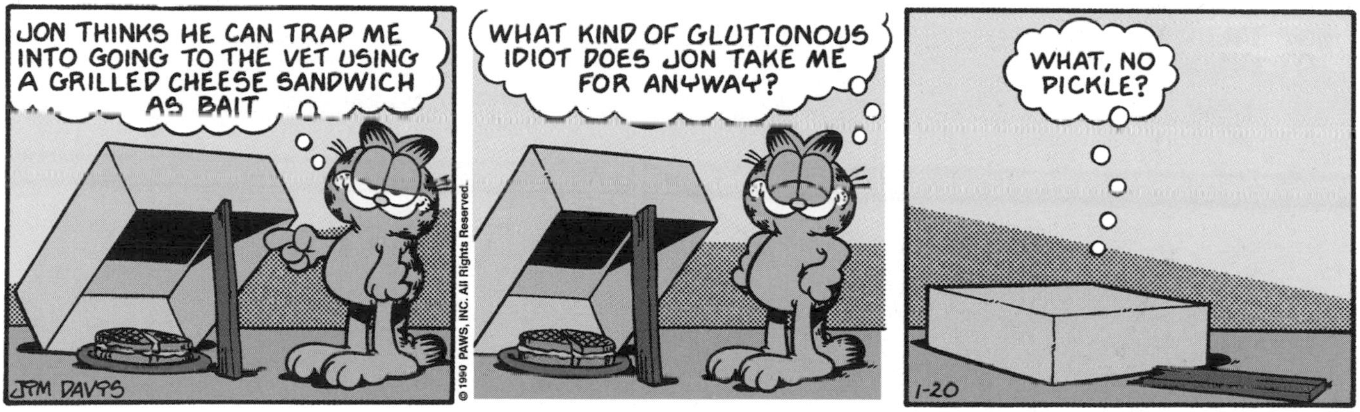
JON THINKS HE CAN TRAP ME INTO GOING TO THE VET USING A GRILLED CHEESE SANDWICH AS BAIT
JPM DAVPS
© 1990 PAWS, INC. All Rights Reserved.
WHAT KIND OF GLUTTONOUS IDIOT DOES JON TAKE ME FOR ANYWAY?
WHAT, NO PICKLE?
1-20

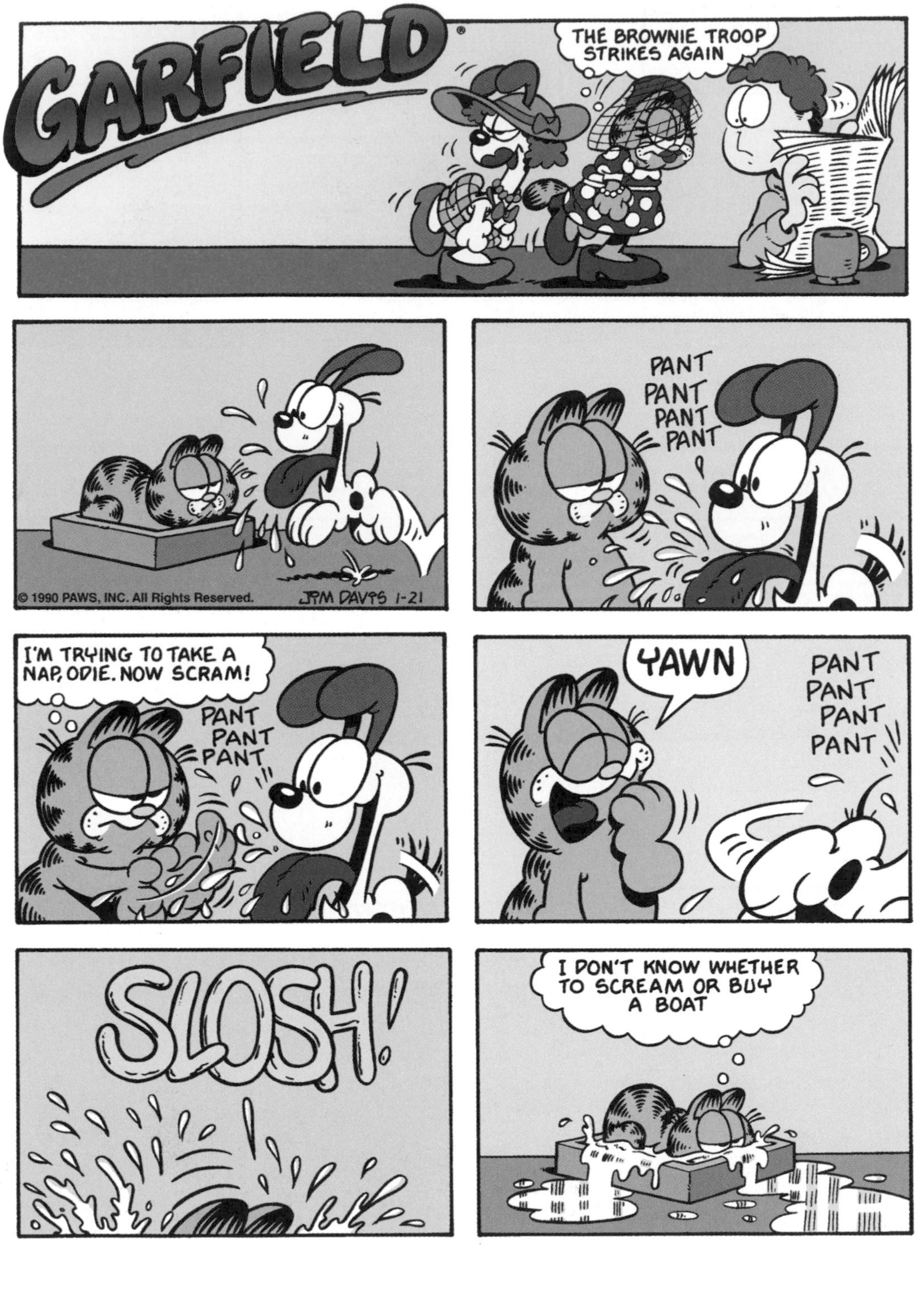
GARFIELD®
THE BROWNIE TROOP STRIKES AGAIN
© 1990 PAWS, INC. All Rights Reserved.
JIM DAVIS 1-21
PANT PANT PANT PANT
I'M TRYING TO TAKE A NAP, ODIE. NOW SCRAM!
PANT PANT PANT
YAWN
PANT PANT PANT PANT
SLOSH!
I DON'T KNOW WHETHER TO SCREAM OR BUY A BOAT

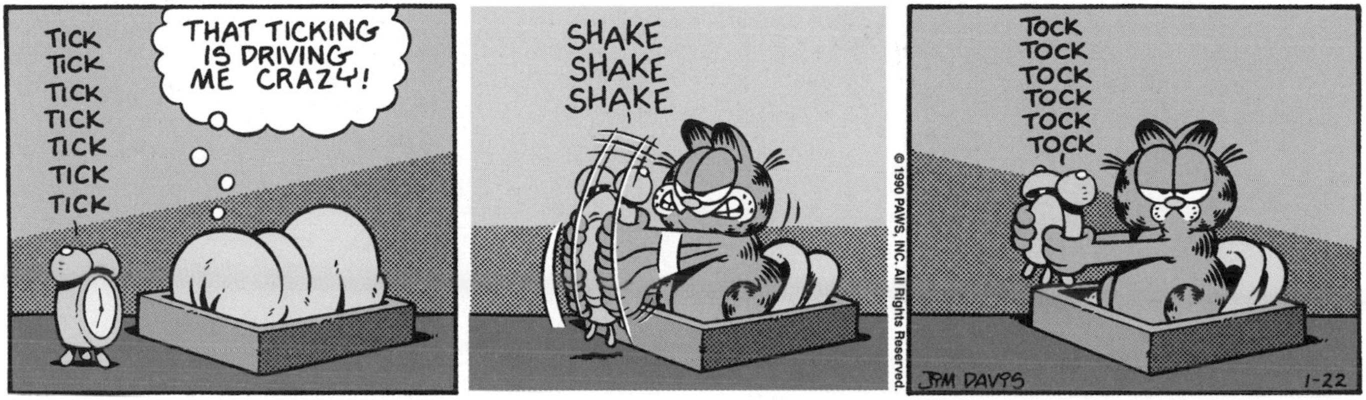
TICK TICK TICK TICK TICK TICK TICK
THAT TICKING IS DRIVING ME CRAZY!
SHAKE SHAKE SHAKE
© 1990 PAWS, INC. All Rights Reserved.
TOCK TOCK TOCK TOCK TOCK TOCK
JIM DAVIS
1-22

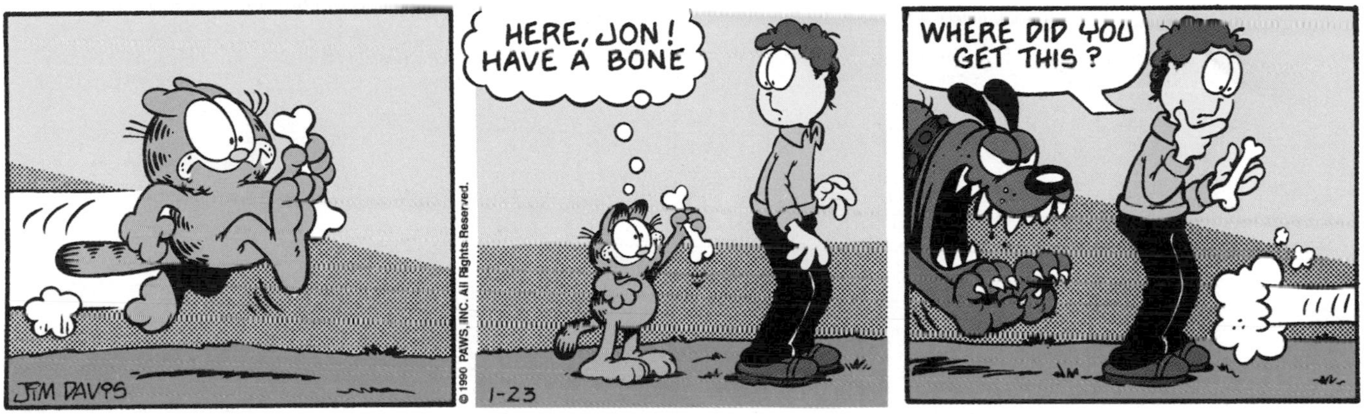
JIM DAVIS
© 1990 PAWS, INC. All Rights Reserved.
HERE, JON! HAVE A BONE
1-23
WHERE DID YOU GET THIS ?

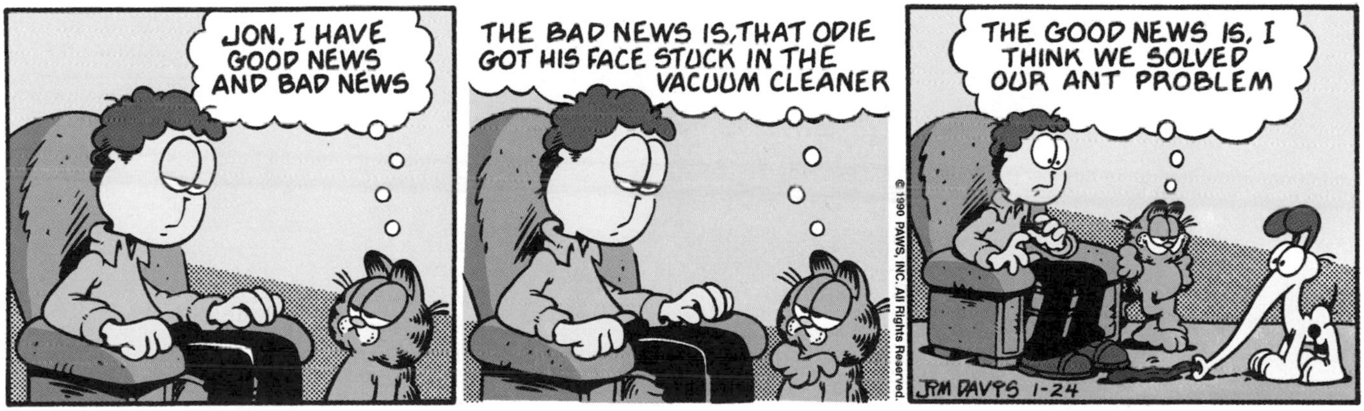
JON, I HAVE GOOD NEWS AND BAD NEWS
THE BAD NEWS IS, THAT ODIE GOT HIS FACE STUCK IN THE VACUUM CLEANER
© 1990 PAWS, INC. All Rights Reserved.
THE GOOD NEWS IS, I THINK WE SOLVED OUR ANT PROBLEM
JIM DAVIS 1-24

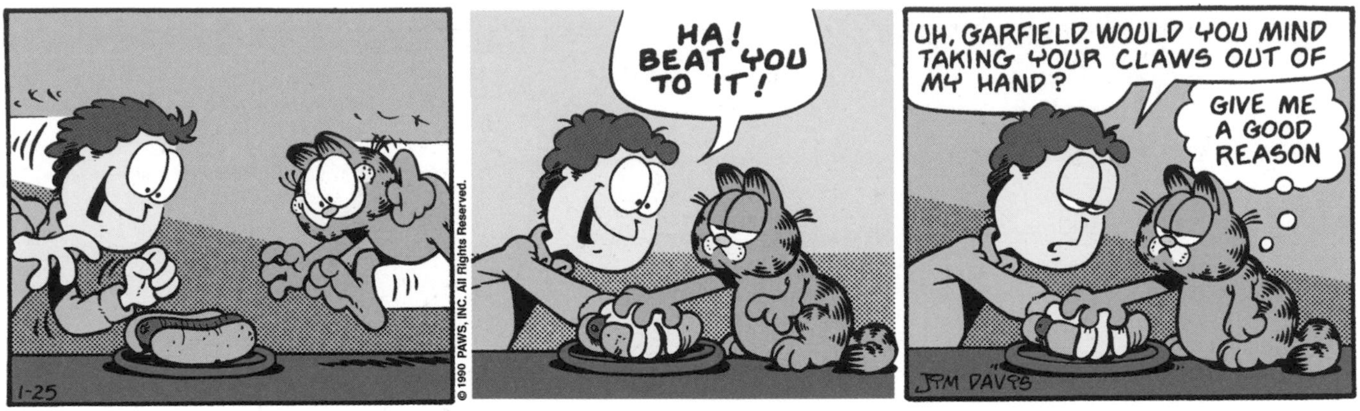
1-25
HA! BEAT YOU TO IT!
UH, GARFIELD. WOULD YOU MIND TAKING YOUR CLAWS OUT OF MY HAND?
GIVE ME A GOOD REASON
JIM DAVIS
© 1990 PAWS, INC. All Rights Reserved.

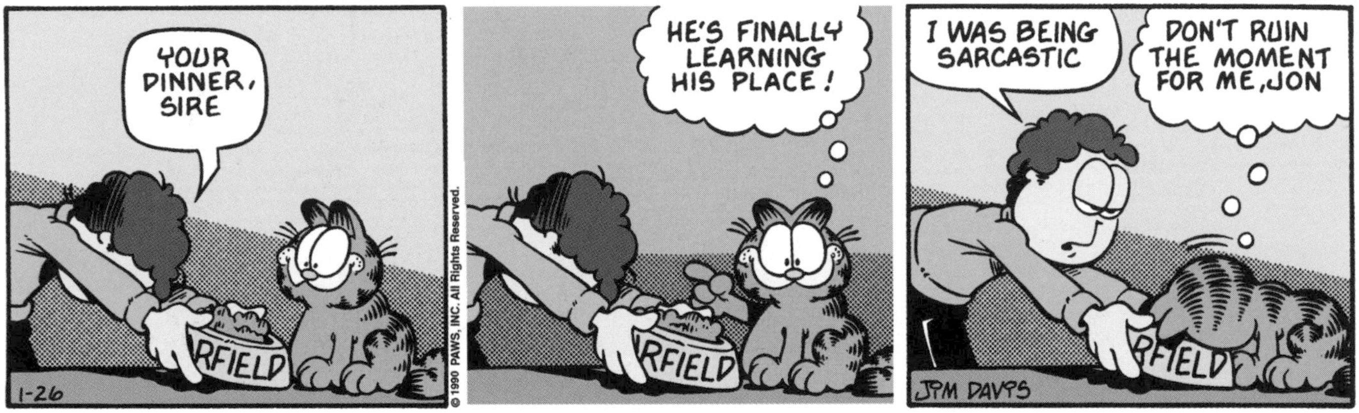
YOUR DINNER, SIRE
RFIELD
1-26
HE'S FINALLY LEARNING HIS PLACE!
I WAS BEING SARCASTIC
DON'T RUIN THE MOMENT FOR ME, JON
JIM DAVIS
© 1990 PAWS, INC. All Rights Reserved.

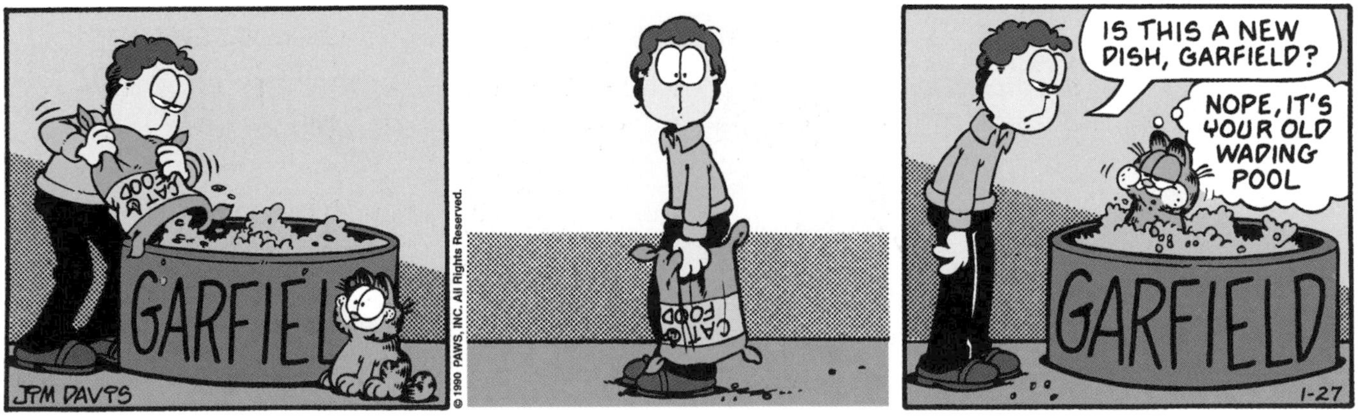
CAT FOOD
GARFIEL
JIM DAVIS
IS THIS A NEW DISH, GARFIELD?
NOPE, IT'S YOUR OLD WADING POOL
GARFIELD
1-27
© 1990 PAWS, INC. All Rights Reserved.

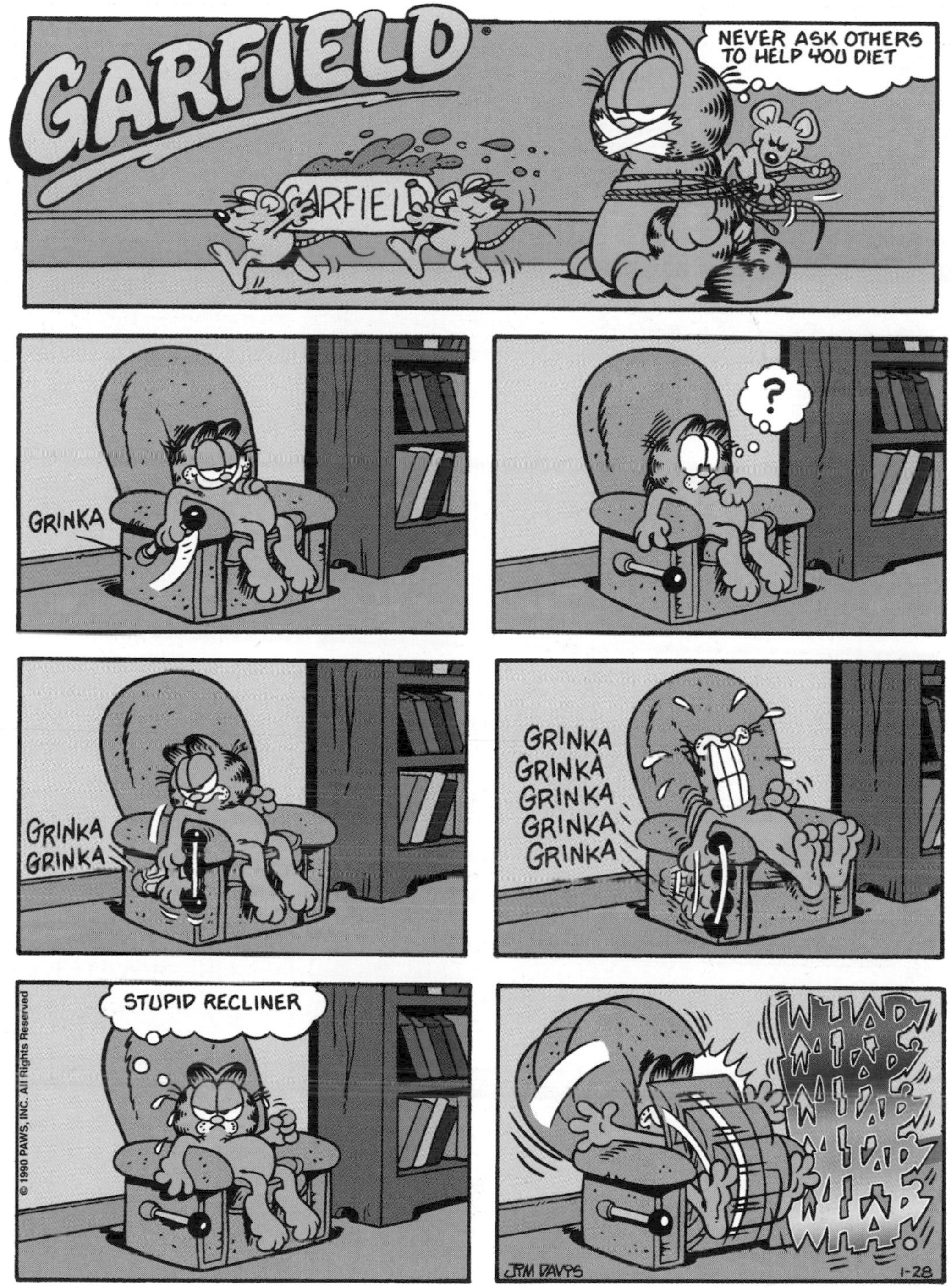
GARFIELD®
GARFIELD
NEVER ASK OTHERS TO HELP YOU DIET
GRINKA
?
GRINKA
GRINKA
GRINKA
GRINKA
GRINKA
GRINKA
GRINKA
© 1990 PAWS, INC. All Rights Reserved
STUPID RECLINER
WHAP
WHAP!
JPM DAVPS
1-28

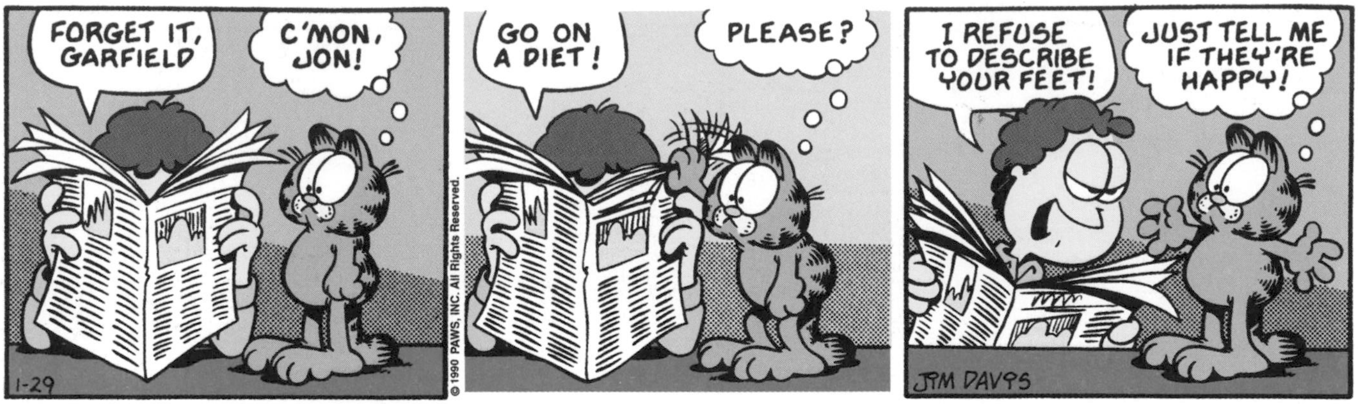
FORGET IT, GARFIELD
C'MON, JON!
1-29
GO ON A DIET!
PLEASE?
© 1990 PAWS, INC. All Rights Reserved.
I REFUSE TO DESCRIBE YOUR FEET!
JUST TELL ME IF THEY'RE HAPPY!

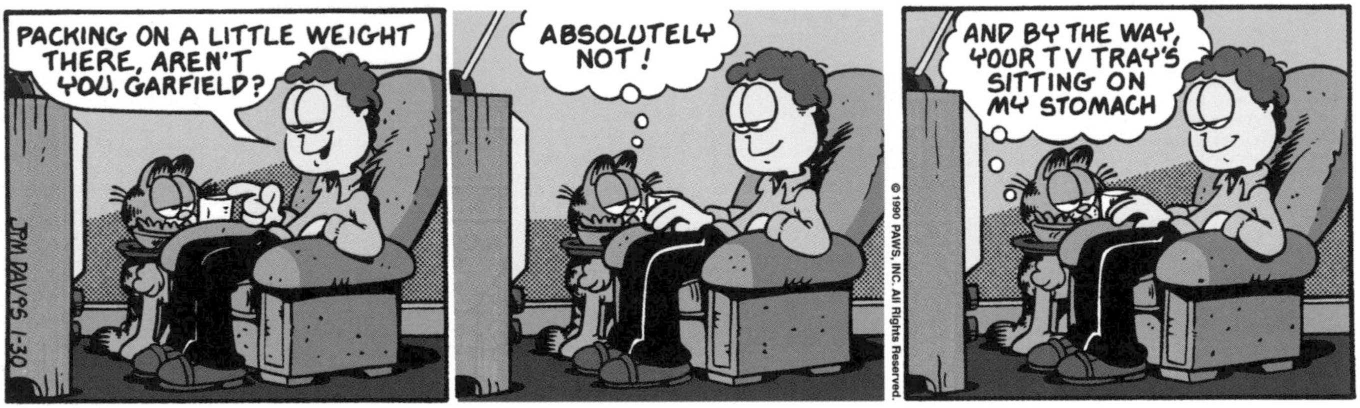
PACKING ON A LITTLE WEIGHT THERE, AREN'T YOU, GARFIELD?
1-30
ABSOLUTELY NOT!
© 1990 PAWS, INC. All Rights Reserved.
AND BY THE WAY, YOUR TV TRAY'S SITTING ON MY STOMACH

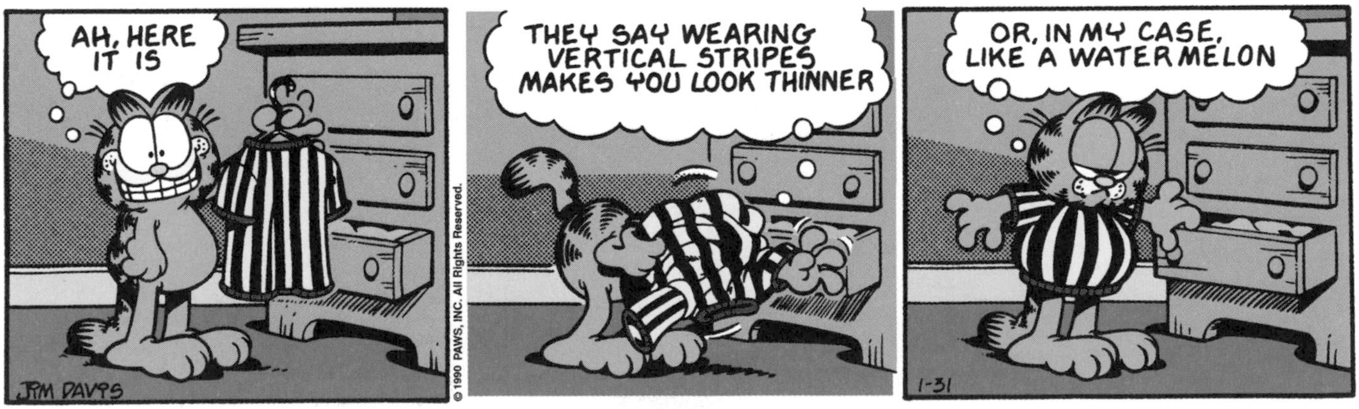
AH, HERE IT IS
© 1990 PAWS, INC. All Rights Reserved.
THEY SAY WEARING VERTICAL STRIPES MAKES YOU LOOK THINNER
OR, IN MY CASE, LIKE A WATERMELON
1-31

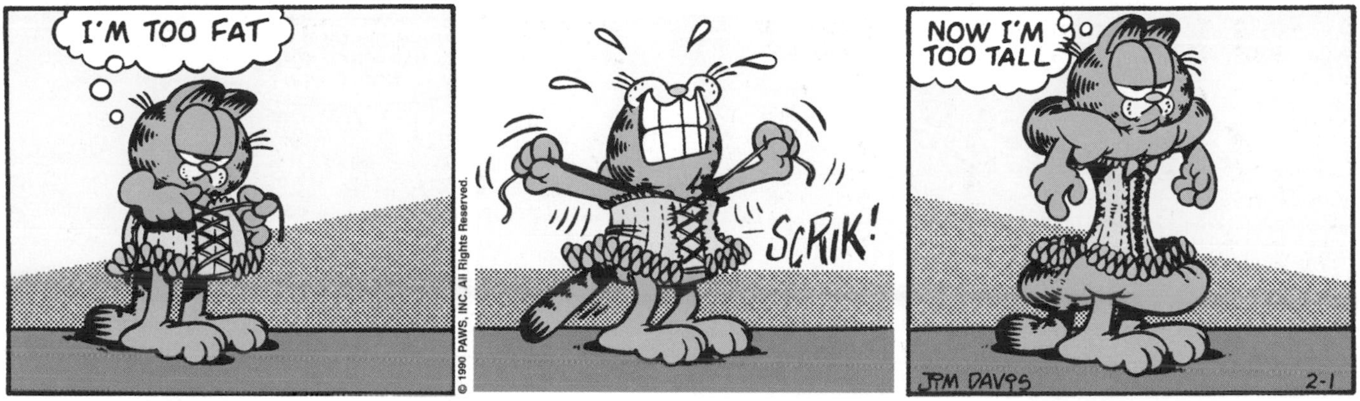
I'M TOO FAT
SCRIK!
NOW I'M TOO TALL
© 1990 PAWS, INC. All Rights Reserved.
JIM DAVIS
2-1

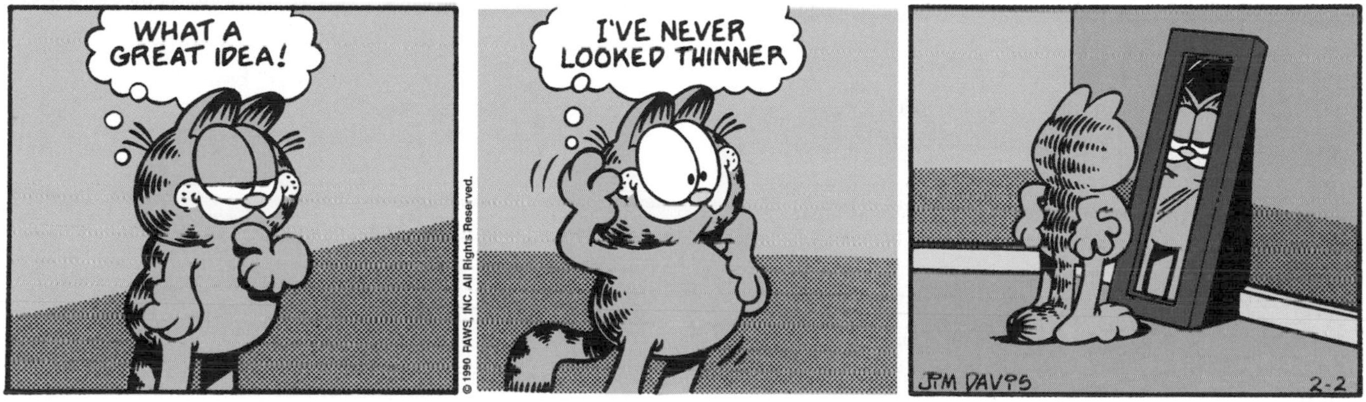
WHAT A GREAT IDEA!
I'VE NEVER LOOKED THINNER
© 1990 PAWS, INC. All Rights Reserved.
JIM DAVIS
2-2

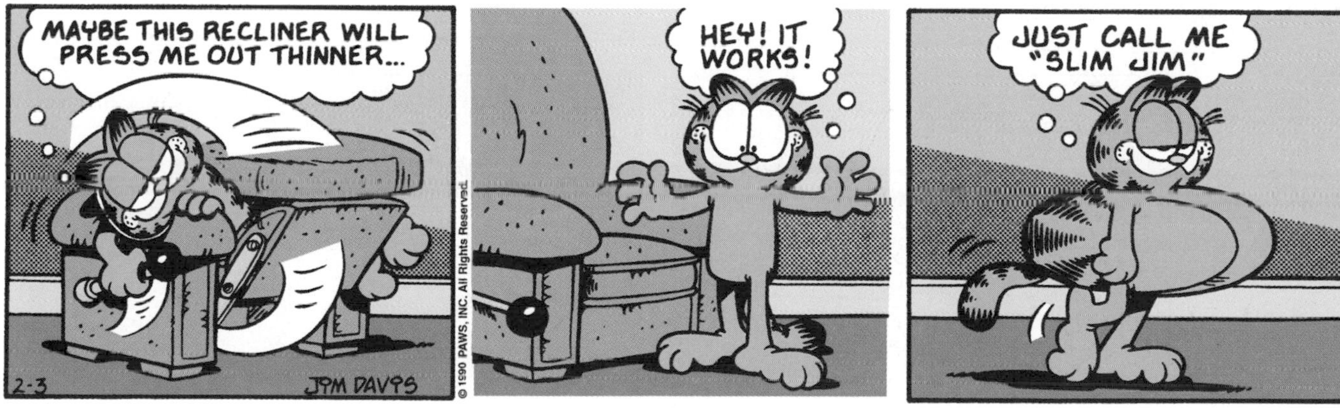
MAYBE THIS RECLINER WILL PRESS ME OUT THINNER...
HEY! IT WORKS!
JUST CALL ME "SLIM JIM"
© 1990 PAWS, INC. All Rights Reserved.
JIM DAVIS
2-3

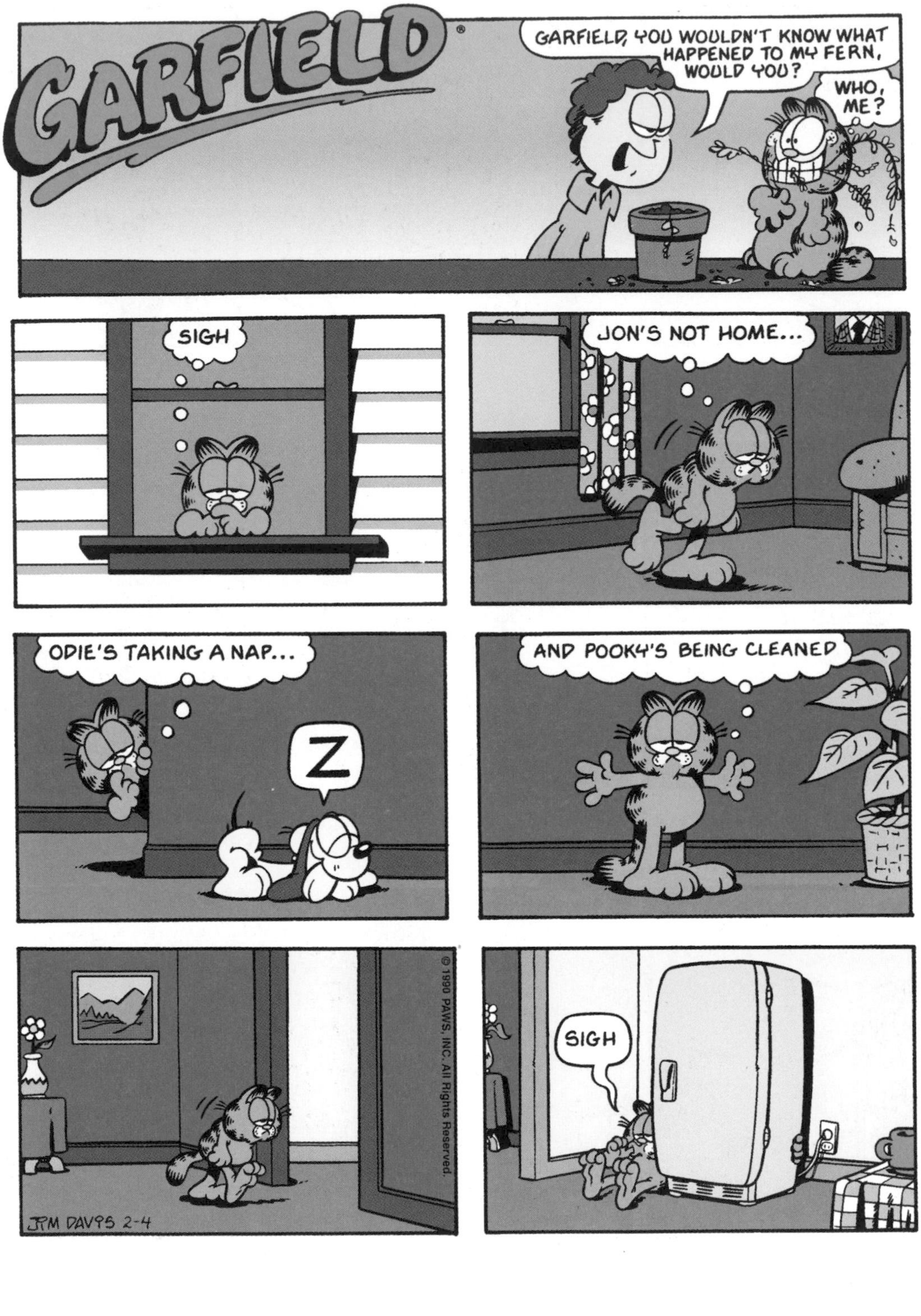
GARFIELD
GARFIELD, YOU WOULDN'T KNOW WHAT HAPPENED TO MY FERN, WOULD YOU?
WHO, ME?
SIGH
JON'S NOT HOME...
ODIE'S TAKING A NAP...
Z
AND POOKY'S BEING CLEANED
© 1990 PAWS, INC. All Rights Reserved.
JIM DAVIS 2-4
SIGH

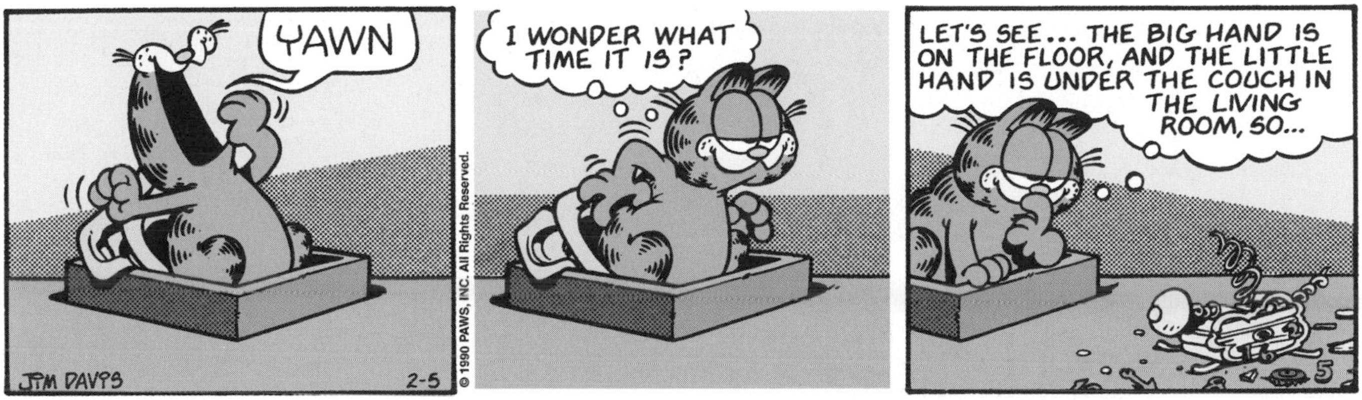
YAWN
JIM DAVIS 2-5
© 1990 PAWS, INC. All Rights Reserved.
I WONDER WHAT TIME IT IS?
LET'S SEE... THE BIG HAND IS ON THE FLOOR, AND THE LITTLE HAND IS UNDER THE COUCH IN THE LIVING ROOM, SO...

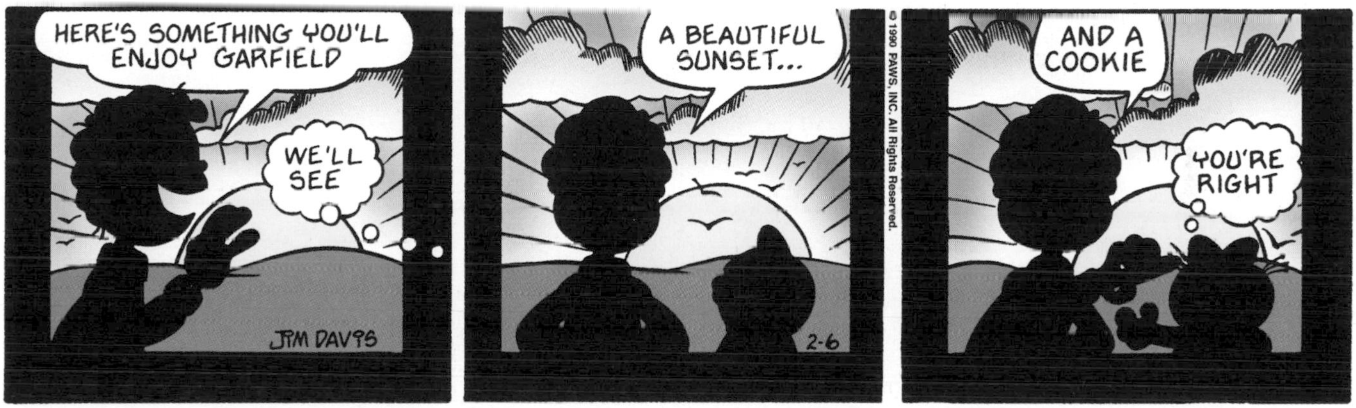
HERE'S SOMETHING YOU'LL ENJOY GARFIELD
WE'LL SEE
JIM DAVIS
A BEAUTIFUL SUNSET...
2-6
© 1990 PAWS, INC. All Rights Reserved.
AND A COOKIE
YOU'RE RIGHT

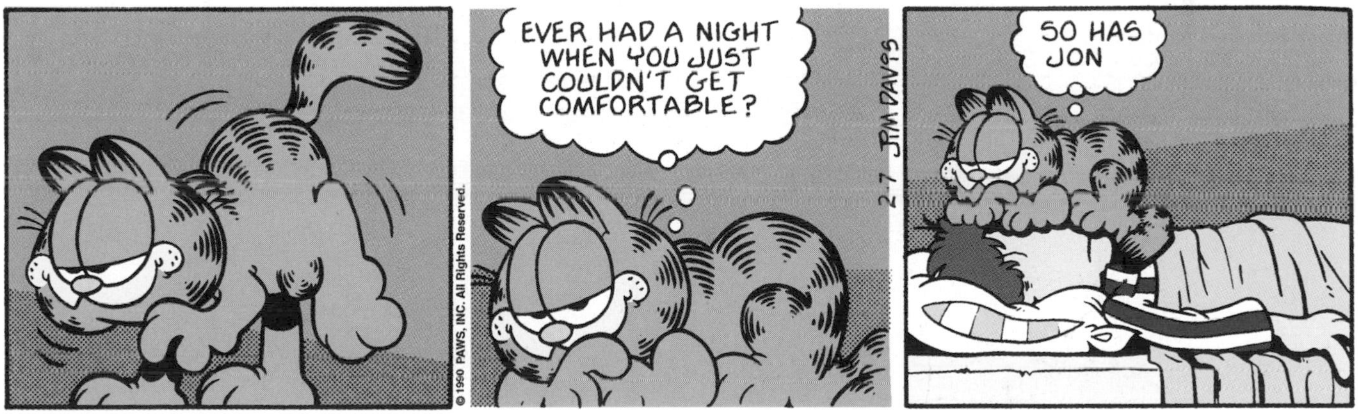
© 1990 PAWS, INC. All Rights Reserved.
EVER HAD A NIGHT WHEN YOU JUST COULDN'T GET COMFORTABLE?
JIM DAVIS 2-7
SO HAS JON

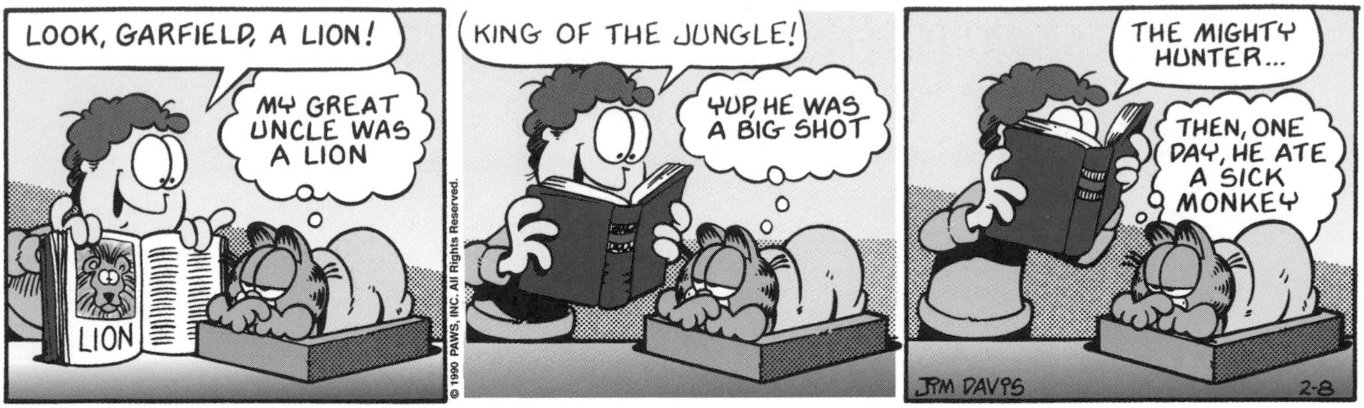
LOOK, GARFIELD, A LION!
MY GREAT UNCLE WAS A LION
LION
KING OF THE JUNGLE!
YUP, HE WAS A BIG SHOT
THE MIGHTY HUNTER...
THEN, ONE DAY, HE ATE A SICK MONKEY
© 1990 PAWS, INC. All Rights Reserved.
JIM DAVIS 2-8

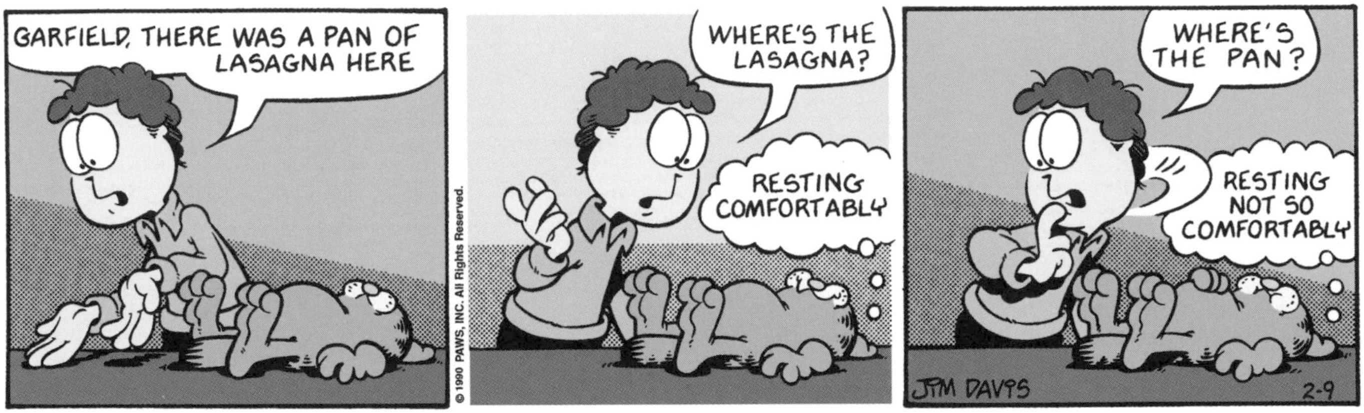
GARFIELD, THERE WAS A PAN OF LASAGNA HERE
WHERE'S THE LASAGNA?
RESTING COMFORTABLY
WHERE'S THE PAN?
RESTING NOT SO COMFORTABLY
© 1990 PAWS, INC. All Rights Reserved.
JIM DAVIS 2-9

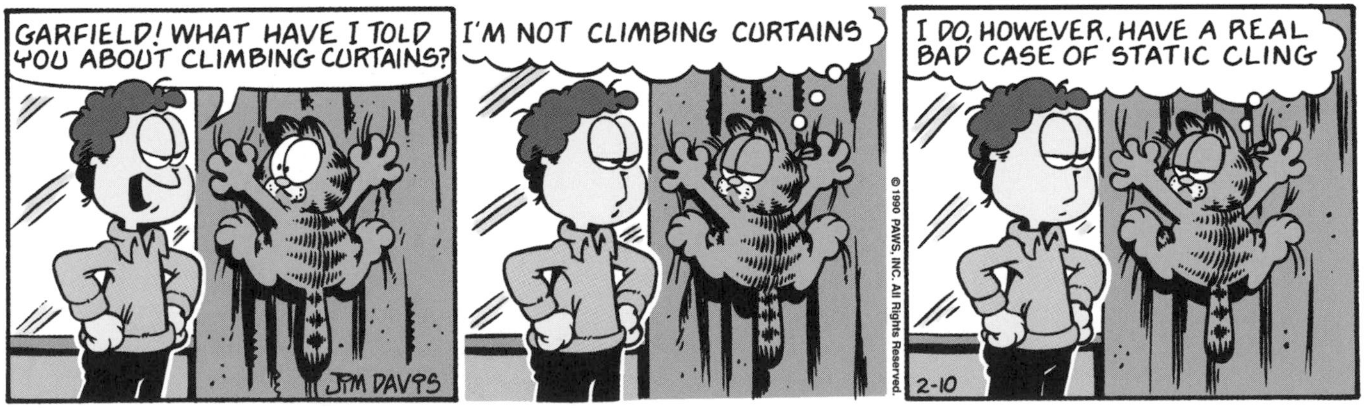
GARFIELD! WHAT HAVE I TOLD YOU ABOUT CLIMBING CURTAINS?
JIM DAVIS
I'M NOT CLIMBING CURTAINS
© 1990 PAWS, INC. All Rights Reserved.
I DO, HOWEVER, HAVE A REAL BAD CASE OF STATIC CLING
2-10

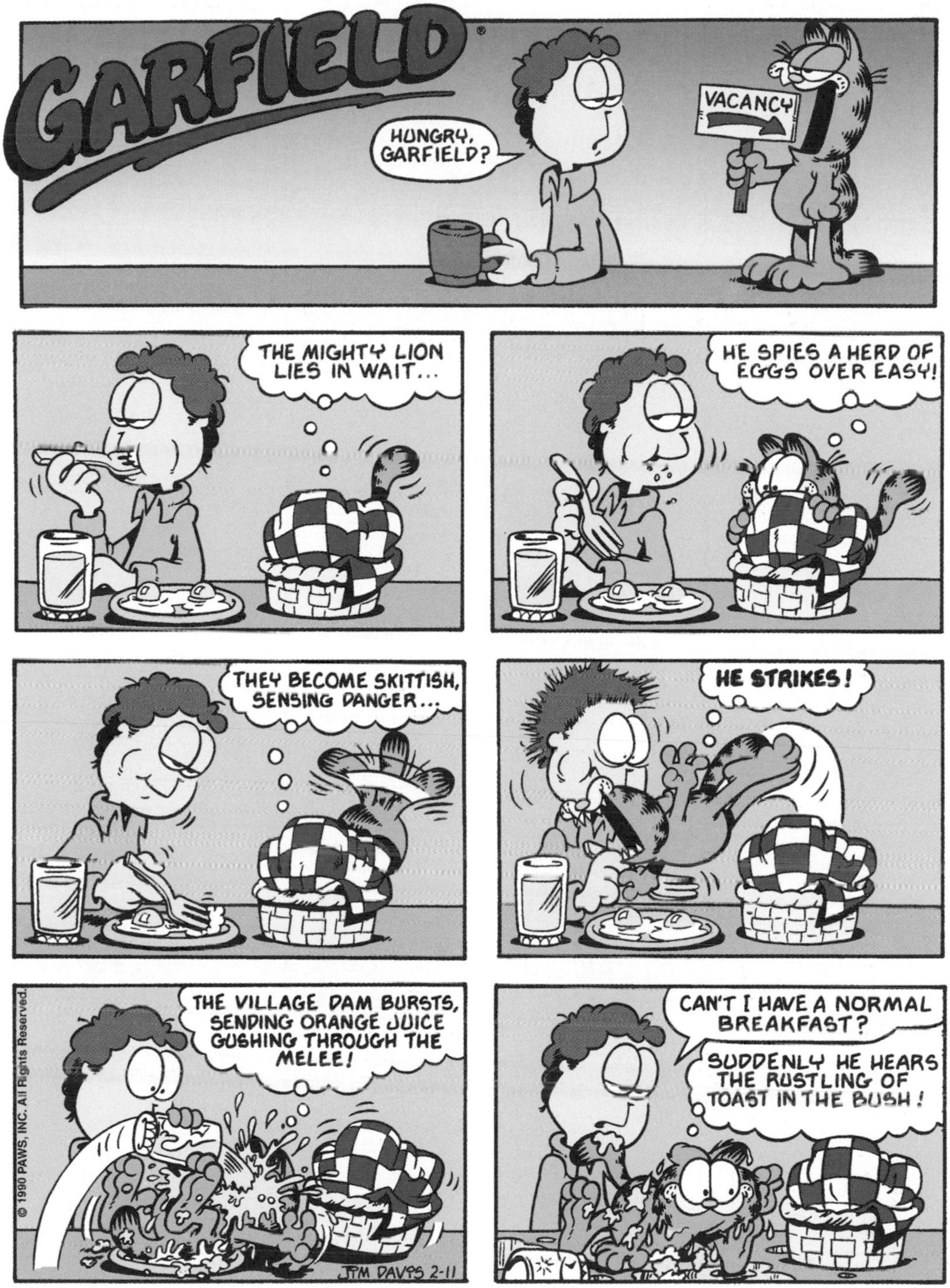
GARFIELD®
HUNGRY, GARFIELD?
VACANCY
THE MIGHTY LION LIES IN WAIT...
HE SPIES A HERD OF EGGS OVER EASY!
THEY BECOME SKITTISH, SENSING DANGER...
HE STRIKES!
THE VILLAGE DAM BURSTS, SENDING ORANGE JUICE GUSHING THROUGH THE MELEE!
© 1990 PAWS, INC. All Rights Reserved.
JIM DAVIS 2-11
CAN'T I HAVE A NORMAL BREAKFAST?
SUDDENLY HE HEARS THE RUSTLING OF TOAST IN THE BUSH!

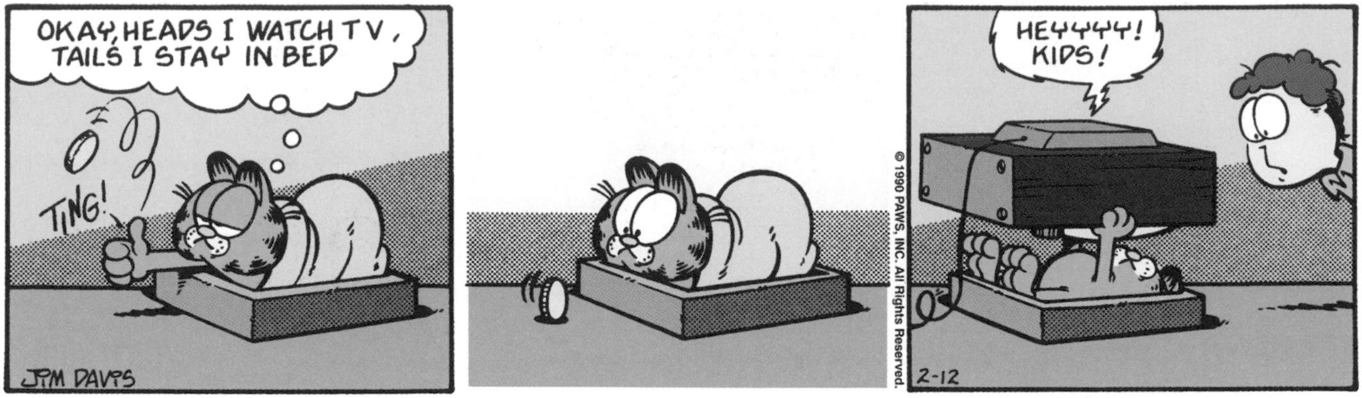
OKAY, HEADS I WATCH TV, TAILS I STAY IN BED
TING!
JIM DAVIS
© 1990 PAWS, INC. All Rights Reserved.
HEYYYY! KIDS!
2-12

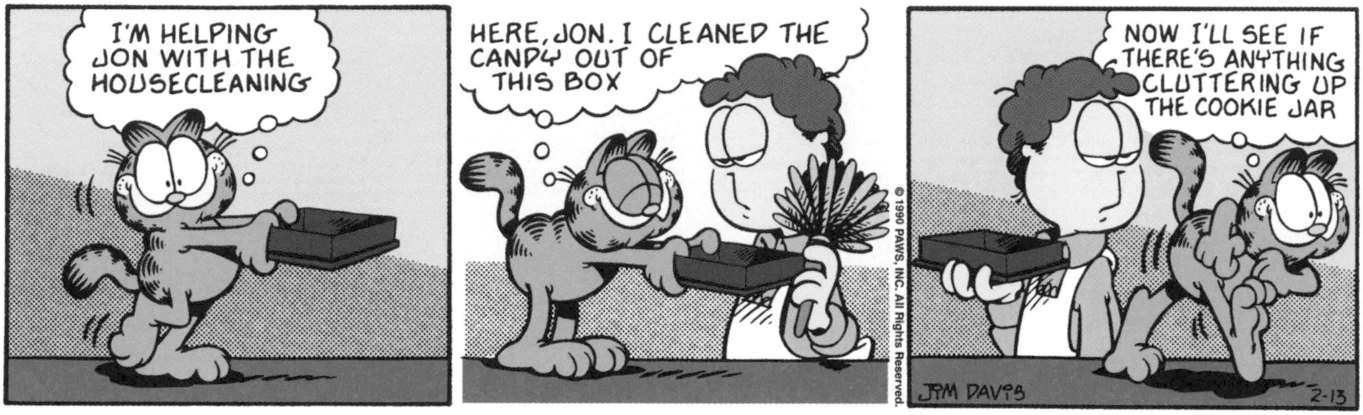
I'M HELPING JON WITH THE HOUSECLEANING
HERE, JON. I CLEANED THE CANDY OUT OF THIS BOX
© 1990 PAWS, INC. All Rights Reserved.
NOW I'LL SEE IF THERE'S ANYTHING CLUTTERING UP THE COOKIE JAR
JIM DAVIS
2-13

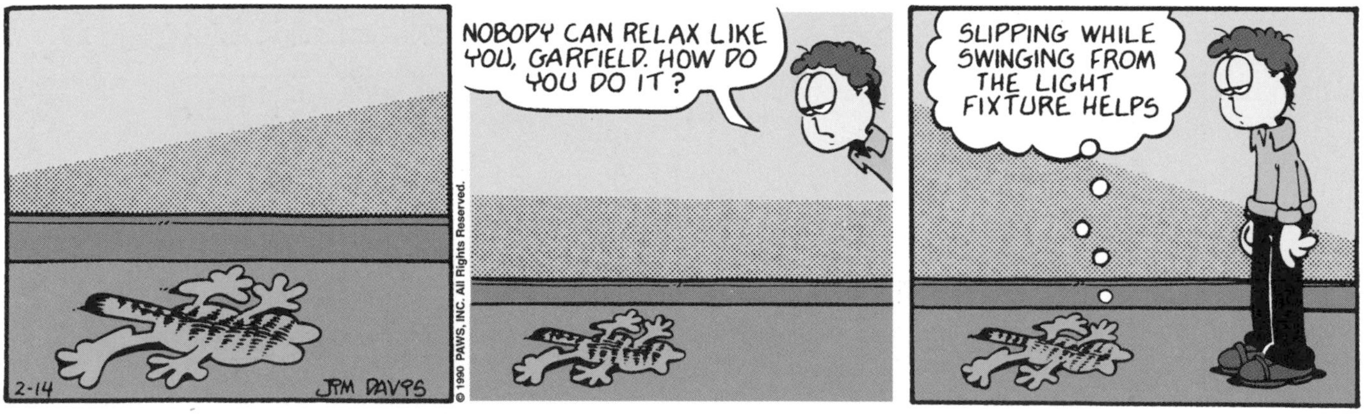
2-14
JIM DAVIS
© 1990 PAWS, INC. All Rights Reserved.
NOBODY CAN RELAX LIKE YOU, GARFIELD. HOW DO YOU DO IT?
SLIPPING WHILE SWINGING FROM THE LIGHT FIXTURE HELPS

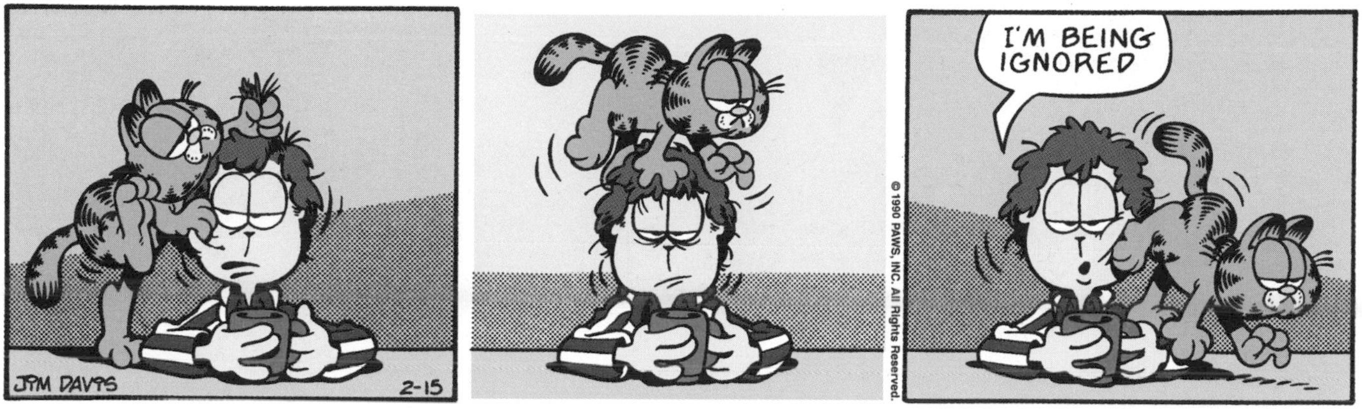
JIM DAVIS
2-15
© 1990 PAWS, INC. All Rights Reserved.
I'M BEING IGNORED

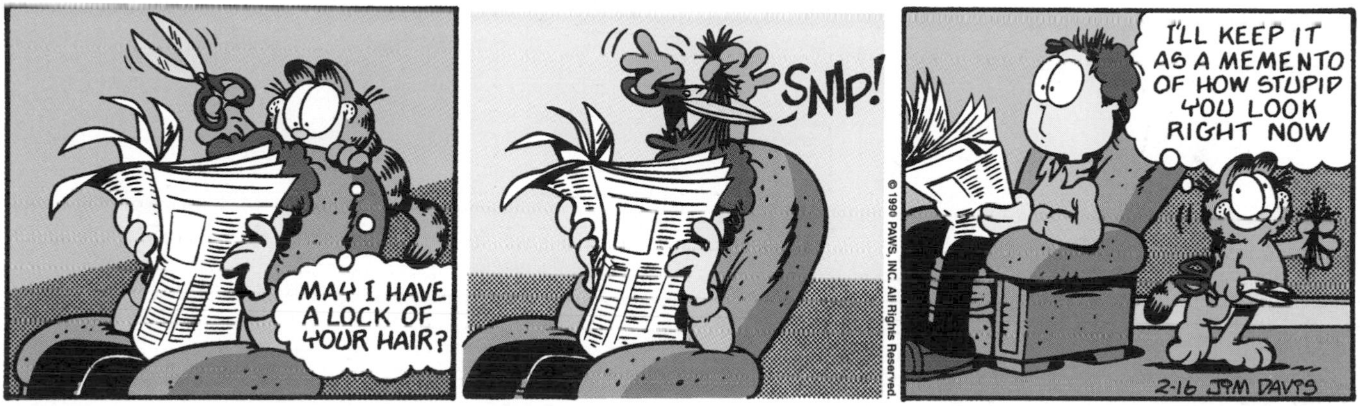
MAY I HAVE A LOCK OF YOUR HAIR?
SNIP!
© 1990 PAWS, INC. All Rights Reserved.
I'LL KEEP IT AS A MEMENTO OF HOW STUPID YOU LOOK RIGHT NOW
2-16 JIM DAVIS

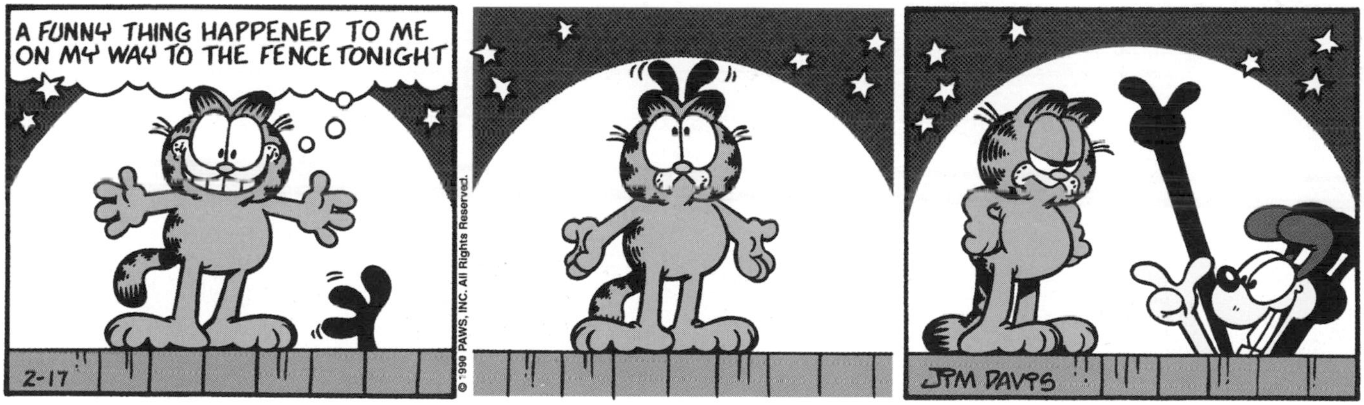
A FUNNY THING HAPPENED TO ME ON MY WAY TO THE FENCE TONIGHT
2-17
© 1990 PAWS, INC. All Rights Reserved.
JIM DAVIS

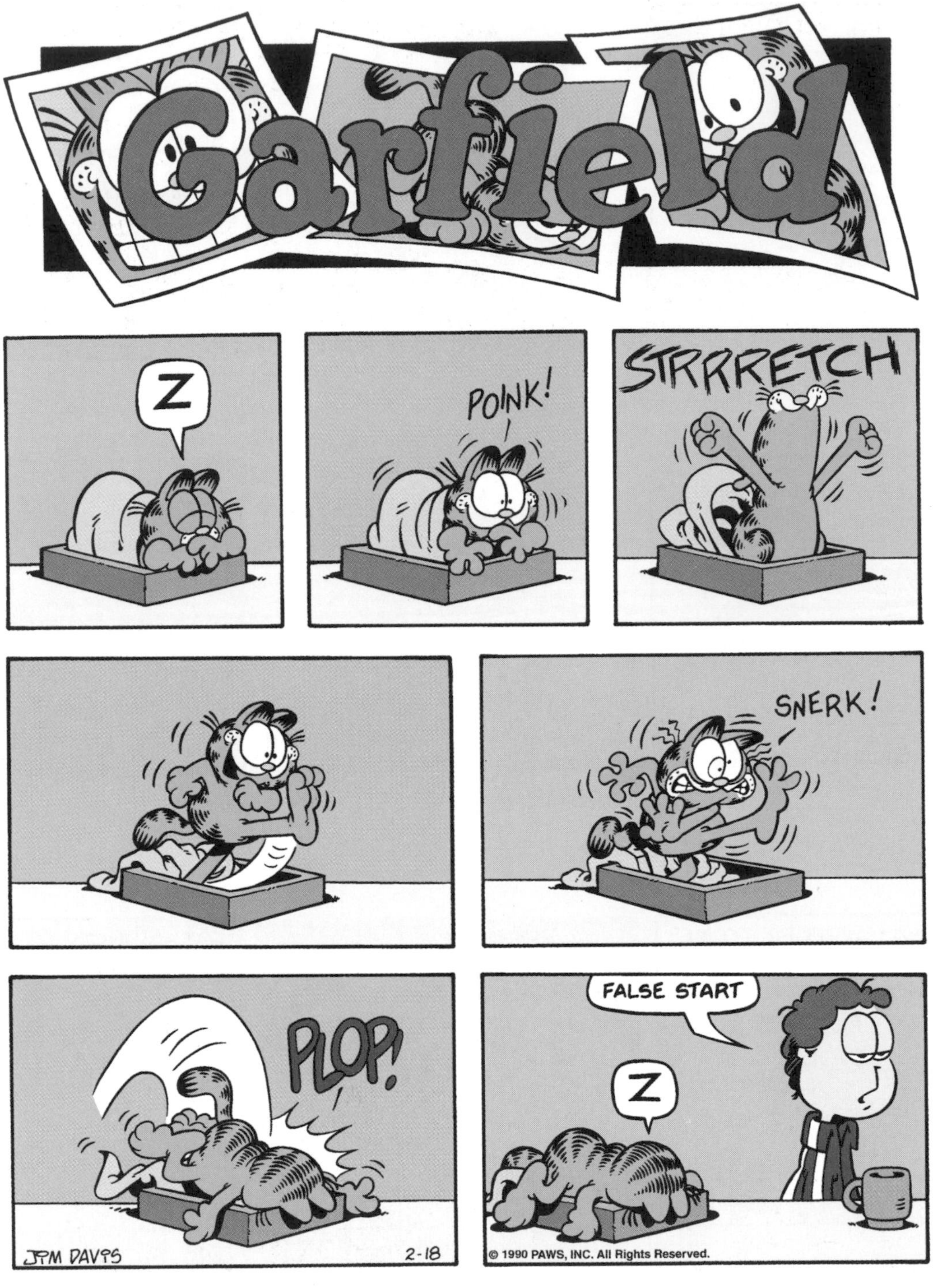
Garfield
Z
POINK!
STRRRETCH
SNERK!
PLOP!
JIM DAVIS
2-18
© 1990 PAWS, INC. All Rights Reserved.
FALSE START
Z

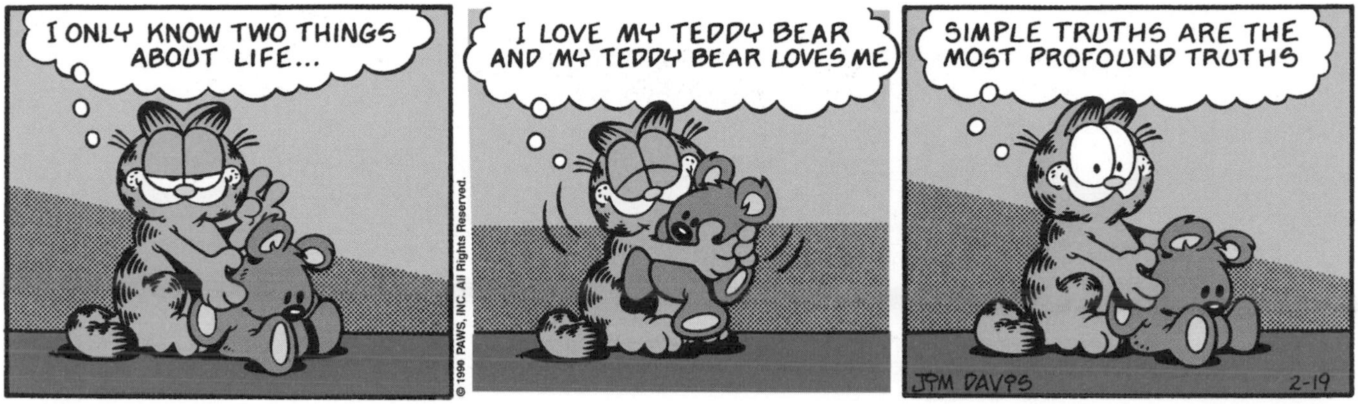
I ONLY KNOW TWO THINGS ABOUT LIFE...
I LOVE MY TEDDY BEAR AND MY TEDDY BEAR LOVES ME
SIMPLE TRUTHS ARE THE MOST PROFOUND TRUTHS
© 1990 PAWS, INC. All Rights Reserved.
JIM DAVIS
2-19

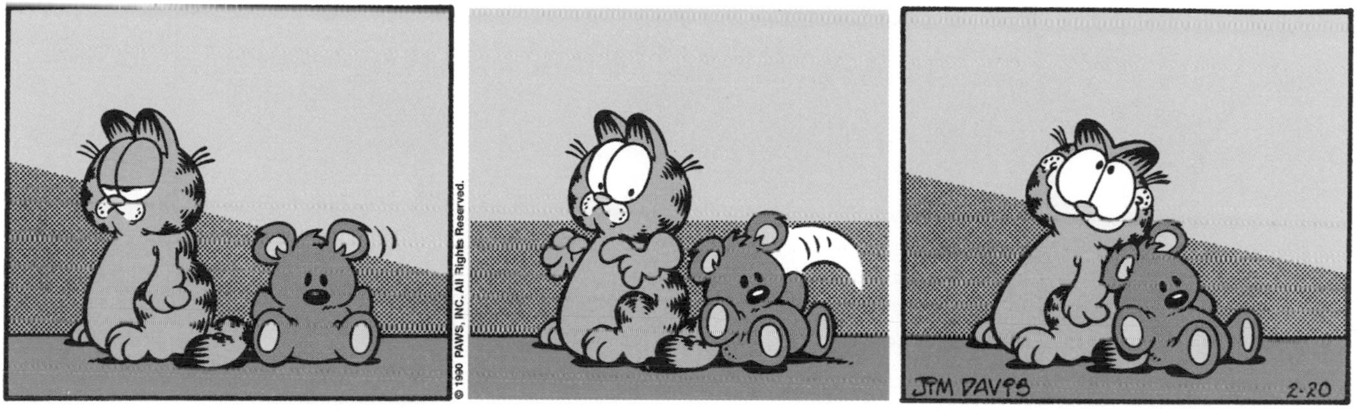
© 1990 PAWS, INC. All Rights Reserved.
JIM DAVIS
2-20

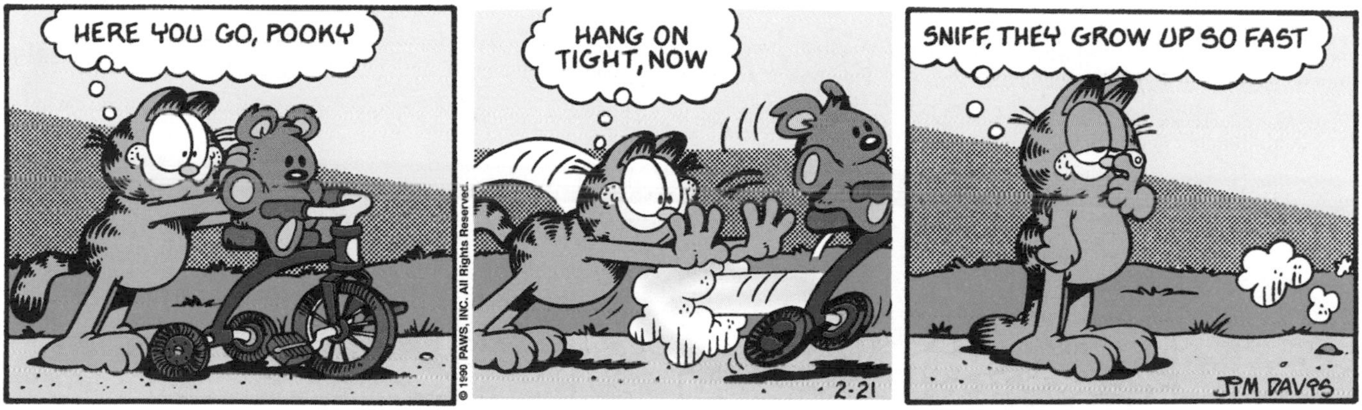
HERE YOU GO, POOKY
HANG ON TIGHT, NOW
SNIFF, THEY GROW UP SO FAST
© 1990 PAWS, INC. All Rights Reserved.
2-21
JIM DAVIS

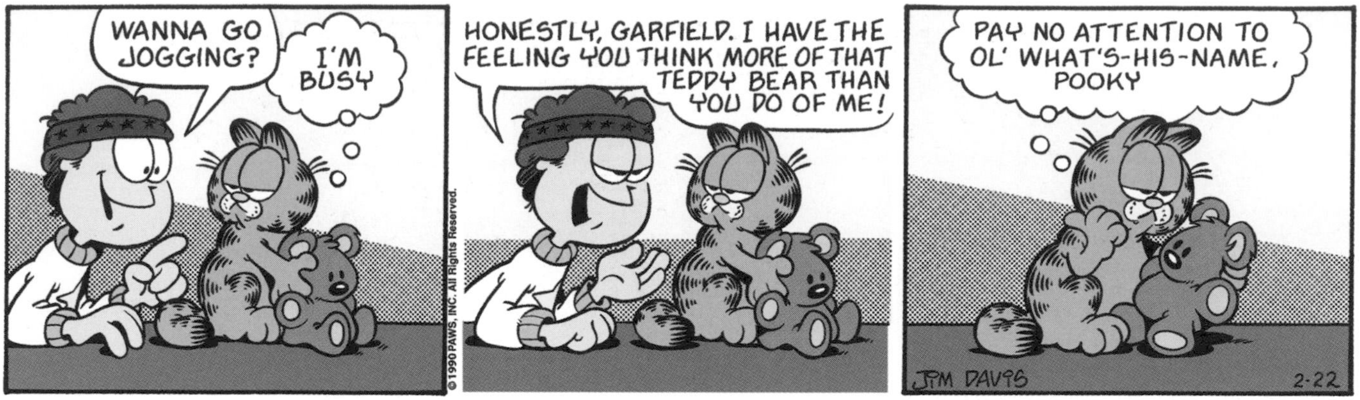
WANNA GO JOGGING?
I'M BUSY
HONESTLY, GARFIELD. I HAVE THE FEELING YOU THINK MORE OF THAT TEDDY BEAR THAN YOU DO OF ME!
PAY NO ATTENTION TO OL' WHAT'S-HIS-NAME, POOKY
JPM DAVPS
2-22
© 1990 PAWS, INC. All Rights Reserved.

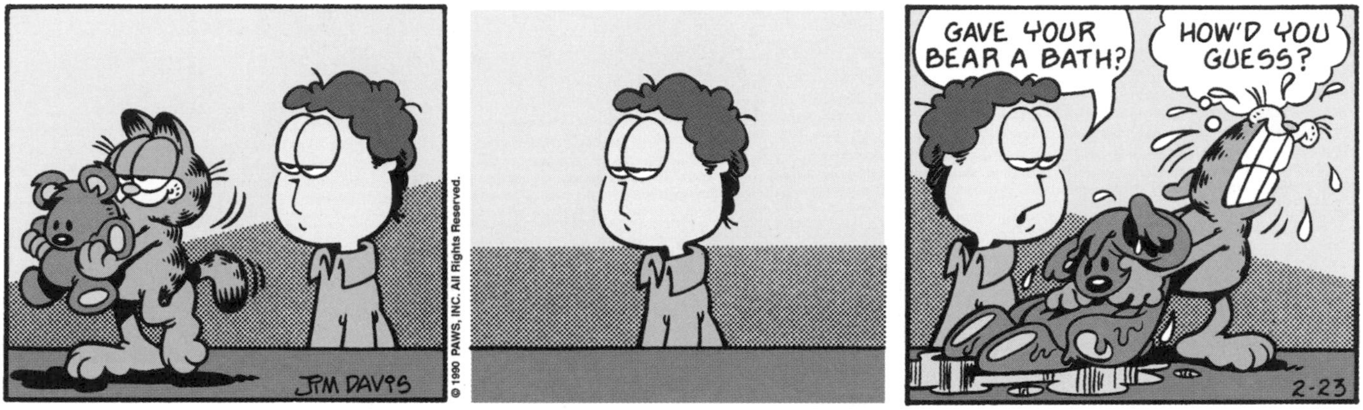
JPM DAVPS
GAVE YOUR BEAR A BATH?
HOW'D YOU GUESS?
2-23
© 1990 PAWS, INC. All Rights Reserved.

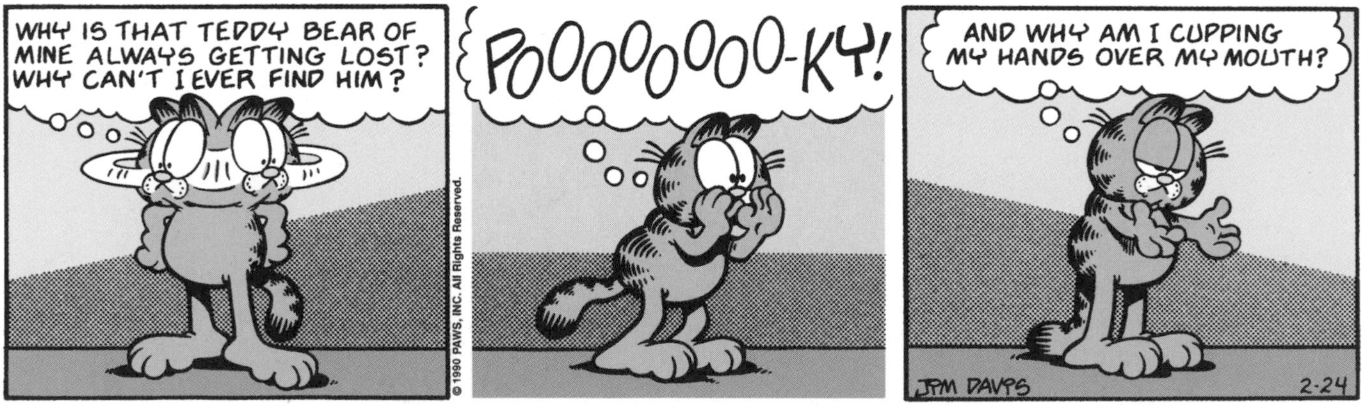
WHY IS THAT TEDDY BEAR OF MINE ALWAYS GETTING LOST? WHY CAN'T I EVER FIND HIM?
POOOOOOOO-KY!
AND WHY AM I CUPPING MY HANDS OVER MY MOUTH?
JPM DAVPS
2-24
© 1990 PAWS, INC. All Rights Reserved.

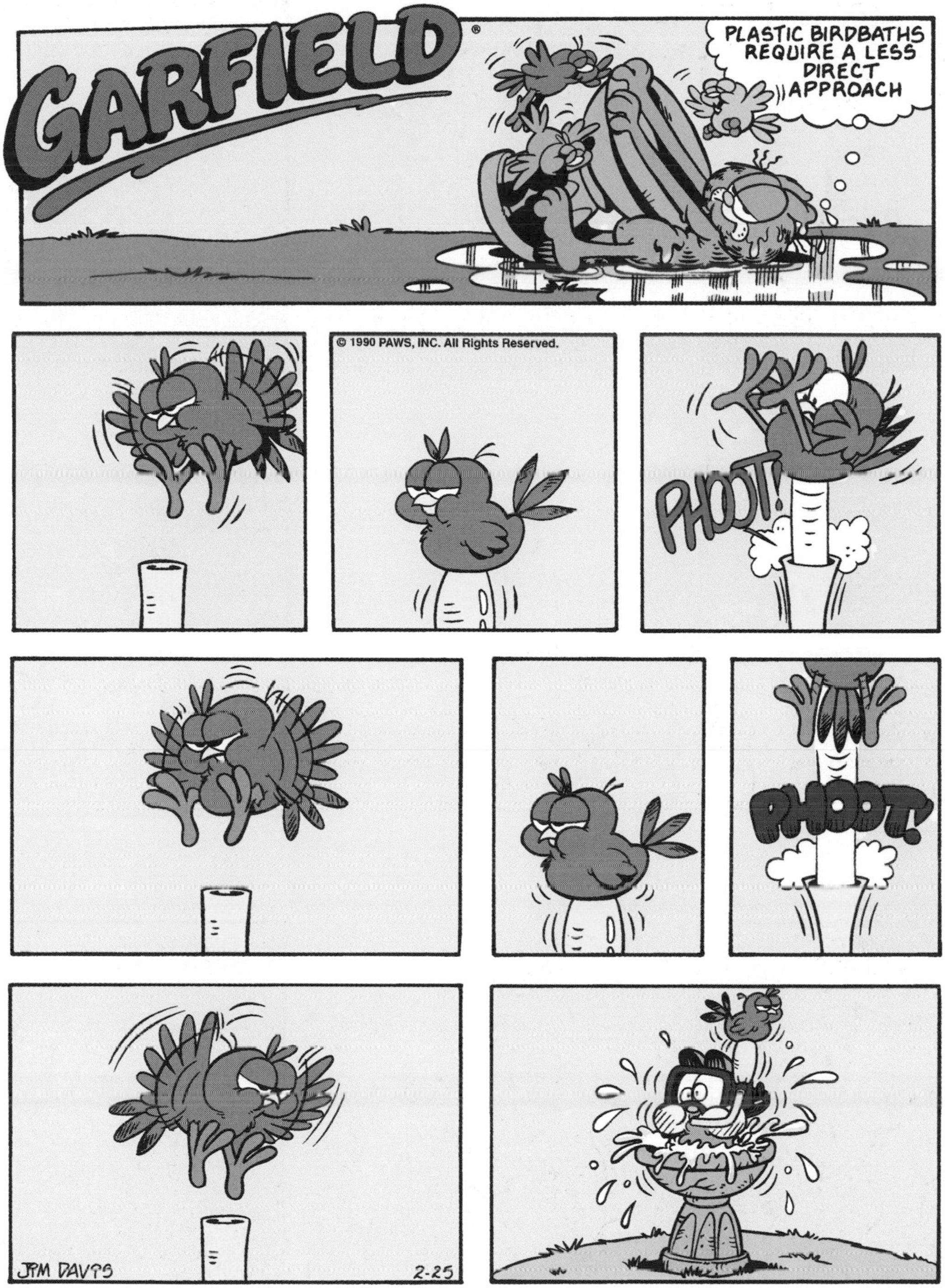
GARFIELD®
PLASTIC BIRDBATHS REQUIRE A LESS DIRECT APPROACH
© 1990 PAWS, INC. All Rights Reserved.
PHOOT!
PHOOT!
JPM DAVPS
2-25

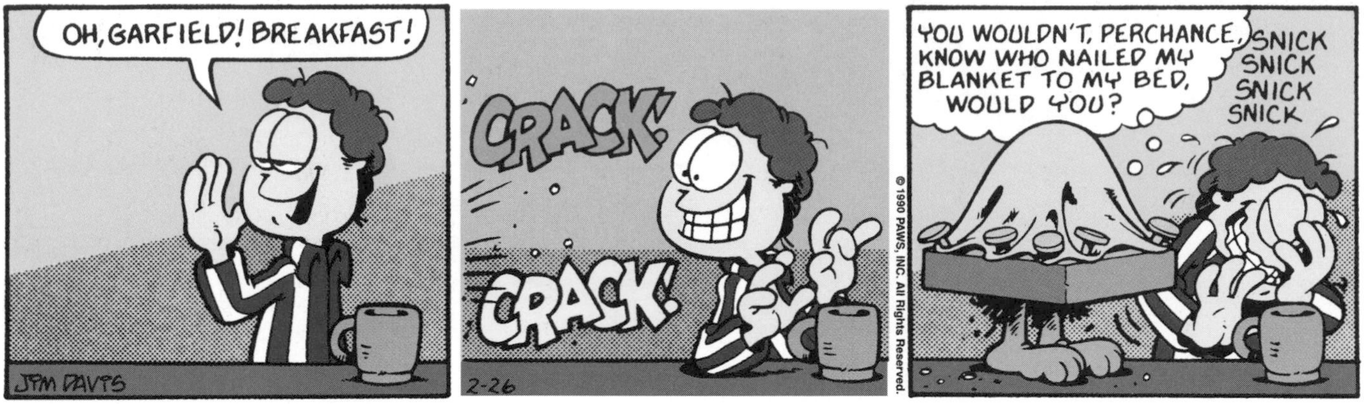
OH, GARFIELD! BREAKFAST!
CRACK!
CRACK!
YOU WOULDN'T, PERCHANCE, KNOW WHO NAILED MY BLANKET TO MY BED, WOULD YOU?
SNICK SNICK SNICK SNICK
JIM DAVIS
2-26
© 1990 PAWS, INC. All Rights Reserved.

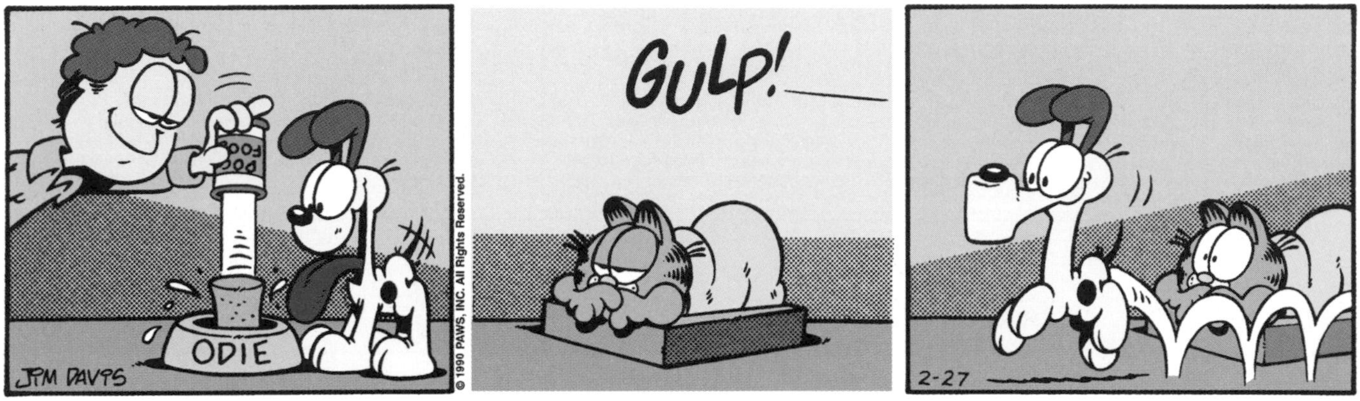
DOG FOOD
ODIE
GULP!
JIM DAVIS
2-27
© 1990 PAWS, INC. All Rights Reserved.

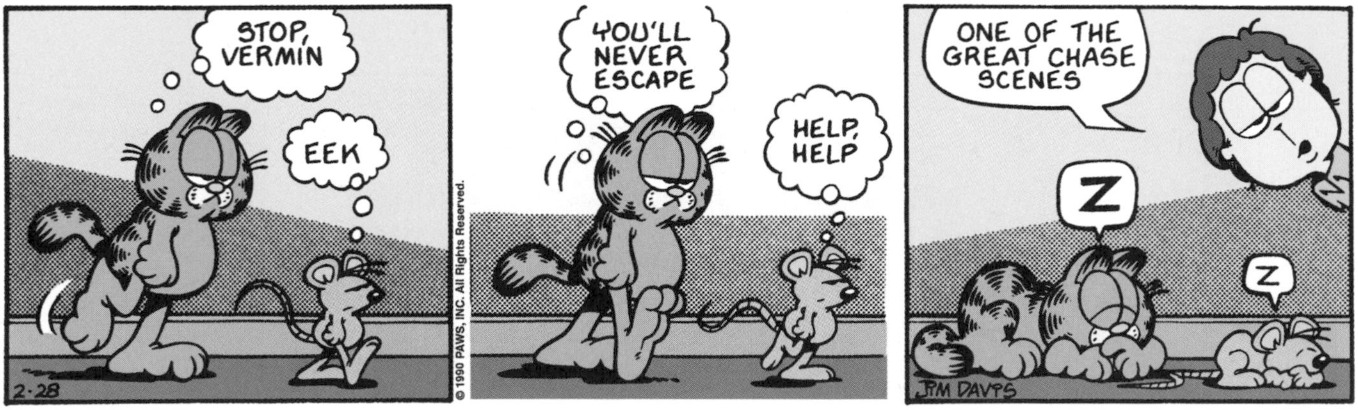
STOP, VERMIN
EEK
YOU'LL NEVER ESCAPE
HELP, HELP
ONE OF THE GREAT CHASE SCENES
Z
Z
2-28
JIM DAVIS
© 1990 PAWS, INC. All Rights Reserved.

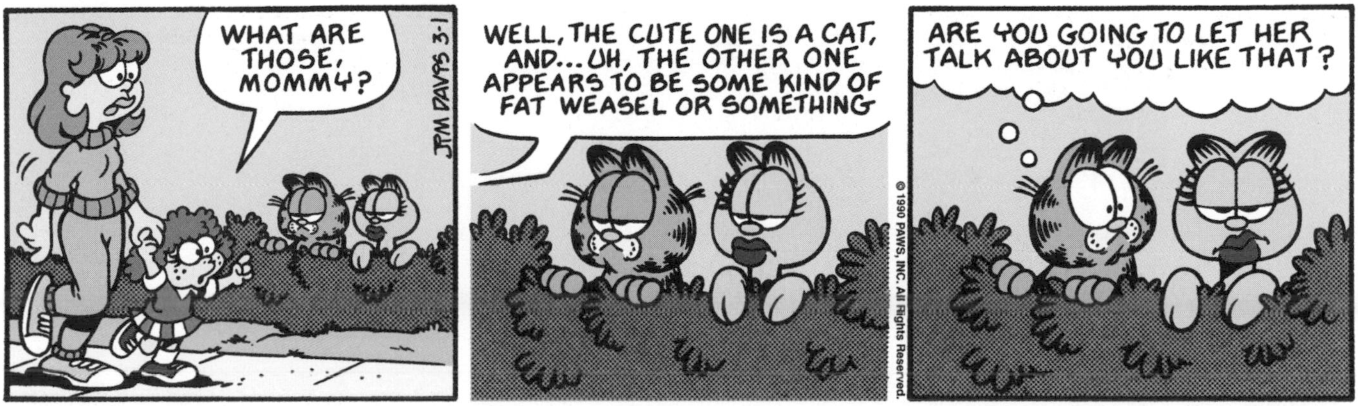
WHAT ARE THOSE, MOMMY?
JIM DAVIS 3-1
WELL, THE CUTE ONE IS A CAT, AND... UH, THE OTHER ONE APPEARS TO BE SOME KIND OF FAT WEASEL OR SOMETHING
© 1990 PAWS, INC. All Rights Reserved.
ARE YOU GOING TO LET HER TALK ABOUT YOU LIKE THAT?

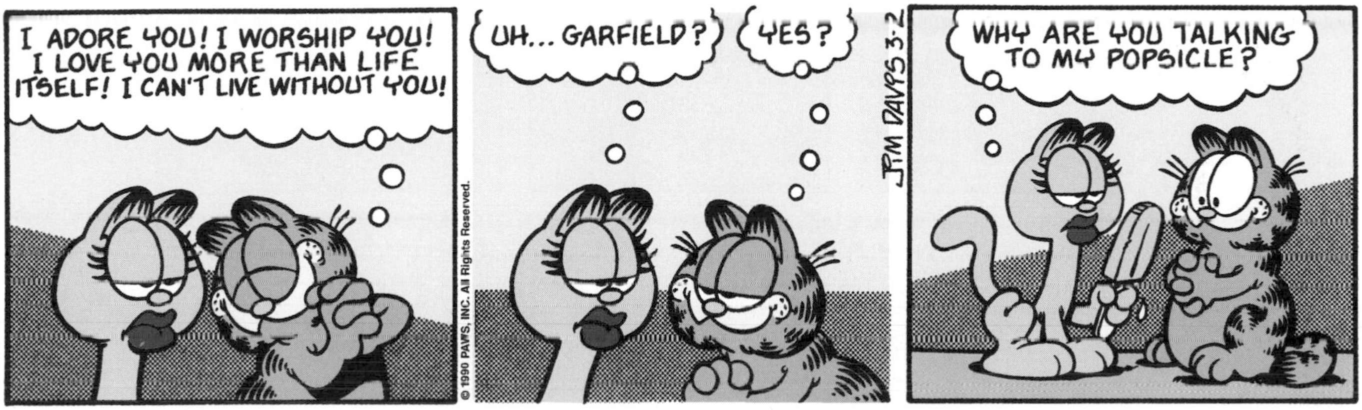
I ADORE YOU! I WORSHIP YOU! I LOVE YOU MORE THAN LIFE ITSELF! I CAN'T LIVE WITHOUT YOU!
© 1990 PAWS, INC. All Rights Reserved.
UH... GARFIELD?
YES?
JIM DAVIS 3-2
WHY ARE YOU TALKING TO MY POPSICLE?

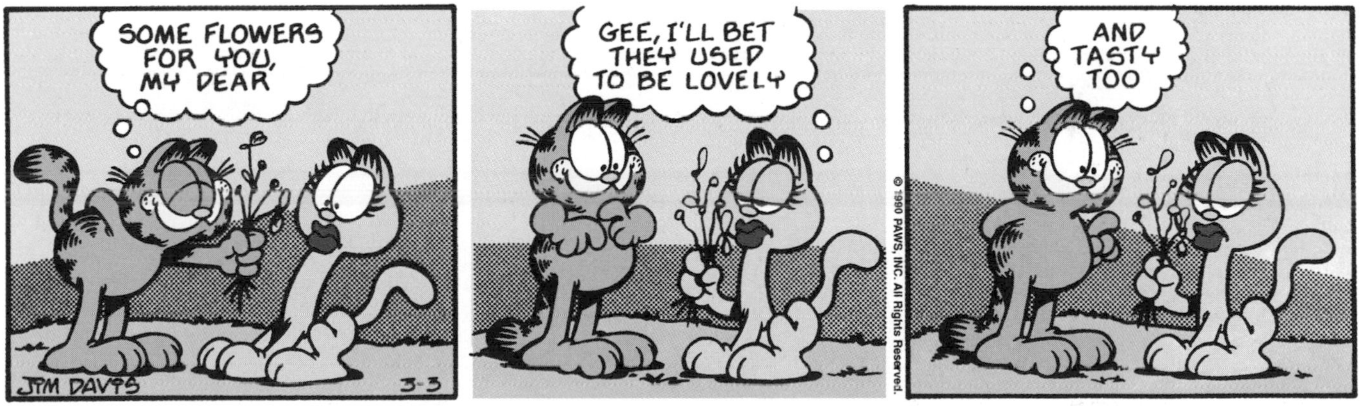
SOME FLOWERS FOR YOU, MY DEAR
JIM DAVIS 3-3
GEE, I'LL BET THEY USED TO BE LOVELY
© 1990 PAWS, INC. All Rights Reserved.
AND TASTY TOO

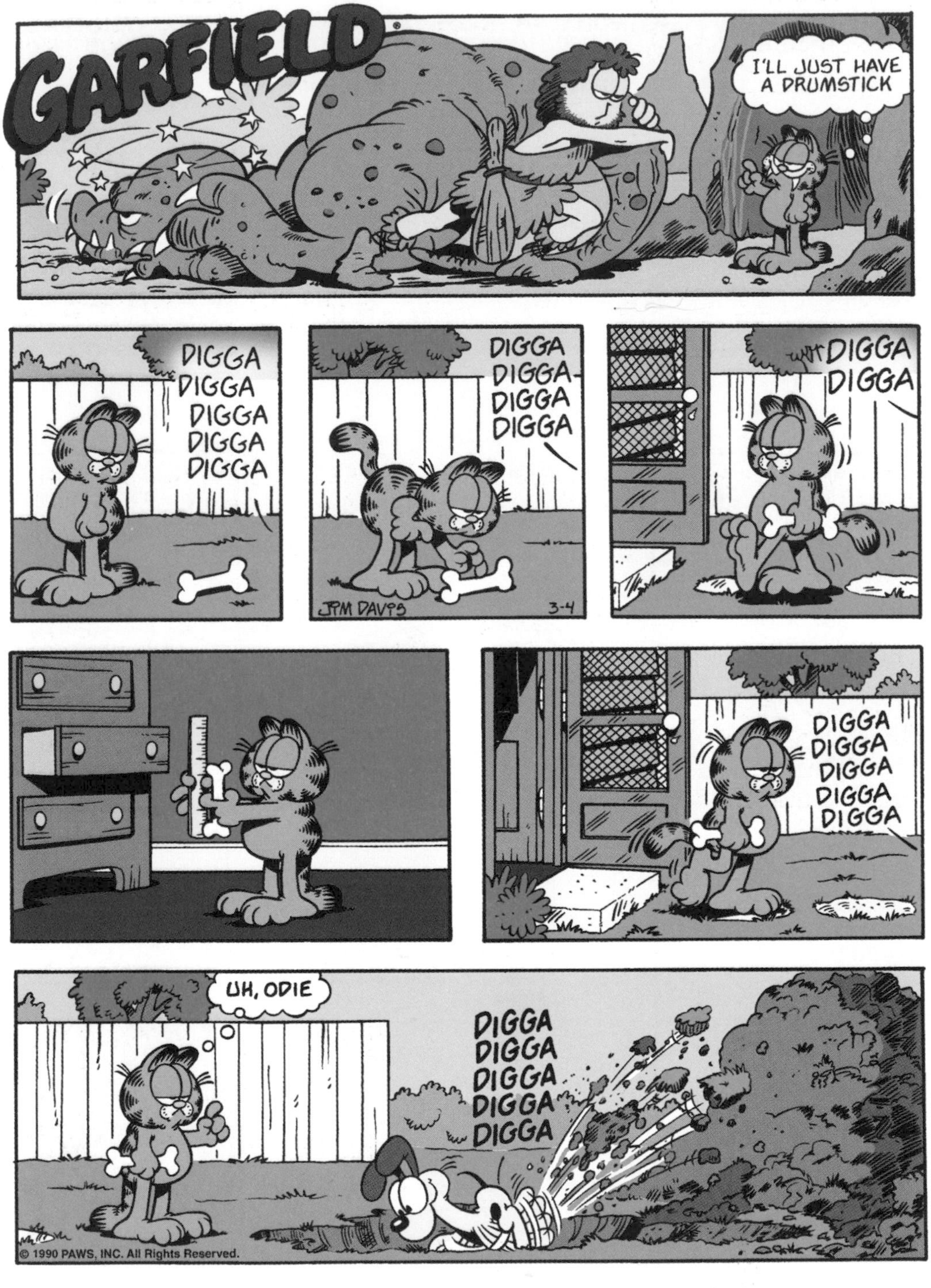
GARFIELD
I'LL JUST HAVE A DRUMSTICK
DIGGA DIGGA DIGGA DIGGA DIGGA
DIGGA DIGGA DIGGA DIGGA
JIM DAVIS
3-4
DIGGA DIGGA
DIGGA DIGGA DIGGA DIGGA DIGGA
UH, ODIE
DIGGA DIGGA DIGGA DIGGA DIGGA
© 1990 PAWS, INC. All Rights Reserved.

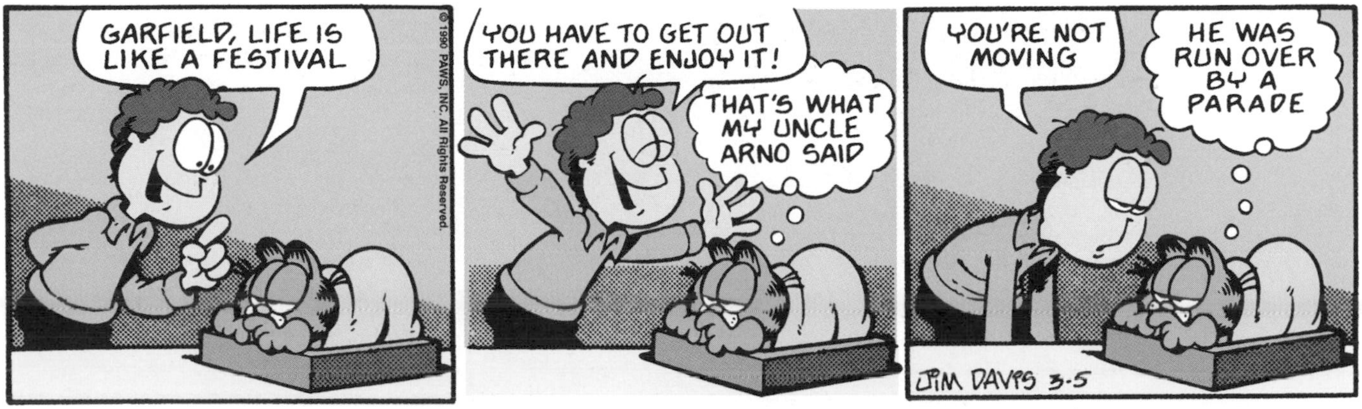
GARFIELD, LIFE IS LIKE A FESTIVAL
© 1990 PAWS, INC. All Rights Reserved.
YOU HAVE TO GET OUT THERE AND ENJOY IT!
THAT'S WHAT MY UNCLE ARNO SAID
YOU'RE NOT MOVING
HE WAS RUN OVER BY A PARADE
JIM DAVIS 3-5

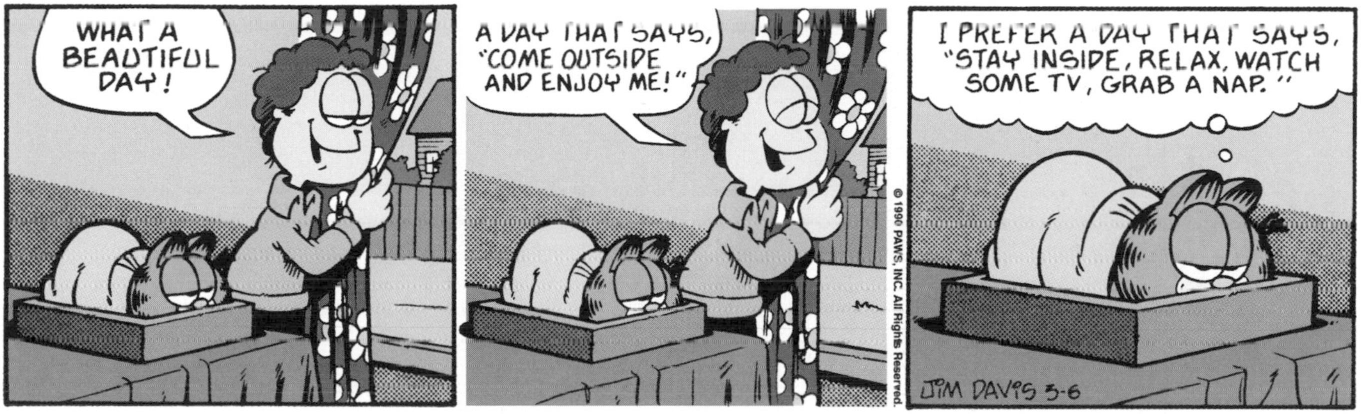
WHAT A BEAUTIFUL DAY!
A DAY THAT SAYS, "COME OUTSIDE AND ENJOY ME!"
© 1990 PAWS, INC. All Rights Reserved.
I PREFER A DAY THAT SAYS, "STAY INSIDE, RELAX, WATCH SOME TV, GRAB A NAP."
JIM DAVIS 3-6

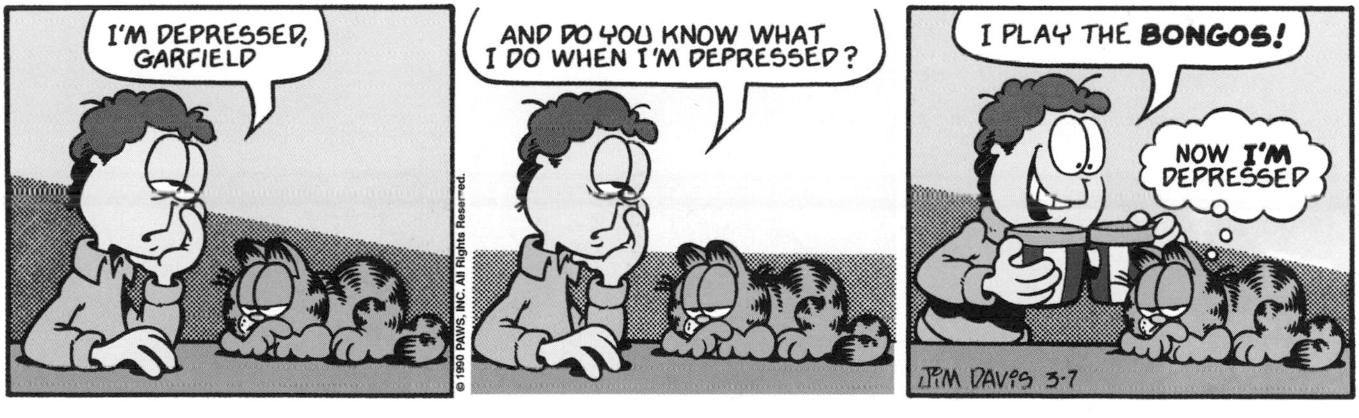
I'M DEPRESSED, GARFIELD
© 1990 PAWS, INC. All Rights Reserved.
AND DO YOU KNOW WHAT I DO WHEN I'M DEPRESSED?
I PLAY THE **BONGOS!**
NOW **I'M** DEPRESSED
JIM DAVIS 3-7

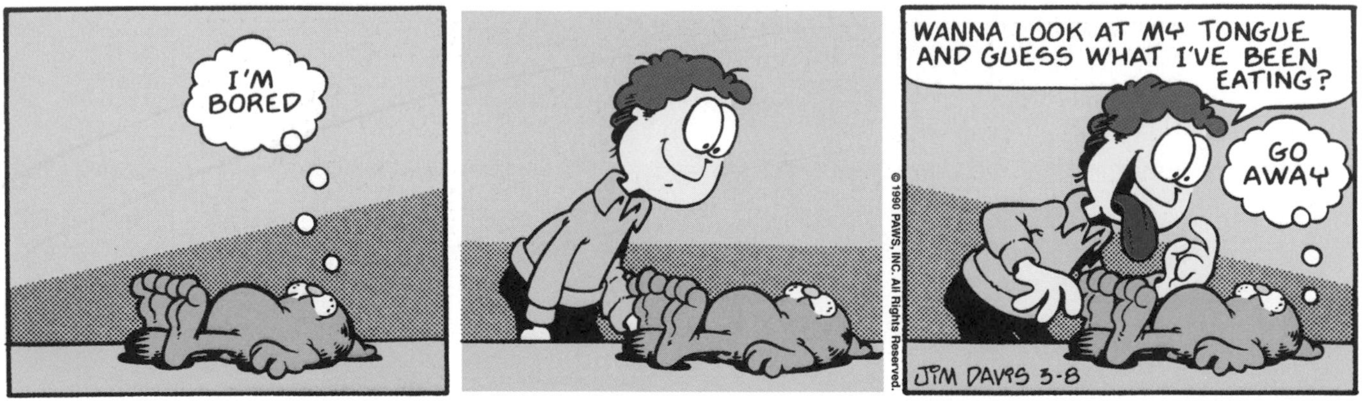
I'M BORED
© 1990 PAWS, INC. All Rights Reserved.
WANNA LOOK AT MY TONGUE AND GUESS WHAT I'VE BEEN EATING?
GO AWAY
JIM DAVIS 3-8

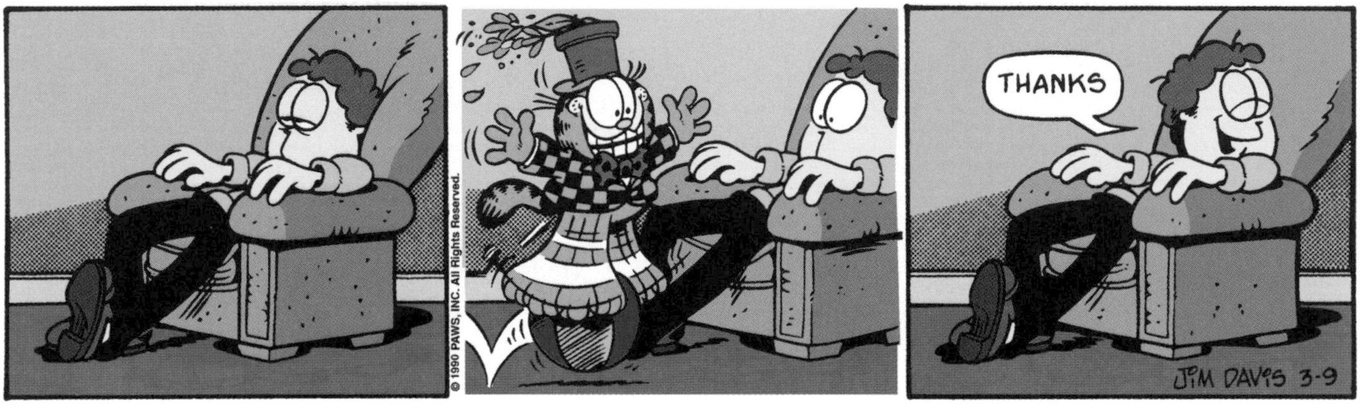
© 1990 PAWS, INC. All Rights Reserved.
THANKS
JIM DAVIS 3-9

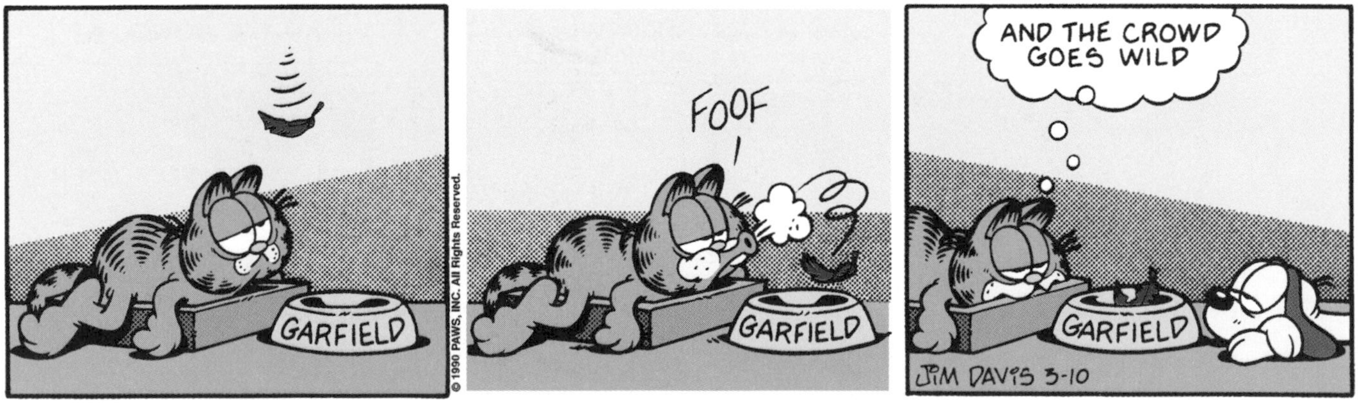
GARFIELD
© 1990 PAWS, INC. All Rights Reserved.
FOOF
GARFIELD
AND THE CROWD GOES WILD
GARFIELD
JIM DAVIS 3-10

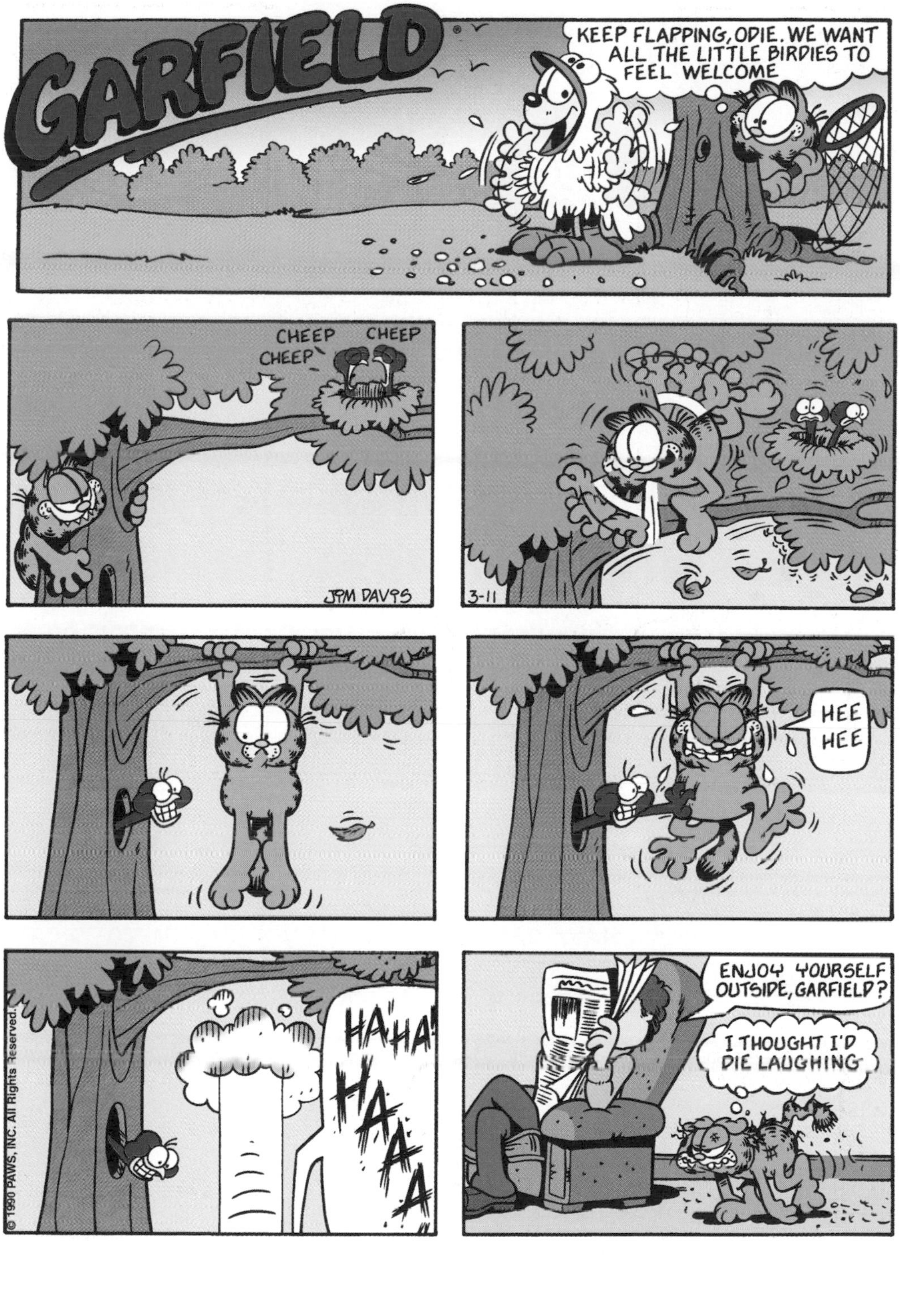
GARFIELD
KEEP FLAPPING, ODIE. WE WANT ALL THE LITTLE BIRDIES TO FEEL WELCOME
CHEEP CHEEP CHEEP
JPM DAVPS
3-11
HEE HEE
HA HA! HA A A
ENJOY YOURSELF OUTSIDE, GARFIELD?
I THOUGHT I'D DIE LAUGHING
© 1990 PAWS, INC. All Rights Reserved.

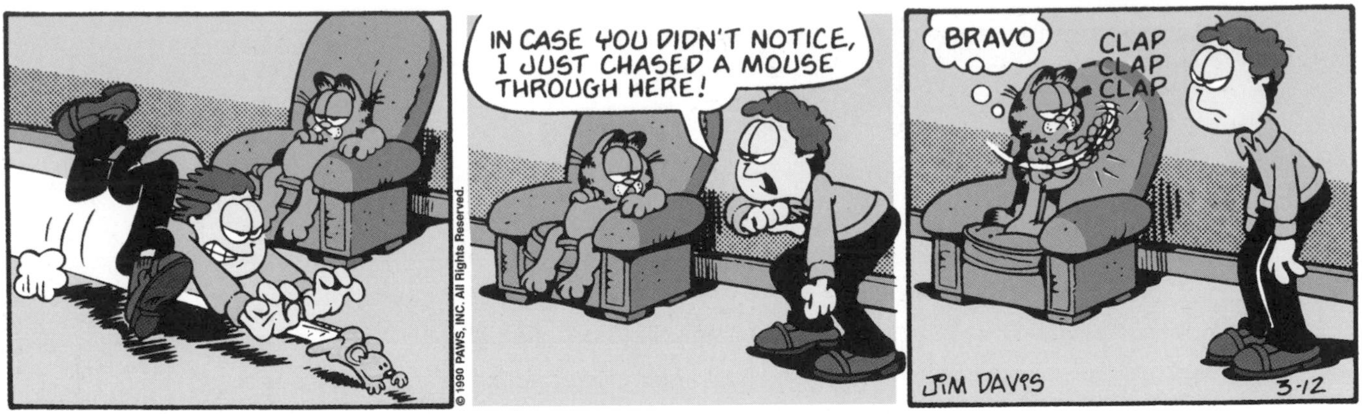
© 1990 PAWS, INC. All Rights Reserved.
IN CASE YOU DIDN'T NOTICE, I JUST CHASED A MOUSE THROUGH HERE!
BRAVO
CLAP CLAP CLAP
JIM DAVIS 3-12

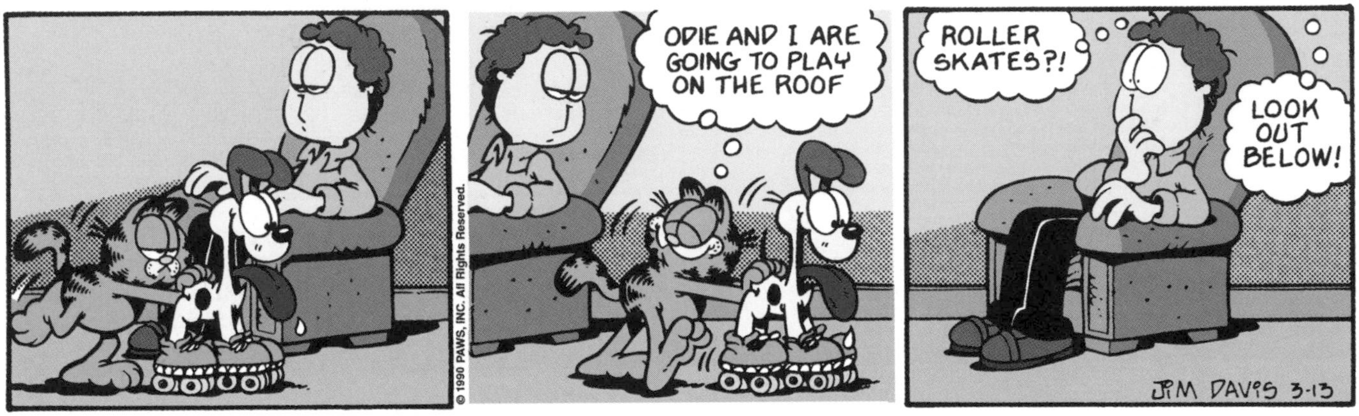
© 1990 PAWS, INC. All Rights Reserved.
ODIE AND I ARE GOING TO PLAY ON THE ROOF
ROLLER SKATES?!
LOOK OUT BELOW!
JIM DAVIS 3-13

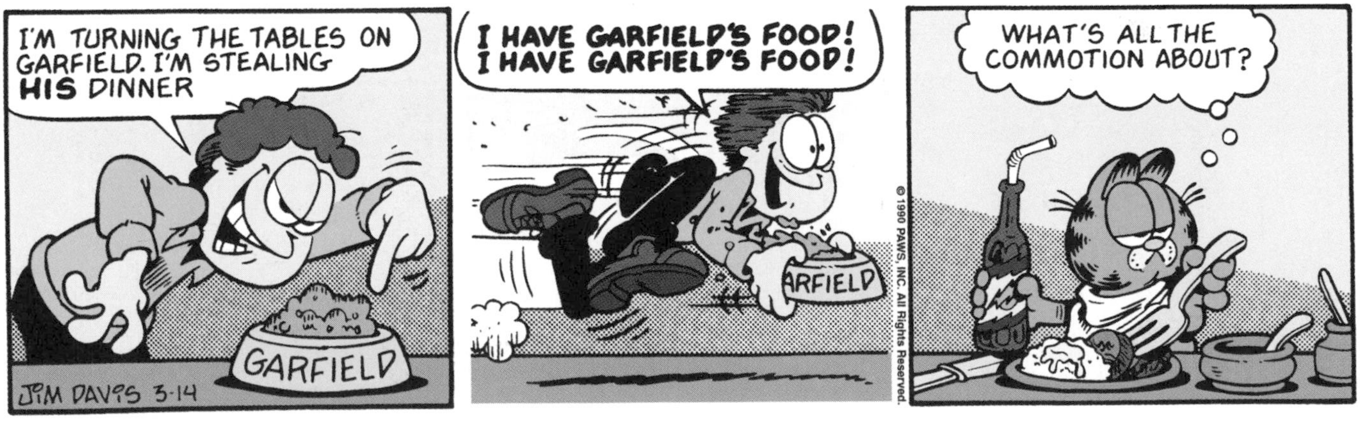
I'M TURNING THE TABLES ON GARFIELD. I'M STEALING **HIS** DINNER
GARFIELD
JIM DAVIS 3-14
I HAVE GARFIELD'S FOOD! I HAVE GARFIELD'S FOOD!
GARFIELD
© 1990 PAWS, INC. All Rights Reserved.
WHAT'S ALL THE COMMOTION ABOUT?

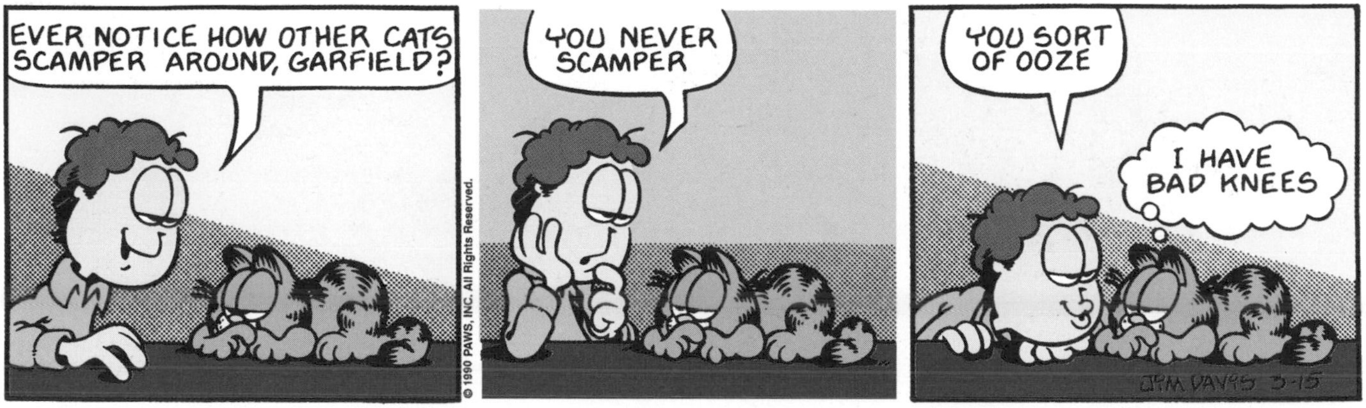
EVER NOTICE HOW OTHER CATS SCAMPER AROUND, GARFIELD?
© 1990 PAWS, INC. All Rights Reserved.
YOU NEVER SCAMPER
YOU SORT OF OOZE
I HAVE BAD KNEES
JIM DAVIS 3-15

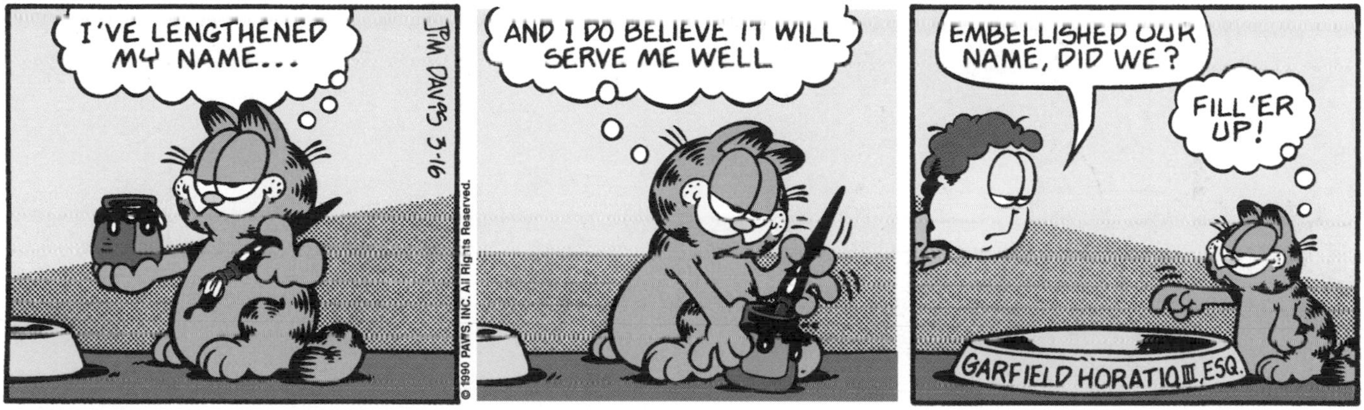
I'VE LENGTHENED MY NAME...
JIM DAVIS 3-16
© 1990 PAWS, INC. All Rights Reserved.
AND I DO BELIEVE IT WILL SERVE ME WELL
EMBELLISHED OUR NAME, DID WE?
FILL'ER UP!
GARFIELD HORATIO III, ESQ.

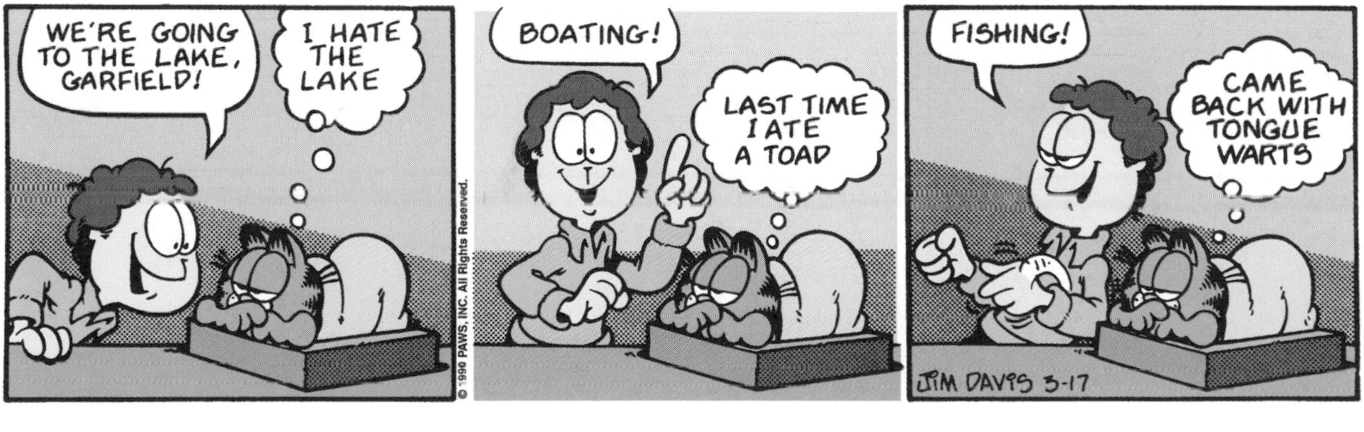
WE'RE GOING TO THE LAKE, GARFIELD!
I HATE THE LAKE
© 1990 PAWS, INC. All Rights Reserved.
BOATING!
LAST TIME I ATE A TOAD
FISHING!
CAME BACK WITH TONGUE WARTS
JIM DAVIS 3-17

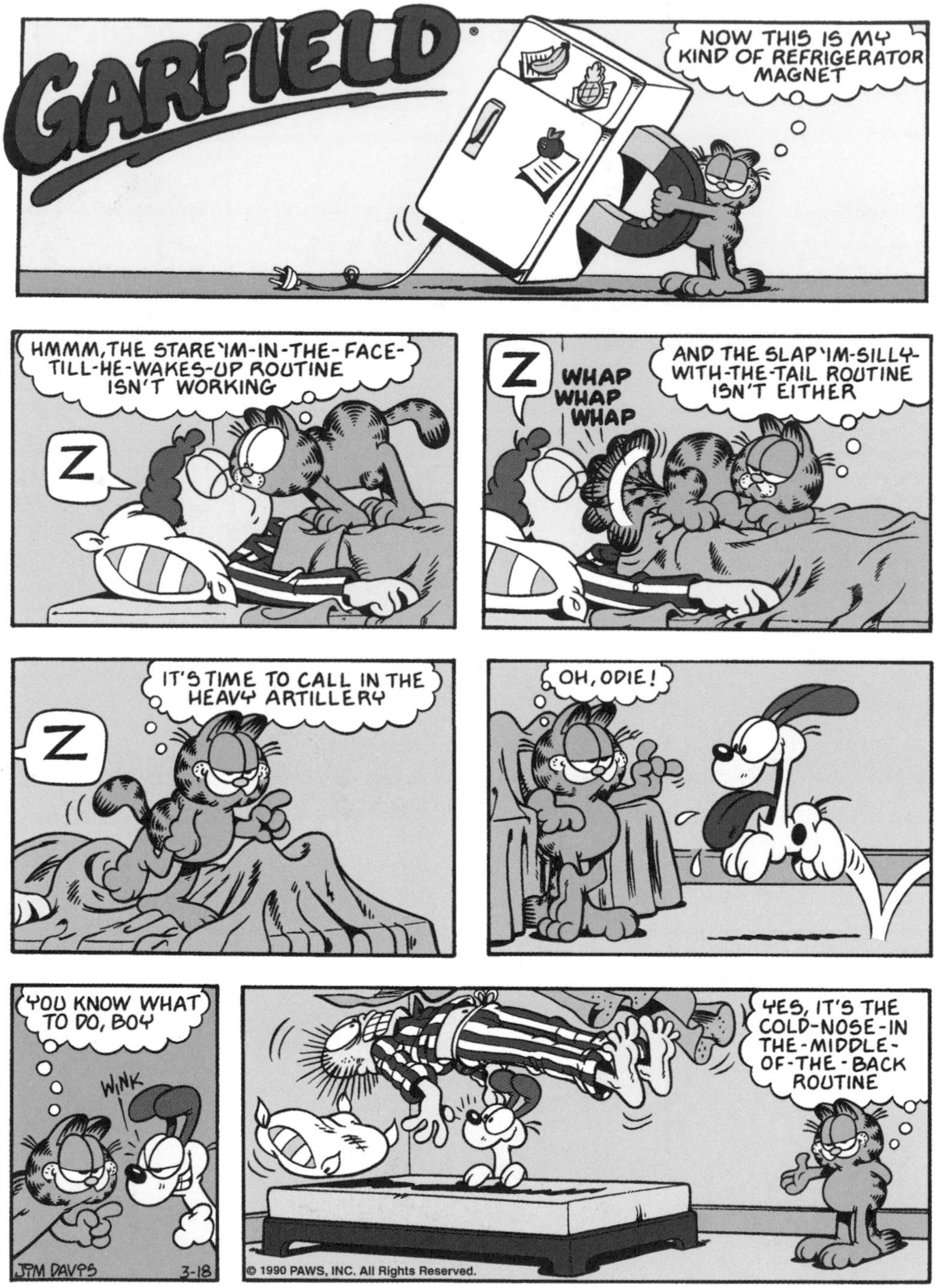
GARFIELD
NOW THIS IS MY KIND OF REFRIGERATOR MAGNET
HMMM, THE STARE 'IM-IN-THE-FACE-TILL-HE-WAKES-UP ROUTINE ISN'T WORKING
Z
Z
WHAP WHAP WHAP
AND THE SLAP 'IM-SILLY-WITH-THE-TAIL ROUTINE ISN'T EITHER
Z
IT'S TIME TO CALL IN THE HEAVY ARTILLERY
OH, ODIE!
YOU KNOW WHAT TO DO, BOY
WINK
YES, IT'S THE COLD-NOSE-IN THE-MIDDLE-OF-THE-BACK ROUTINE
JIM DAVIS 3-18
© 1990 PAWS, INC. All Rights Reserved.

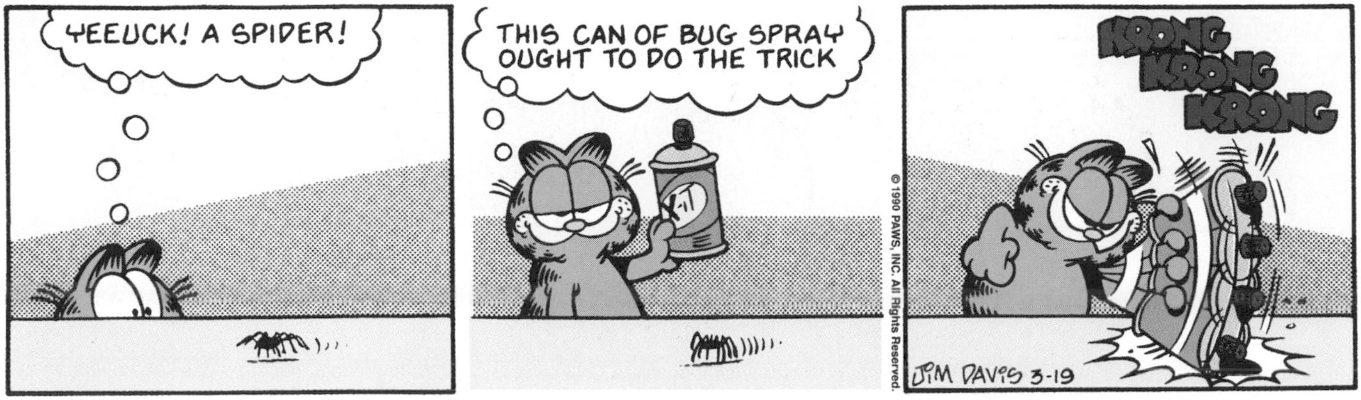
YEEUCK! A SPIDER!
THIS CAN OF BUG SPRAY OUGHT TO DO THE TRICK
KRONG KRONG KRONG
© 1990 PAWS, INC. All Rights Reserved.
JIM DAVIS 3-19

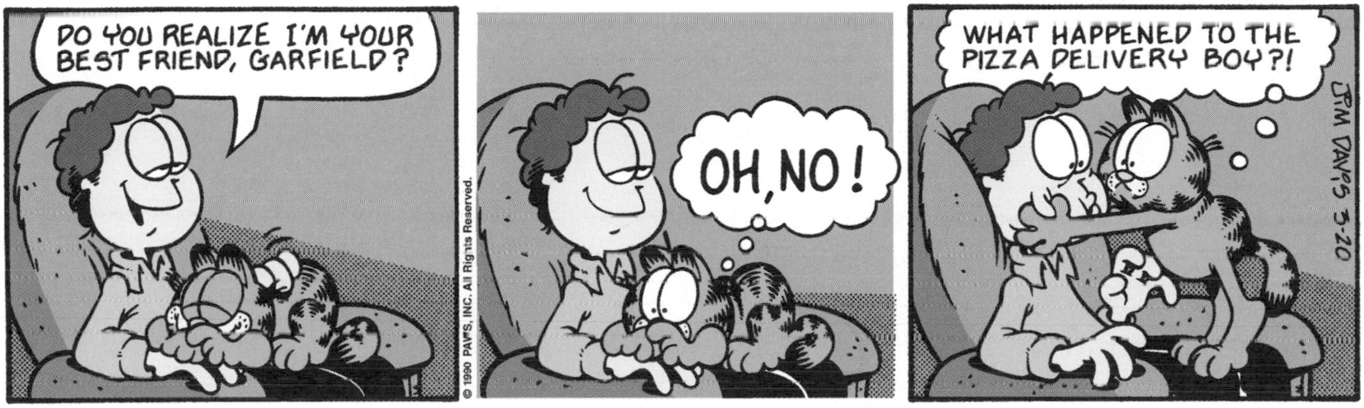
DO YOU REALIZE I'M YOUR BEST FRIEND, GARFIELD?
© 1990 PAWS, INC. All Rights Reserved.
OH, NO!
WHAT HAPPENED TO THE PIZZA DELIVERY BOY?!
JIM DAVIS 3-20

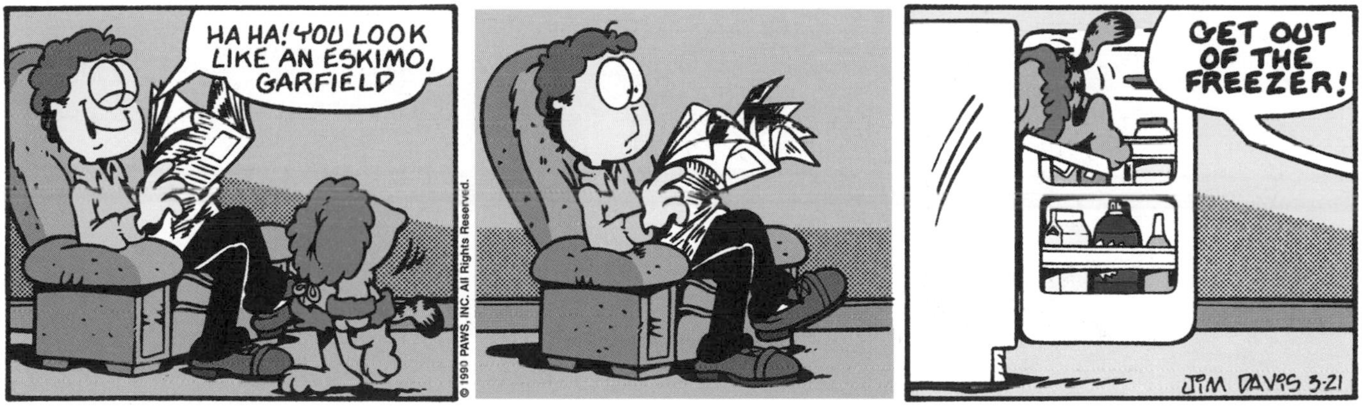
HA HA! YOU LOOK LIKE AN ESKIMO, GARFIELD
© 1990 PAWS, INC. All Rights Reserved.
GET OUT OF THE FREEZER!
JIM DAVIS 3-21

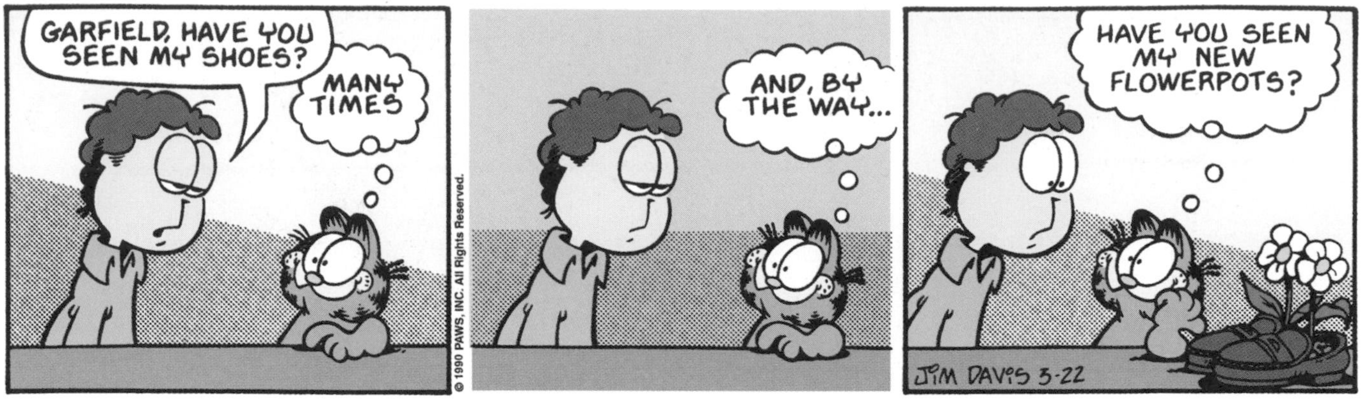
GARFIELD, HAVE YOU SEEN MY SHOES?
MANY TIMES
AND, BY THE WAY...
HAVE YOU SEEN MY NEW FLOWERPOTS?
© 1990 PAWS, INC. All Rights Reserved.
JIM DAVIS 3-22

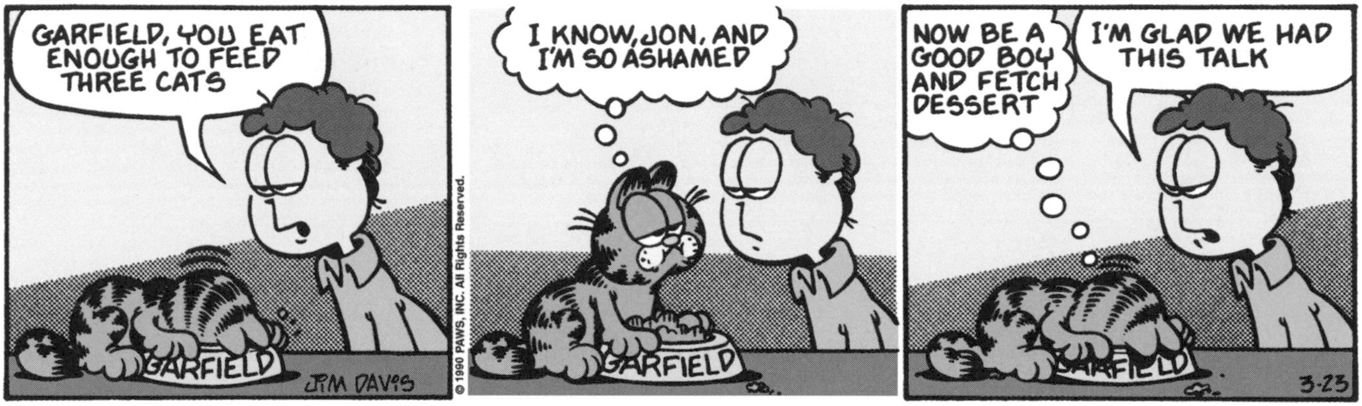
GARFIELD, YOU EAT ENOUGH TO FEED THREE CATS
GARFIELD
JIM DAVIS
© 1990 PAWS, INC. All Rights Reserved.
I KNOW, JON, AND I'M SO ASHAMED
GARFIELD
NOW BE A GOOD BOY AND FETCH DESSERT
I'M GLAD WE HAD THIS TALK
GARFIELD
3-23

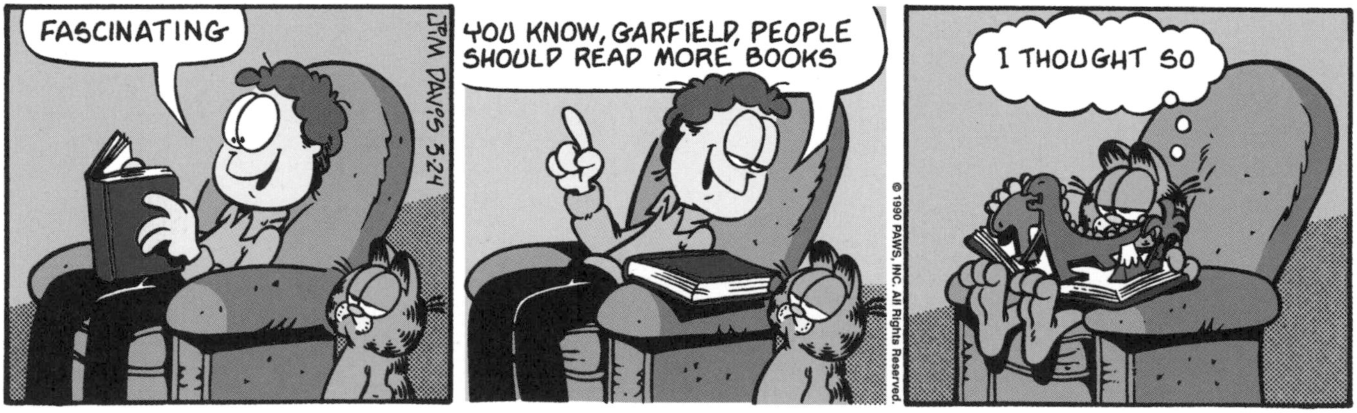
FASCINATING
JIM DAVIS 3-24
YOU KNOW, GARFIELD, PEOPLE SHOULD READ MORE BOOKS
© 1990 PAWS, INC. All Rights Reserved.
I THOUGHT SO

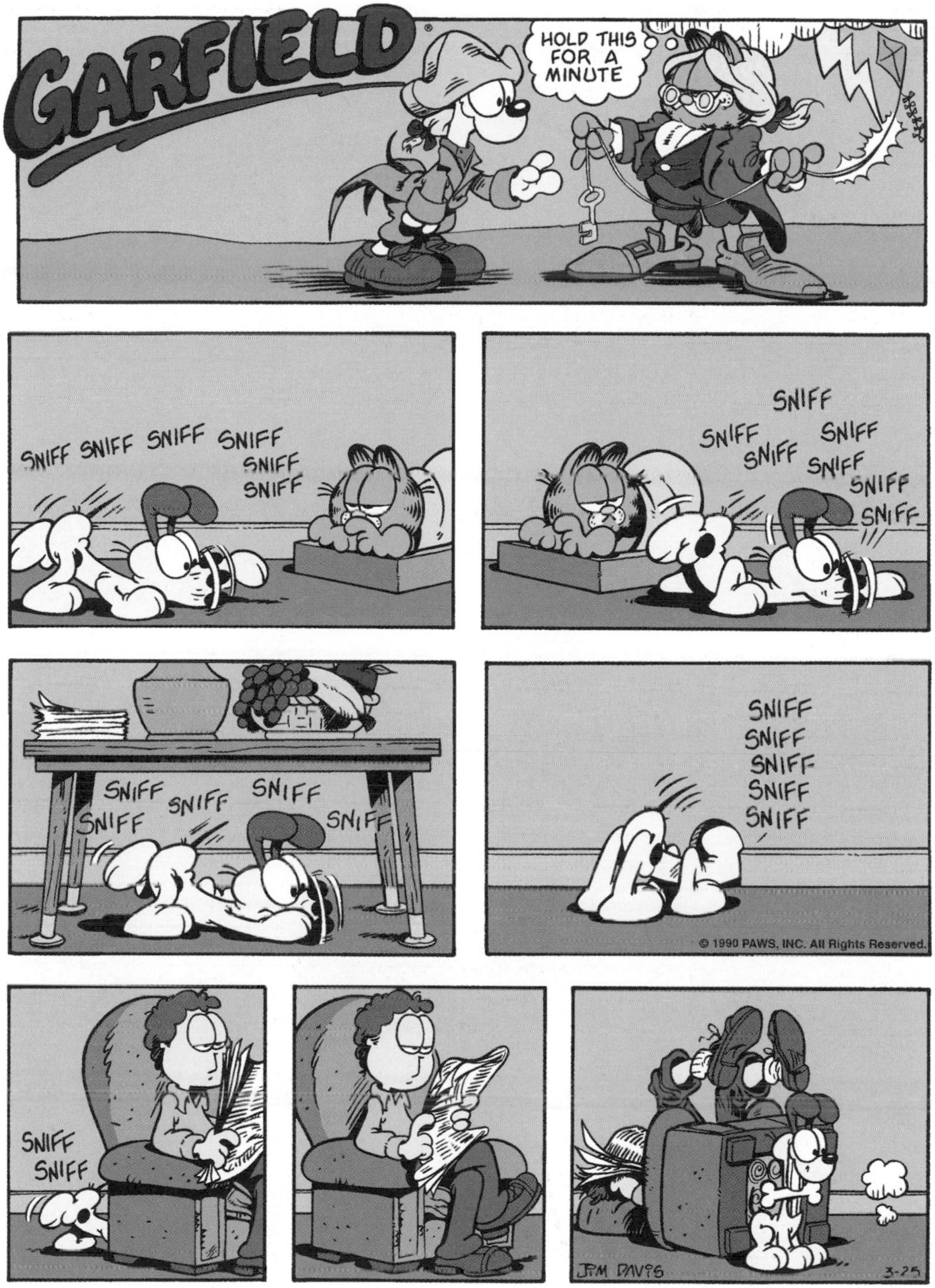
GARFIELD
HOLD THIS FOR A MINUTE
SNIFF SNIFF SNIFF SNIFF SNIFF SNIFF
SNIFF SNIFF SNIFF SNIFF SNIFF SNIFF SNIFF
SNIFF SNIFF SNIFF SNIFF SNIFF
SNIFF SNIFF SNIFF SNIFF SNIFF
© 1990 PAWS, INC. All Rights Reserved.
SNIFF SNIFF
JIM DAVIS 3-25

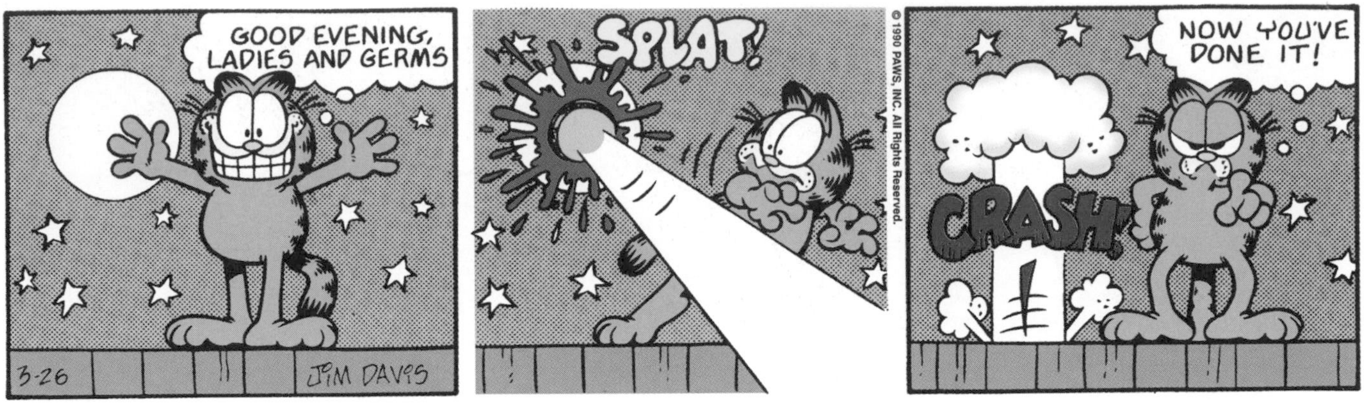
GOOD EVENING, LADIES AND GERMS
3-26
JIM DAVIS
SPLAT!
© 1990 PAWS, INC. All Rights Reserved.
CRASH!
NOW YOU'VE DONE IT!

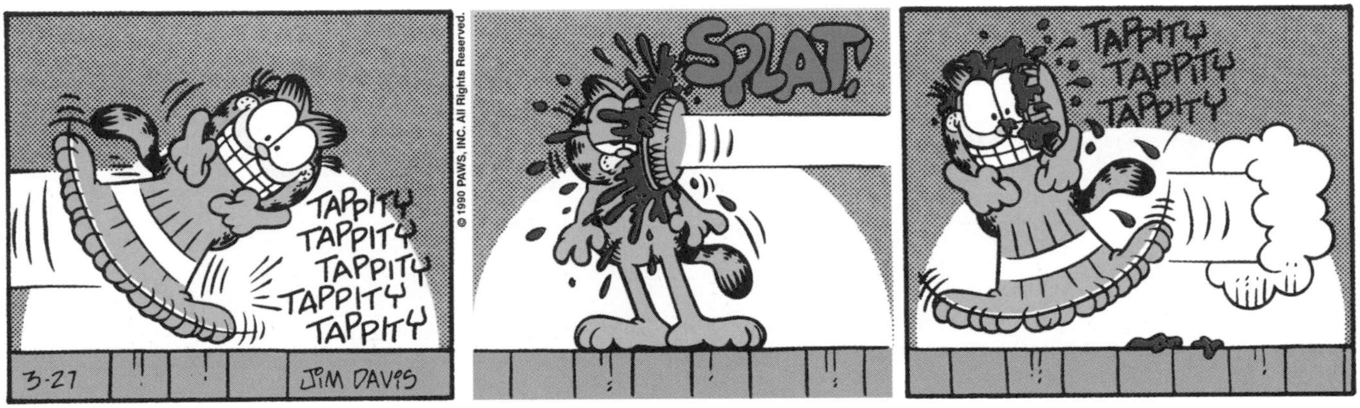
TAPPITY TAPPITY TAPPITY TAPPITY TAPPITY TAPPITY
3-27
JIM DAVIS
© 1990 PAWS, INC. All Rights Reserved.
SPLAT!
TAPPITY TAPPITY TAPPITY

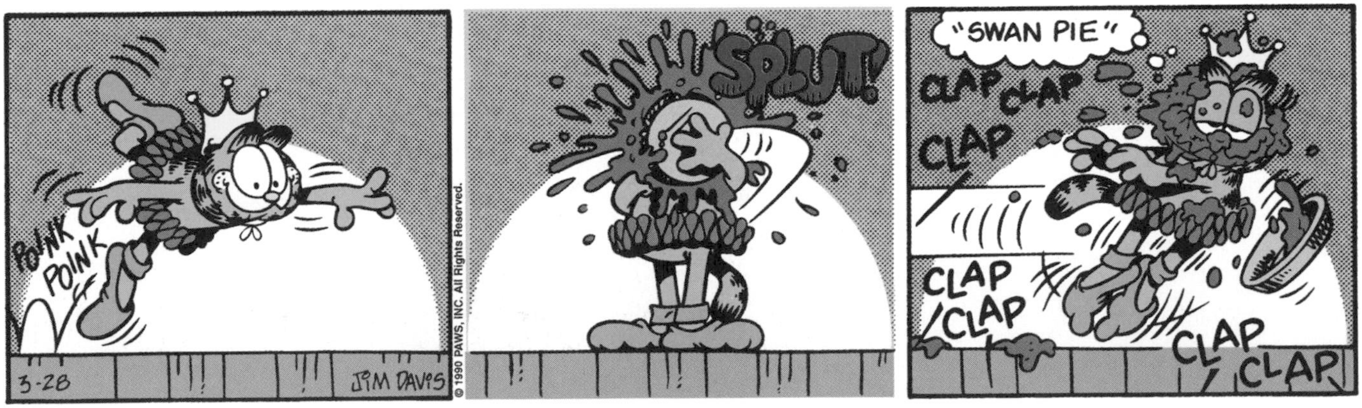
POINK POINK
3-28
JIM DAVIS
© 1990 PAWS, INC. All Rights Reserved.
SPLUT!
"SWAN PIE"
CLAP CLAP CLAP
CLAP CLAP
CLAP CLAP

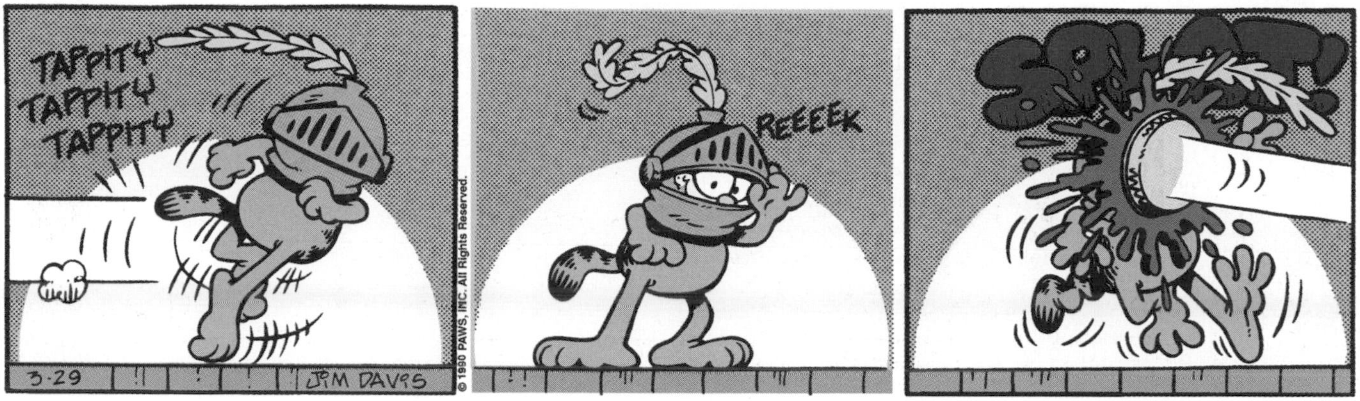
TAPPITY
TAPPITY
TAPPITY
3-29
JIM DAVIS
© 1990 PAWS, INC. All Rights Reserved.
REEEEK
SPLAT!

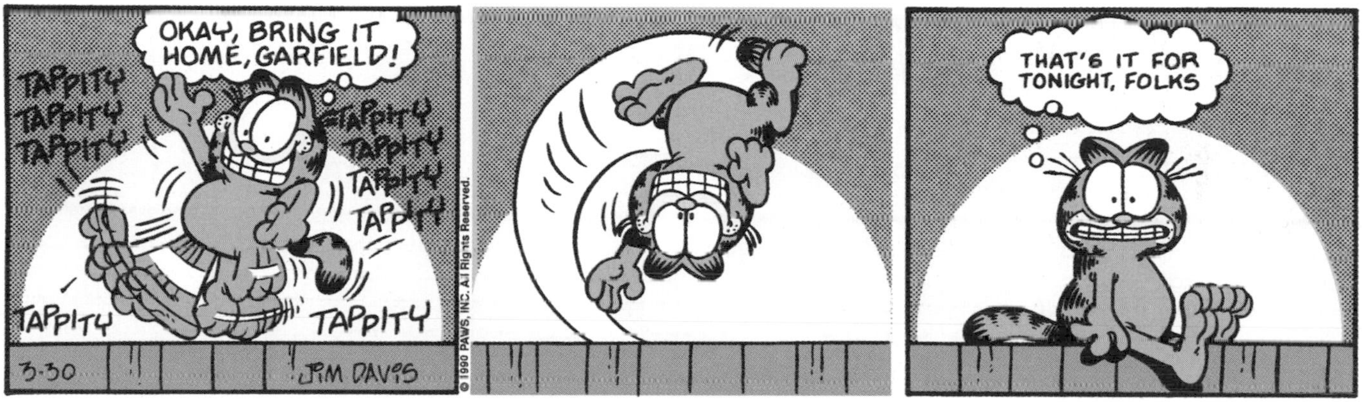
OKAY, BRING IT HOME, GARFIELD!
TAPPITY
TAPPITY
TAPPITY
TAPPITY
TAPPITY
TAPPITY
TAPPITY
TAPPITY
TAPPITY
3-30
JIM DAVIS
© 1990 PAWS, INC. All Rights Reserved.
THAT'S IT FOR TONIGHT, FOLKS

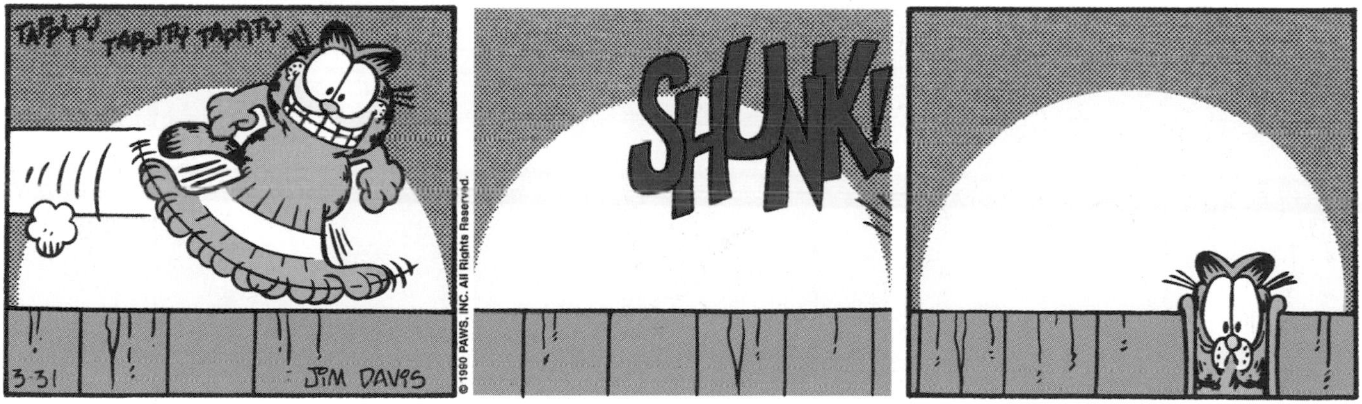
TAPPITY TAPPITY TAPPITY
3-31
JIM DAVIS
© 1990 PAWS, INC. All Rights Reserved.
SHUNK!

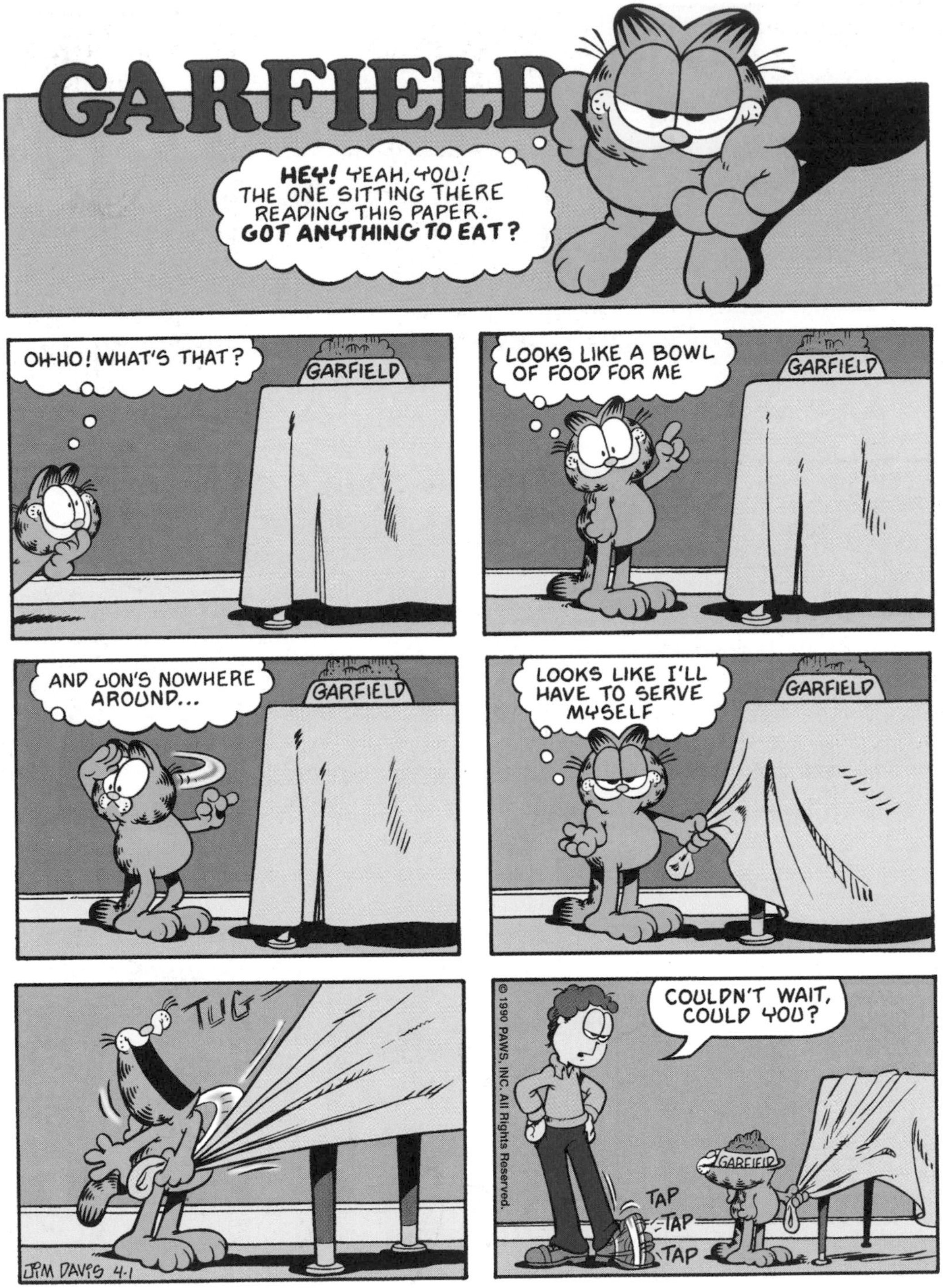
GARFIELD
HEY! YEAH, YOU!
THE ONE SITTING THERE
READING THIS PAPER.
GOT ANYTHING TO EAT?
OH-HO! WHAT'S THAT?
GARFIELD
LOOKS LIKE A BOWL
OF FOOD FOR ME
GARFIELD
AND JON'S NOWHERE
AROUND...
GARFIELD
LOOKS LIKE I'LL
HAVE TO SERVE
MYSELF
GARFIELD
TUG
JIM DAVIS 4-1
© 1990 PAWS, INC. All Rights Reserved.
COULDN'T WAIT,
COULD YOU?
GARFIELD
TAP
TAP
TAP

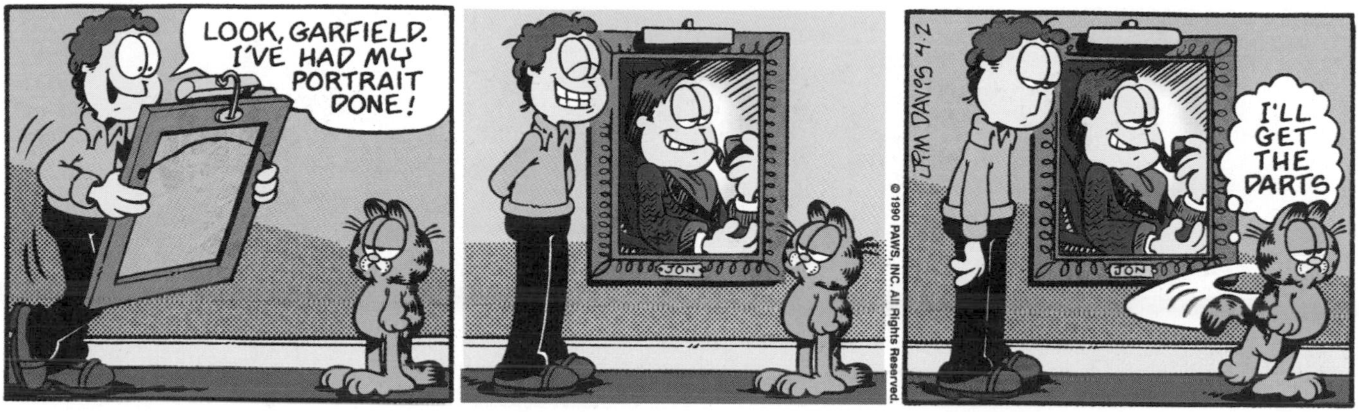
LOOK, GARFIELD. I'VE HAD MY PORTRAIT DONE!
JON
JIM DAVIS 4-2
© 1990 PAWS, INC. All Rights Reserved.
I'LL GET THE DARTS

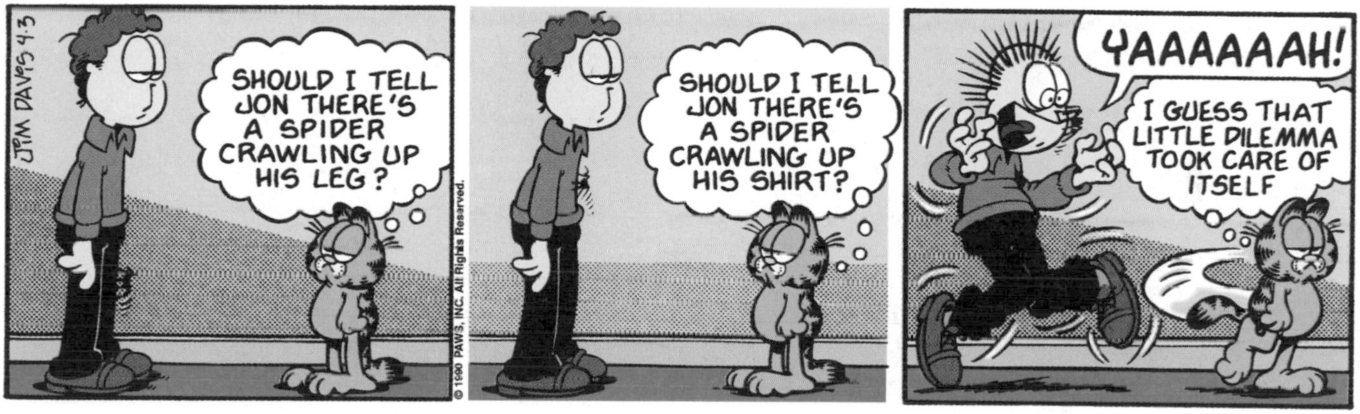
JIM DAVIS 4-3
SHOULD I TELL JON THERE'S A SPIDER CRAWLING UP HIS LEG?
© 1990 PAWS, INC. All Rights Reserved.
SHOULD I TELL JON THERE'S A SPIDER CRAWLING UP HIS SHIRT?
YAAAAAAH!
I GUESS THAT LITTLE DILEMMA TOOK CARE OF ITSELF

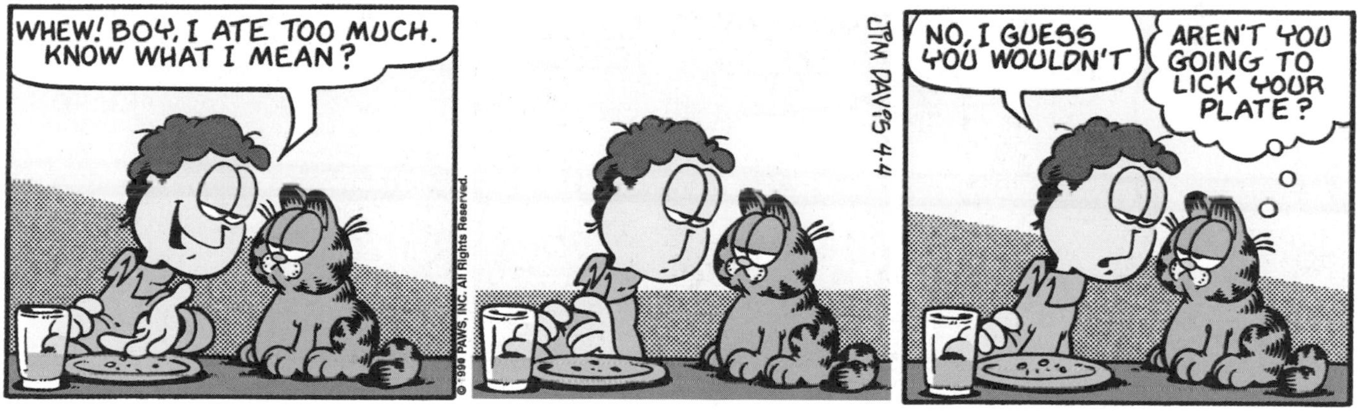
WHEW! BOY, I ATE TOO MUCH. KNOW WHAT I MEAN?
© 1990 PAWS, INC. All Rights Reserved.
JIM DAVIS 4-4
NO, I GUESS YOU WOULDN'T
AREN'T YOU GOING TO LICK YOUR PLATE?

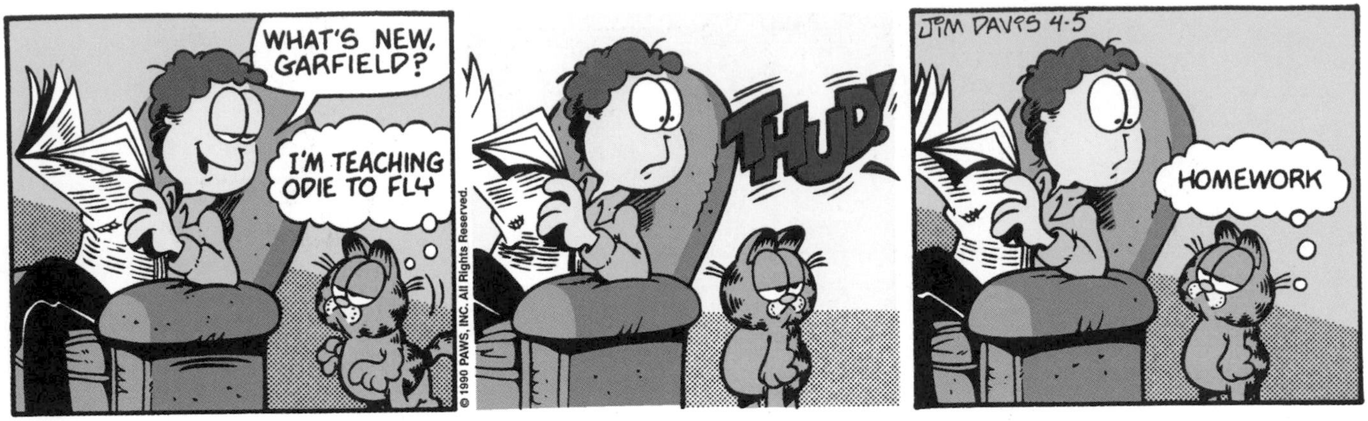
WHAT'S NEW, GARFIELD?
I'M TEACHING ODIE TO FLY
© 1990 PAWS, INC. All Rights Reserved.
THUD!
JIM DAVIS 4-5
HOMEWORK

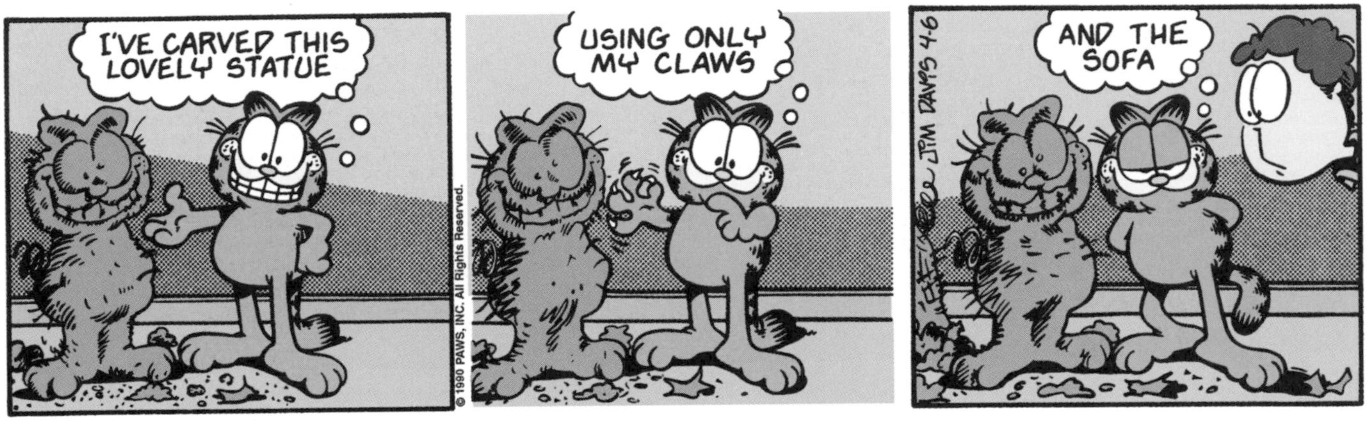
I'VE CARVED THIS LOVELY STATUE
© 1990 PAWS, INC. All Rights Reserved.
USING ONLY MY CLAWS
JIM DAVIS 4-6
AND THE SOFA

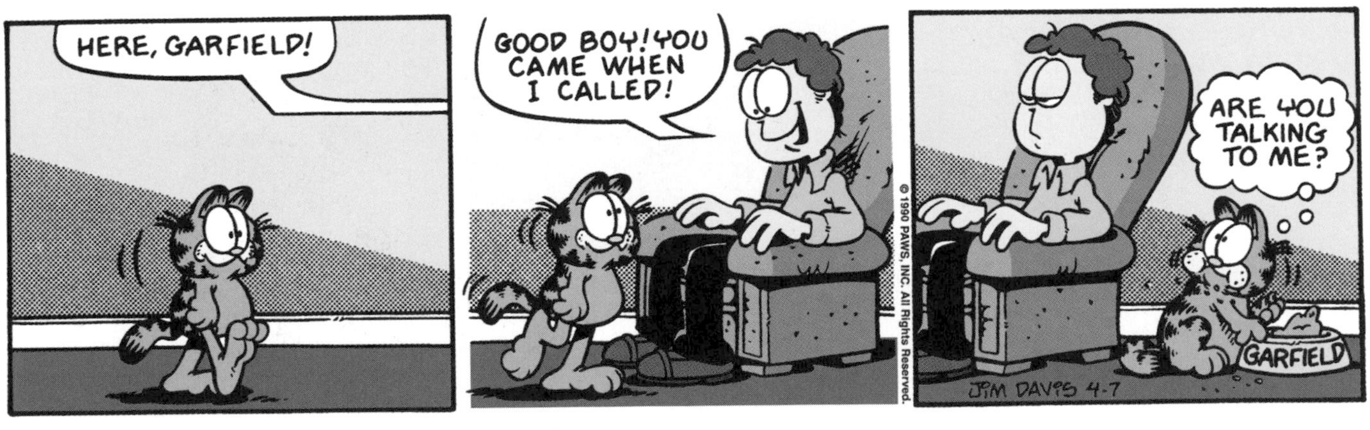
HERE, GARFIELD!
GOOD BOY! YOU CAME WHEN I CALLED!
© 1990 PAWS, INC. All Rights Reserved.
ARE YOU TALKING TO ME?
GARFIELD
JIM DAVIS 4-7

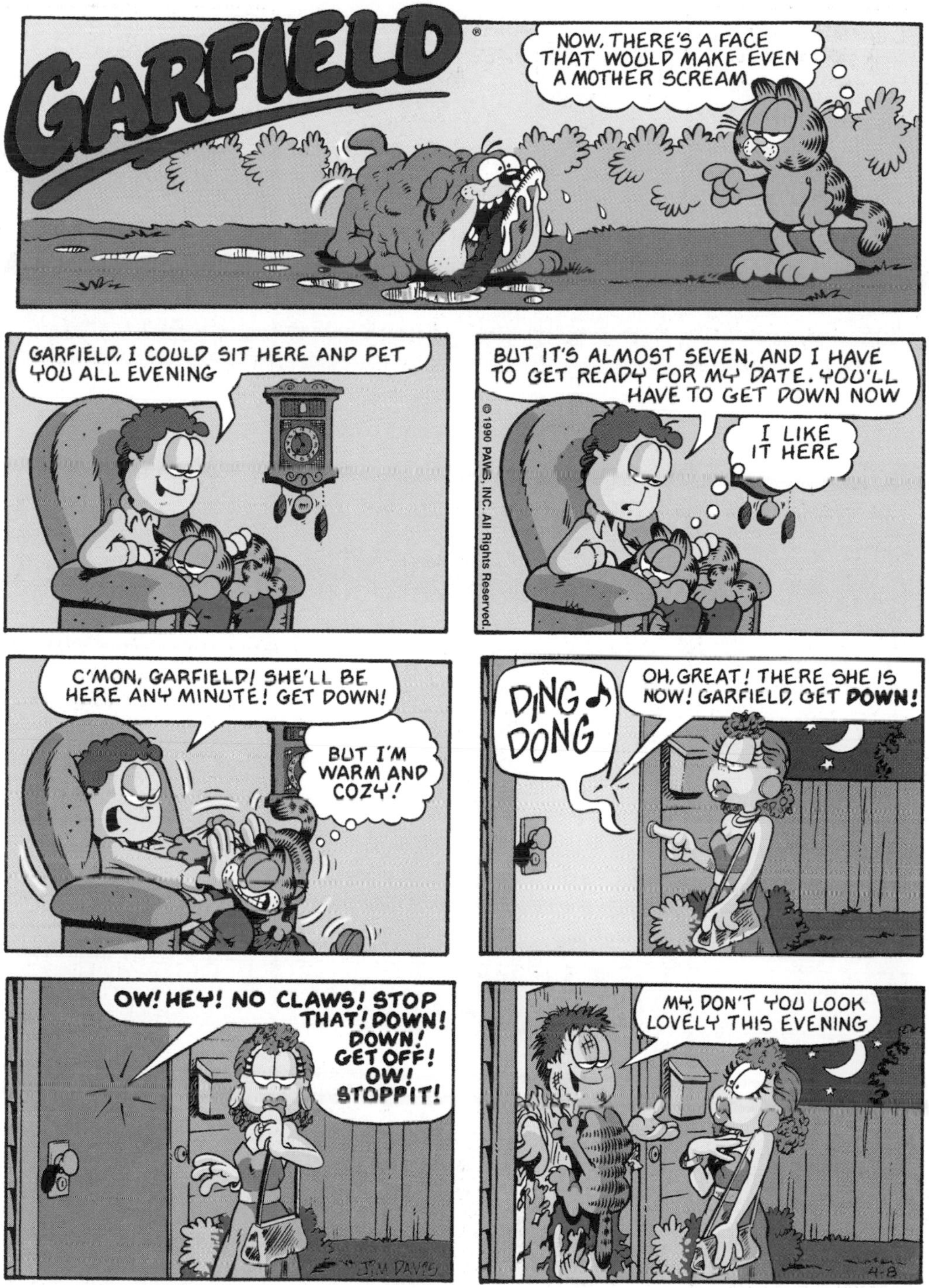
GARFIELD®
NOW, THERE'S A FACE THAT WOULD MAKE EVEN A MOTHER SCREAM
GARFIELD, I COULD SIT HERE AND PET YOU ALL EVENING
BUT IT'S ALMOST SEVEN, AND I HAVE TO GET READY FOR MY DATE. YOU'LL HAVE TO GET DOWN NOW
I LIKE IT HERE
© 1990 PAWS, INC. All Rights Reserved.
C'MON, GARFIELD! SHE'LL BE HERE ANY MINUTE! GET DOWN!
BUT I'M WARM AND COZY!
DING DONG
OH, GREAT! THERE SHE IS NOW! GARFIELD, GET DOWN!
OW! HEY! NO CLAWS! STOP THAT! DOWN! DOWN! GET OFF! OW! STOPPIT!
JIM DAVIS
MY, DON'T YOU LOOK LOVELY THIS EVENING
4-8

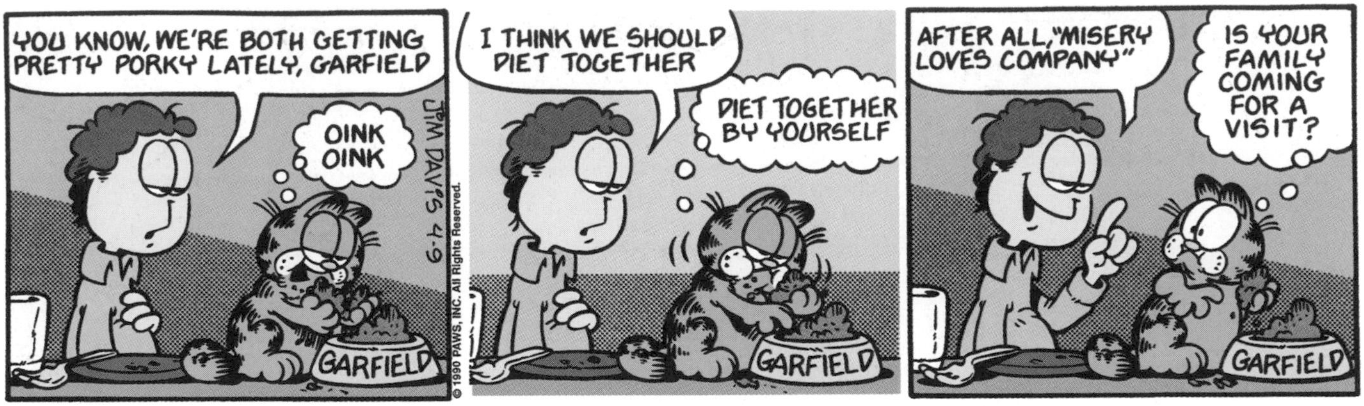
YOU KNOW, WE'RE BOTH GETTING PRETTY PORKY LATELY, GARFIELD
OINK OINK
JIM DAVIS 4-9
© 1990 PAWS, INC. All Rights Reserved.
GARFIELD
I THINK WE SHOULD DIET TOGETHER
DIET TOGETHER BY YOURSELF
GARFIELD
AFTER ALL, "MISERY LOVES COMPANY"
IS YOUR FAMILY COMING FOR A VISIT?
GARFIELD

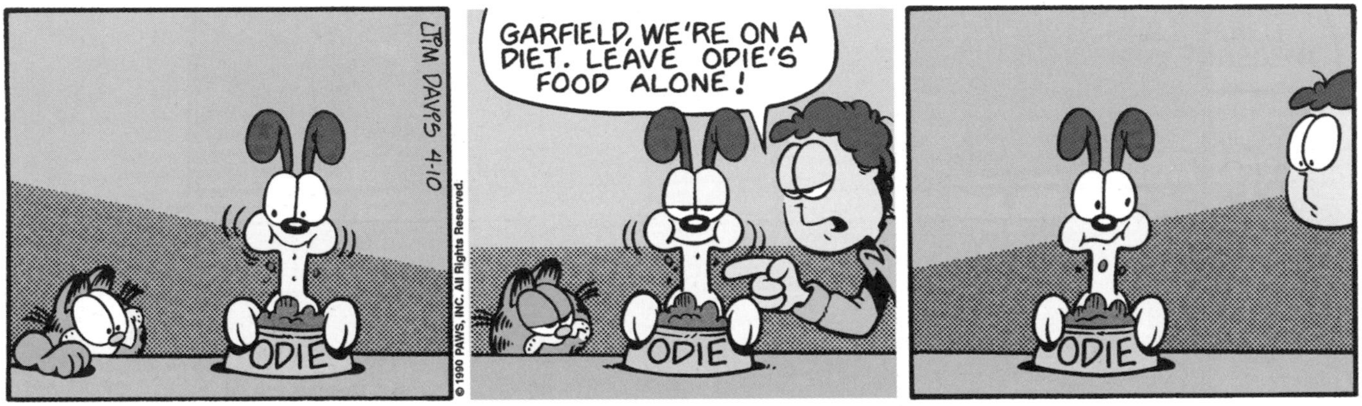
JIM DAVIS 4-10
ODIE
© 1990 PAWS, INC. All Rights Reserved.
GARFIELD, WE'RE ON A DIET. LEAVE ODIE'S FOOD ALONE!
ODIE
ODIE

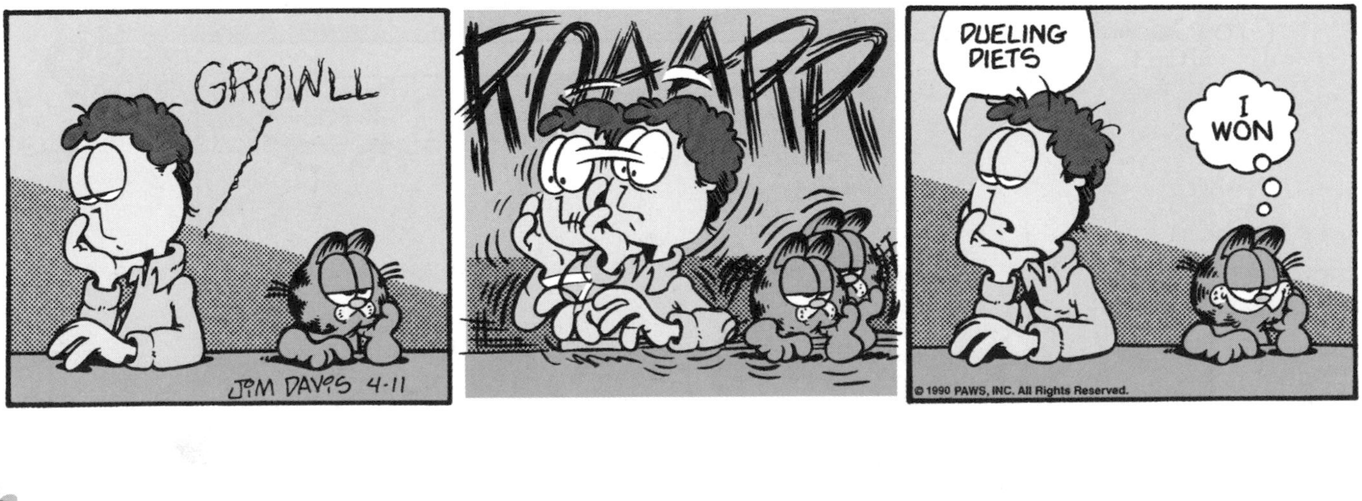
GROWLL
JIM DAVIS 4-11
ROAARR
DUELING DIETS
I WON
© 1990 PAWS, INC. All Rights Reserved.

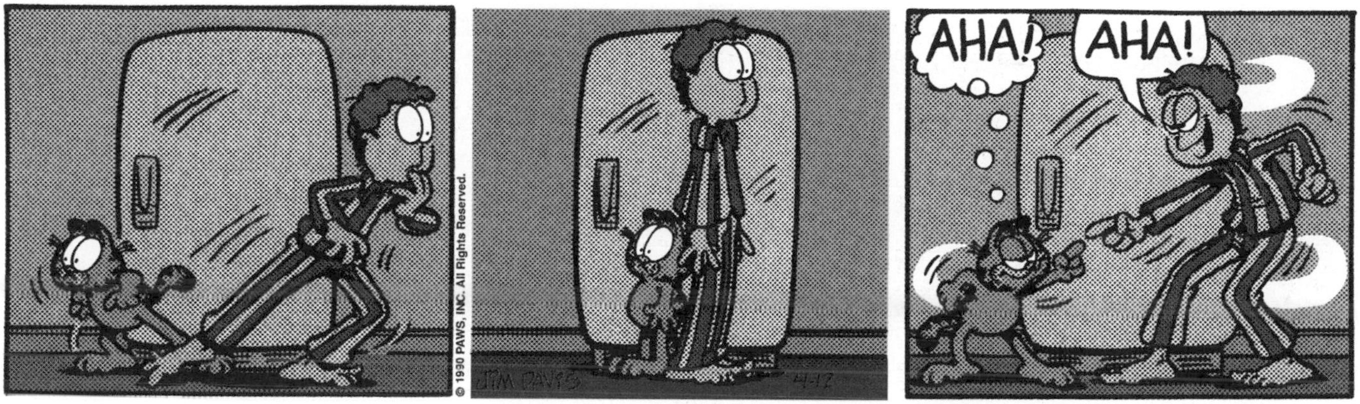
AHA!
AHA!
JIM DAVIS 4-12

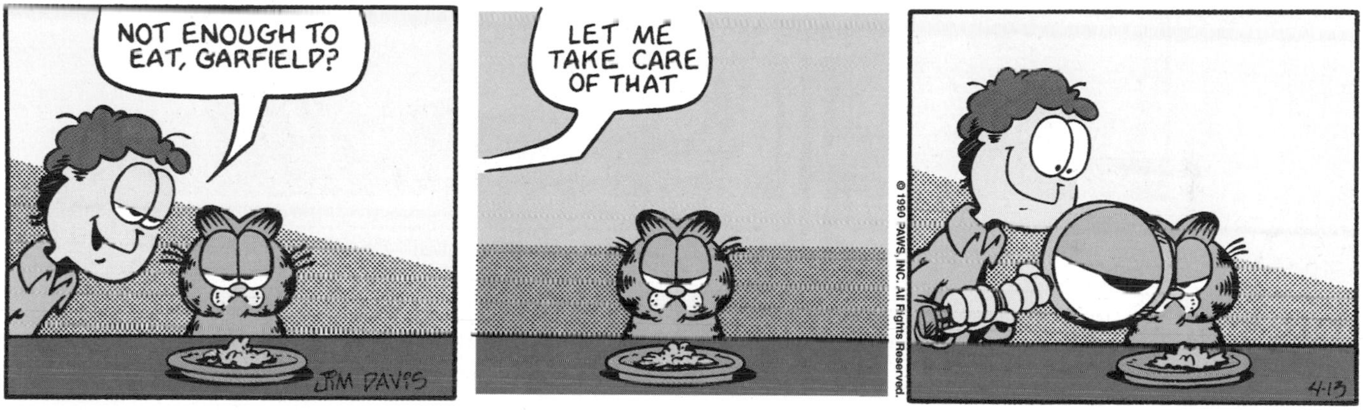
NOT ENOUGH TO EAT, GARFIELD?
LET ME TAKE CARE OF THAT
JIM DAVIS
4-13

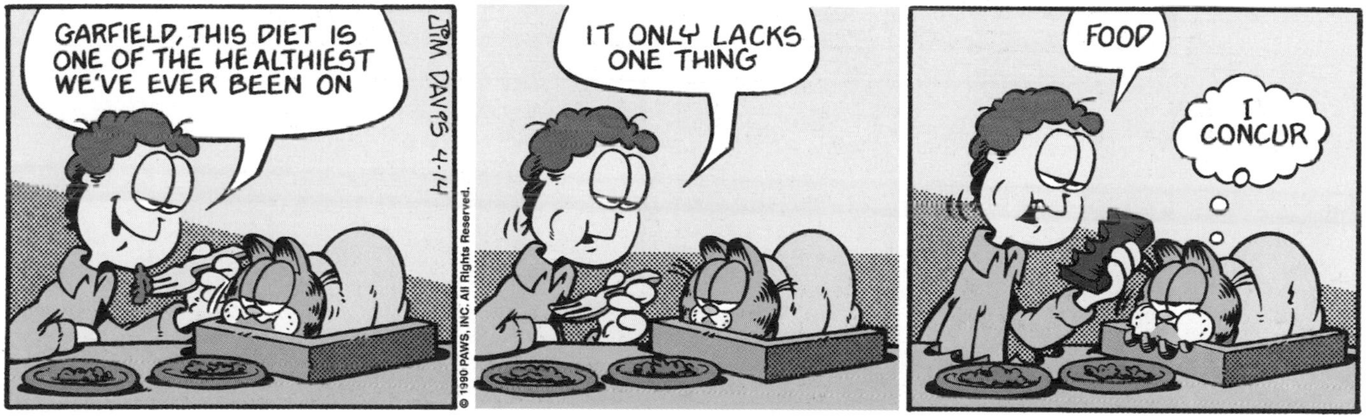
GARFIELD, THIS DIET IS ONE OF THE HEALTHIEST WE'VE EVER BEEN ON
JIM DAVIS 4-14
IT ONLY LACKS ONE THING
FOOD
I CONCUR

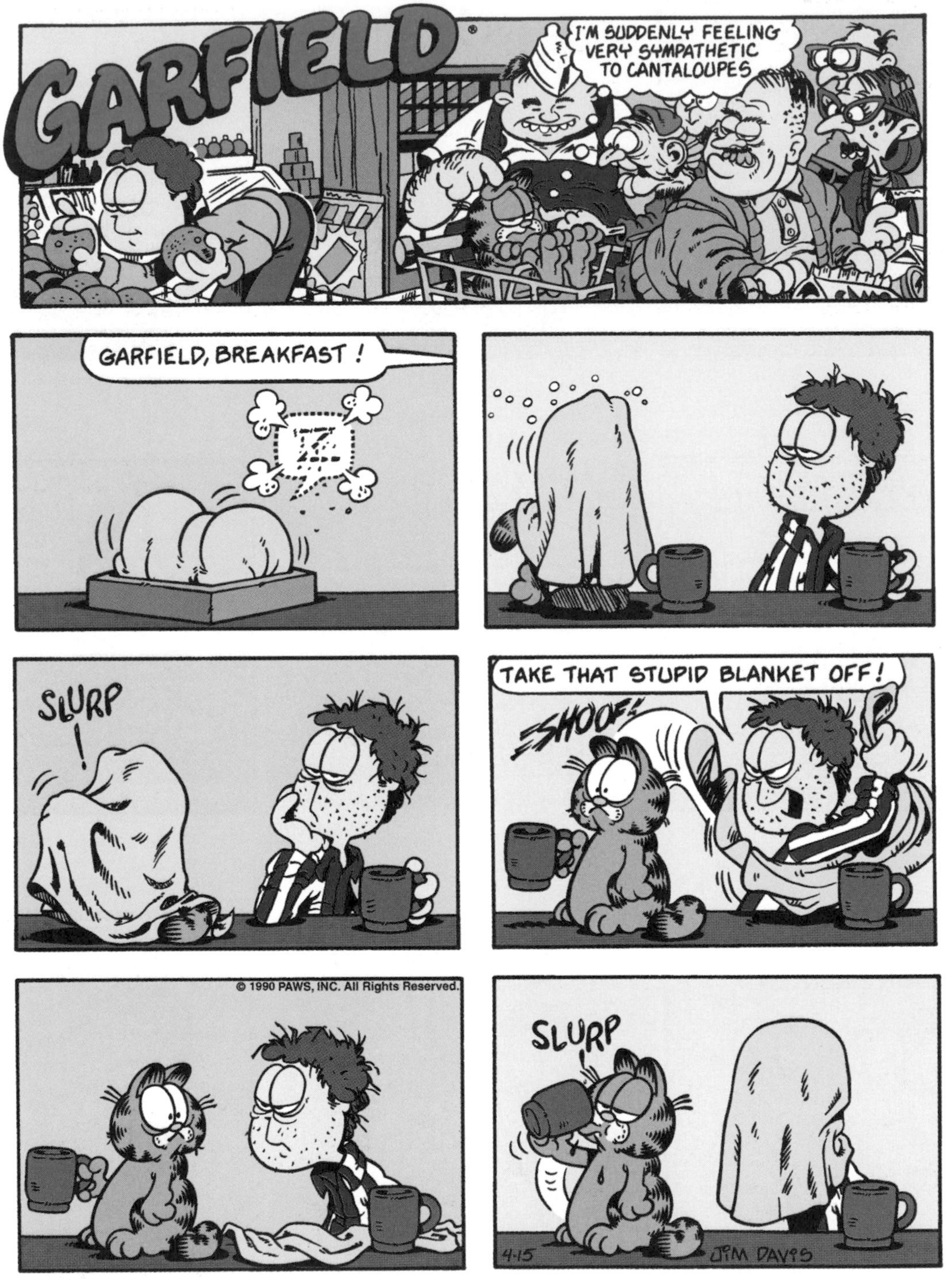
GARFIELD
I'M SUDDENLY FEELING VERY SYMPATHETIC TO CANTALOUPES
GARFIELD, BREAKFAST!
Z
SLURP
TAKE THAT STUPID BLANKET OFF!
SHOOF!
© 1990 PAWS, INC. All Rights Reserved.
SLURP
4-15
JIM DAVIS

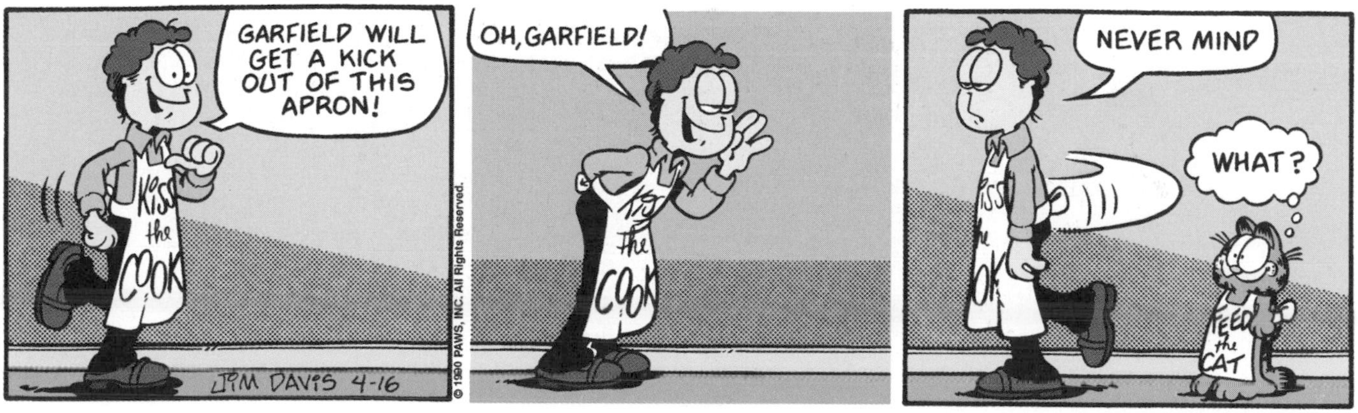
GARFIELD WILL GET A KICK OUT OF THIS APRON!
KISS the COOK
JIM DAVIS 4-16
© 1990 PAWS, INC. All Rights Reserved.
OH, GARFIELD!
NEVER MIND
WHAT?
FEED the CAT

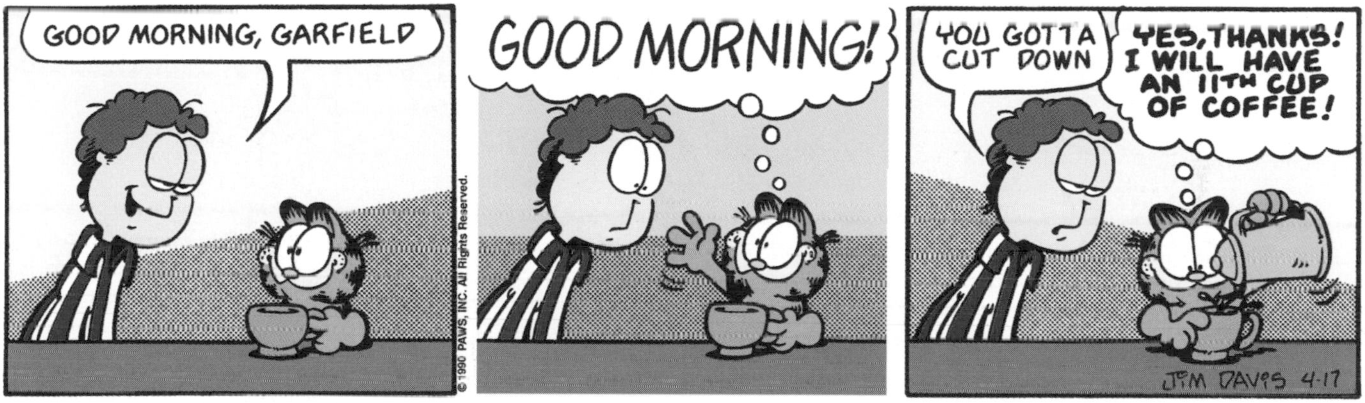
GOOD MORNING, GARFIELD
© 1990 PAWS, INC. All Rights Reserved.
GOOD MORNING!
YOU GOTTA CUT DOWN
YES, THANKS! I WILL HAVE AN 11TH CUP OF COFFEE!
JIM DAVIS 4-17

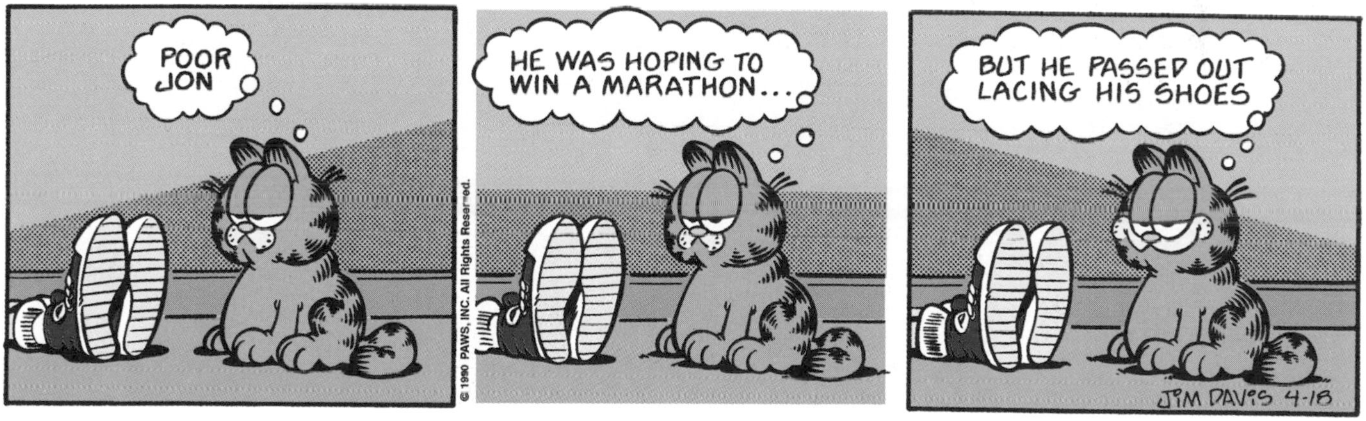
POOR JON
© 1990 PAWS, INC. All Rights Reserved.
HE WAS HOPING TO WIN A MARATHON...
BUT HE PASSED OUT LACING HIS SHOES
JIM DAVIS 4-18

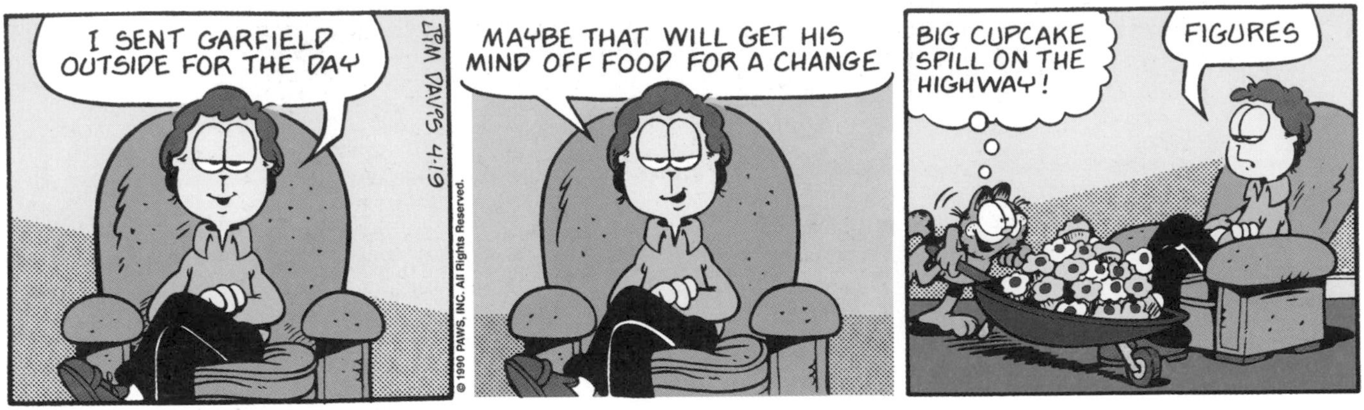
I SENT GARFIELD OUTSIDE FOR THE DAY
JPM DAVIS 4-19
© 1990 PAWS, INC. All Rights Reserved.
MAYBE THAT WILL GET HIS MIND OFF FOOD FOR A CHANGE
BIG CUPCAKE SPILL ON THE HIGHWAY!
FIGURES

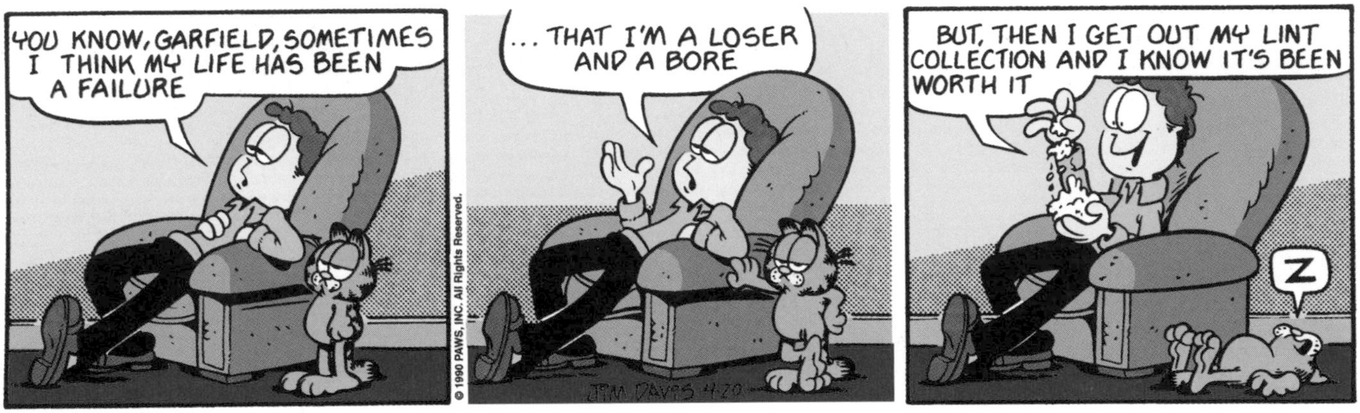
YOU KNOW, GARFIELD, SOMETIMES I THINK MY LIFE HAS BEEN A FAILURE
© 1990 PAWS, INC. All Rights Reserved.
. . . THAT I'M A LOSER AND A BORE
JPM DAVIS 4-20
BUT, THEN I GET OUT MY LINT COLLECTION AND I KNOW IT'S BEEN WORTH IT
Z

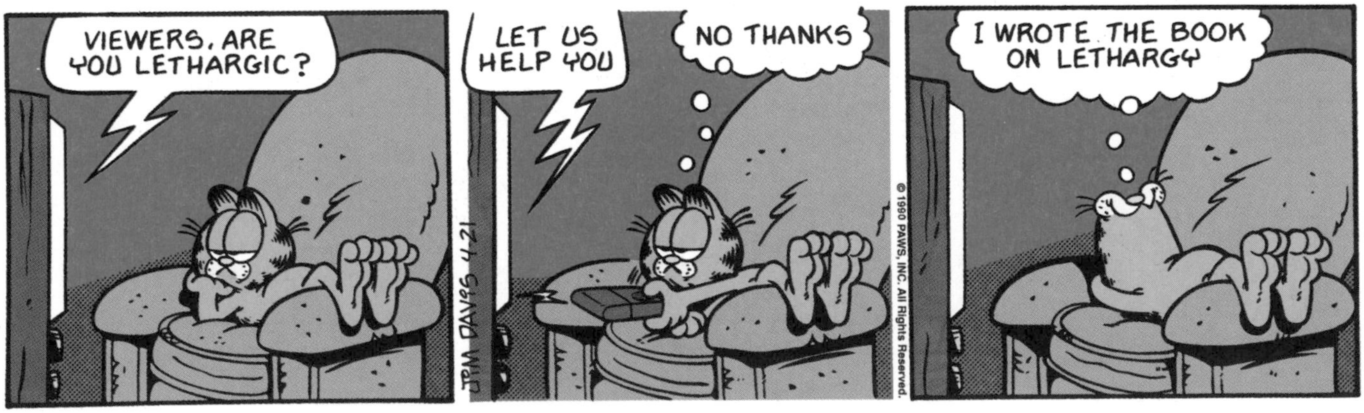
VIEWERS, ARE YOU LETHARGIC?
JPM DAVIS 4-21
LET US HELP YOU
NO THANKS
© 1990 PAWS, INC. All Rights Reserved.
I WROTE THE BOOK ON LETHARGY

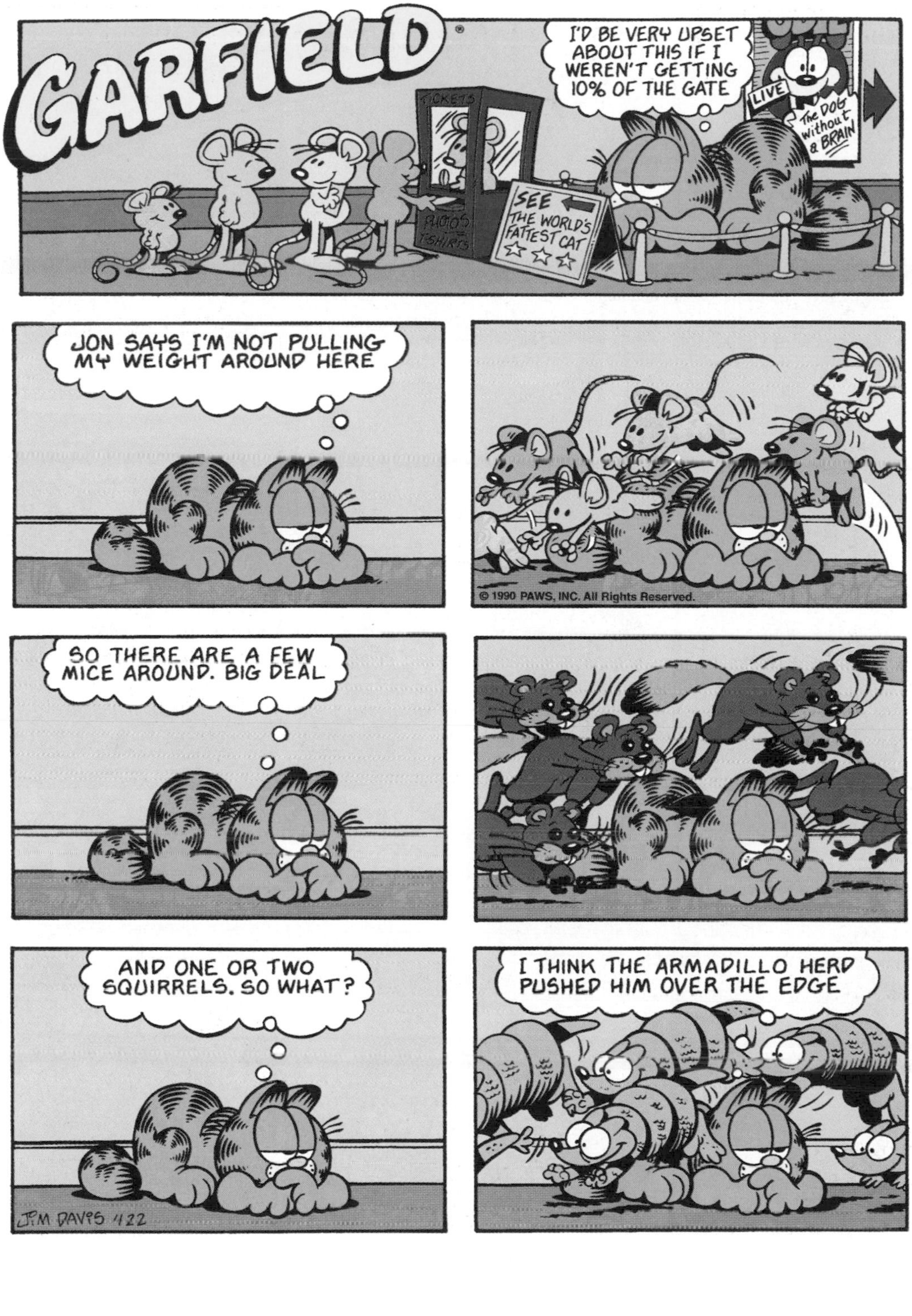
GARFIELD
I'D BE VERY UPSET ABOUT THIS IF I WEREN'T GETTING 10% OF THE GATE
TICKETS
PHOTOS T-SHIRTS
SEE THE WORLD'S FATTEST CAT
LIVE
The DOG without a BRAIN
JON SAYS I'M NOT PULLING MY WEIGHT AROUND HERE
© 1990 PAWS, INC. All Rights Reserved.
SO THERE ARE A FEW MICE AROUND. BIG DEAL
AND ONE OR TWO SQUIRRELS. SO WHAT?
I THINK THE ARMADILLO HERD PUSHED HIM OVER THE EDGE
JIM DAVIS 4-22

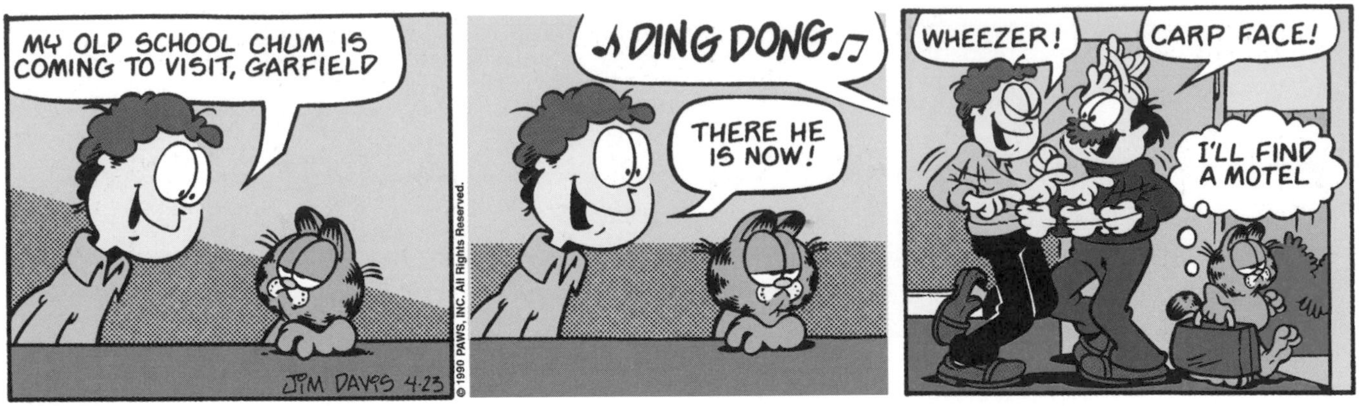
MY OLD SCHOOL CHUM IS COMING TO VISIT, GARFIELD
JIM DAVIS 4-23
© 1990 PAWS, INC. All Rights Reserved.
DING DONG
THERE HE IS NOW!
WHEEZER!
CARP FACE!
I'LL FIND A MOTEL

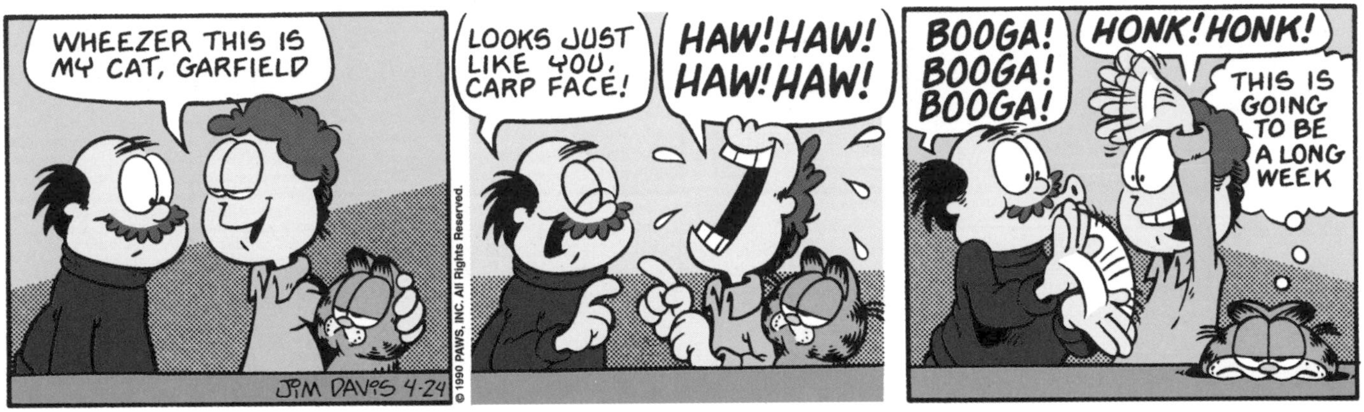
WHEEZER THIS IS MY CAT, GARFIELD
JIM DAVIS 4-24
© 1990 PAWS, INC. All Rights Reserved.
LOOKS JUST LIKE YOU, CARP FACE!
HAW! HAW! HAW! HAW!
BOOGA! BOOGA! BOOGA!
HONK! HONK!
THIS IS GOING TO BE A LONG WEEK

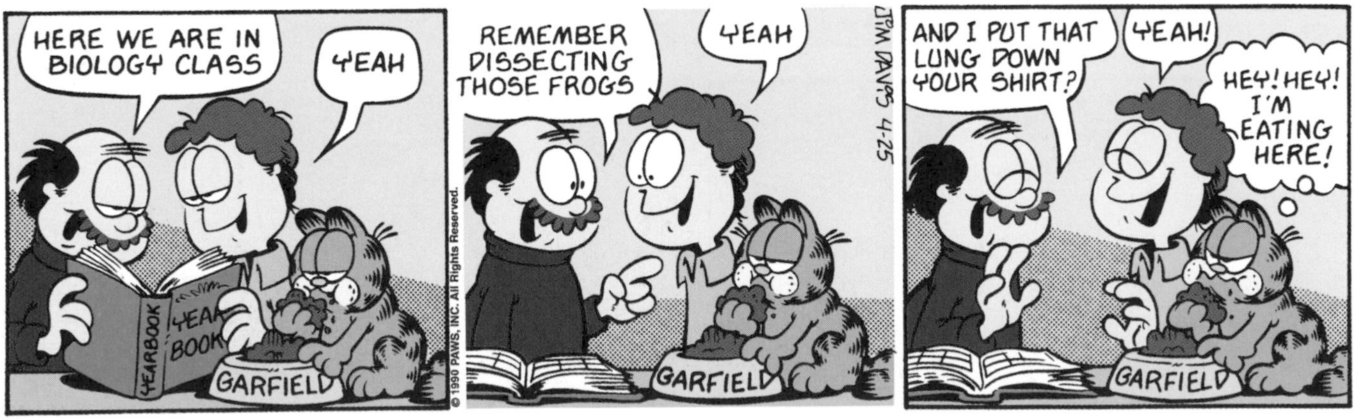
HERE WE ARE IN BIOLOGY CLASS
YEAH
YEARBOOK
YEARBOOK
GARFIELD
© 1990 PAWS, INC. All Rights Reserved.
REMEMBER DISSECTING THOSE FROGS
YEAH
JIM DAVIS 4-25
GARFIELD
AND I PUT THAT LUNG DOWN YOUR SHIRT?
YEAH!
HEY! HEY! I'M EATING HERE!
GARFIELD

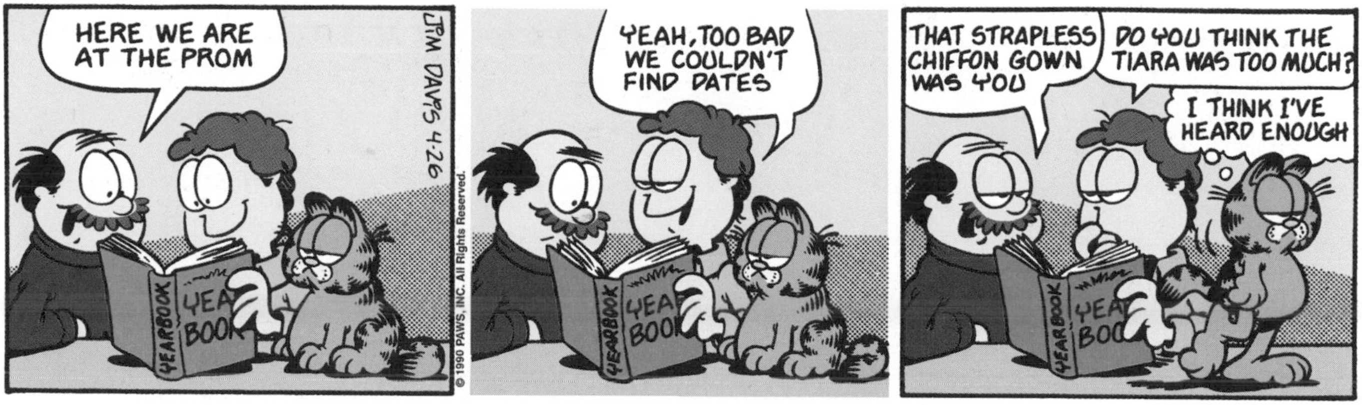
HERE WE ARE AT THE PROM
JIM DAVIS 4-26
© 1990 PAWS, INC. All Rights Reserved.
YEAH, TOO BAD WE COULDN'T FIND DATES
THAT STRAPLESS CHIFFON GOWN WAS YOU
DO YOU THINK THE TIARA WAS TOO MUCH?
I THINK I'VE HEARD ENOUGH

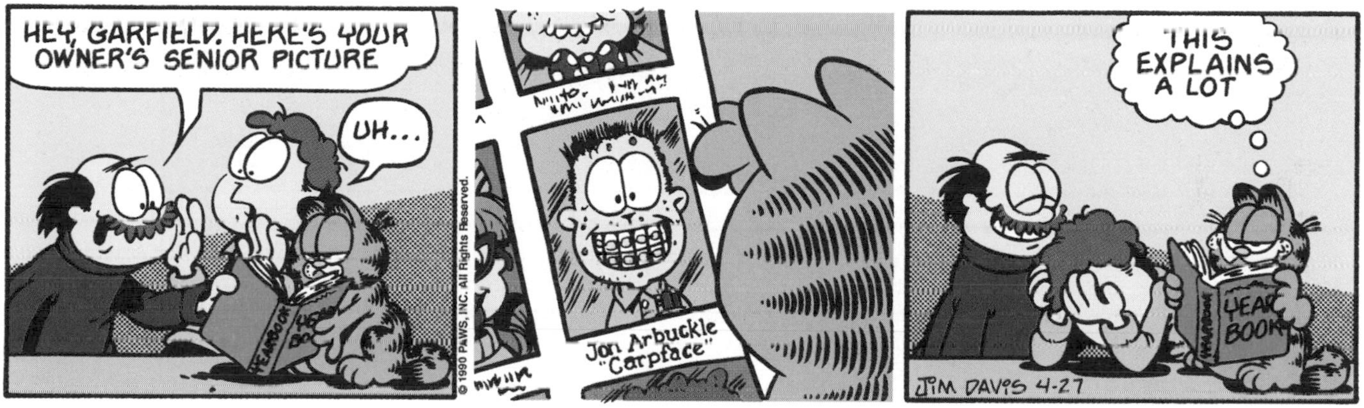
HEY, GARFIELD. HERE'S YOUR OWNER'S SENIOR PICTURE
UH...
© 1990 PAWS, INC. All Rights Reserved.
Jon Arbuckle "Carpface"
THIS EXPLAINS A LOT
JIM DAVIS 4-27

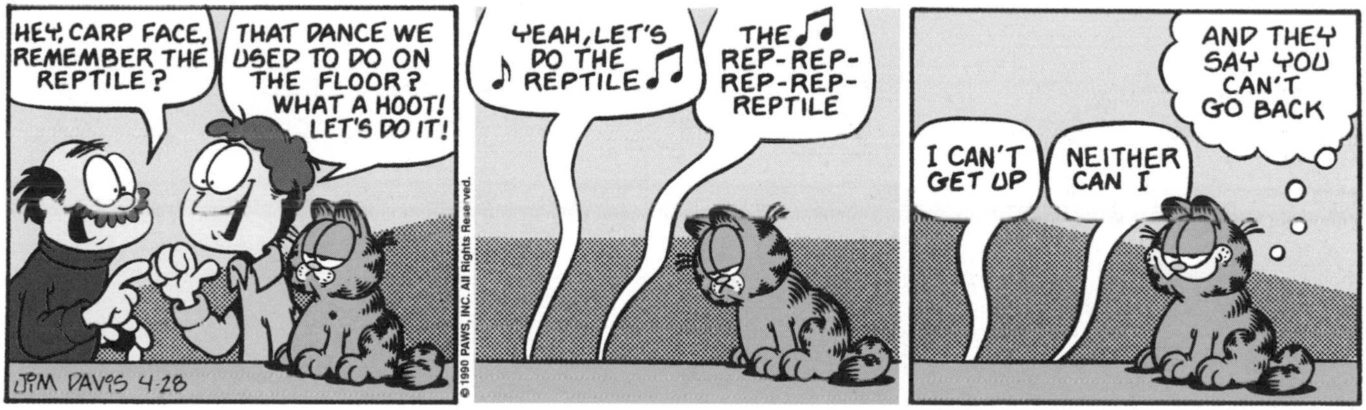
HEY, CARP FACE, REMEMBER THE REPTILE?
THAT DANCE WE USED TO DO ON THE FLOOR? WHAT A HOOT! LET'S DO IT!
JIM DAVIS 4-28
© 1990 PAWS, INC. All Rights Reserved.
YEAH, LET'S ♪ DO THE REPTILE ♫
THE ♫ REP-REP-REP-REP-REPTILE
I CAN'T GET UP
NEITHER CAN I
AND THEY SAY YOU CAN'T GO BACK

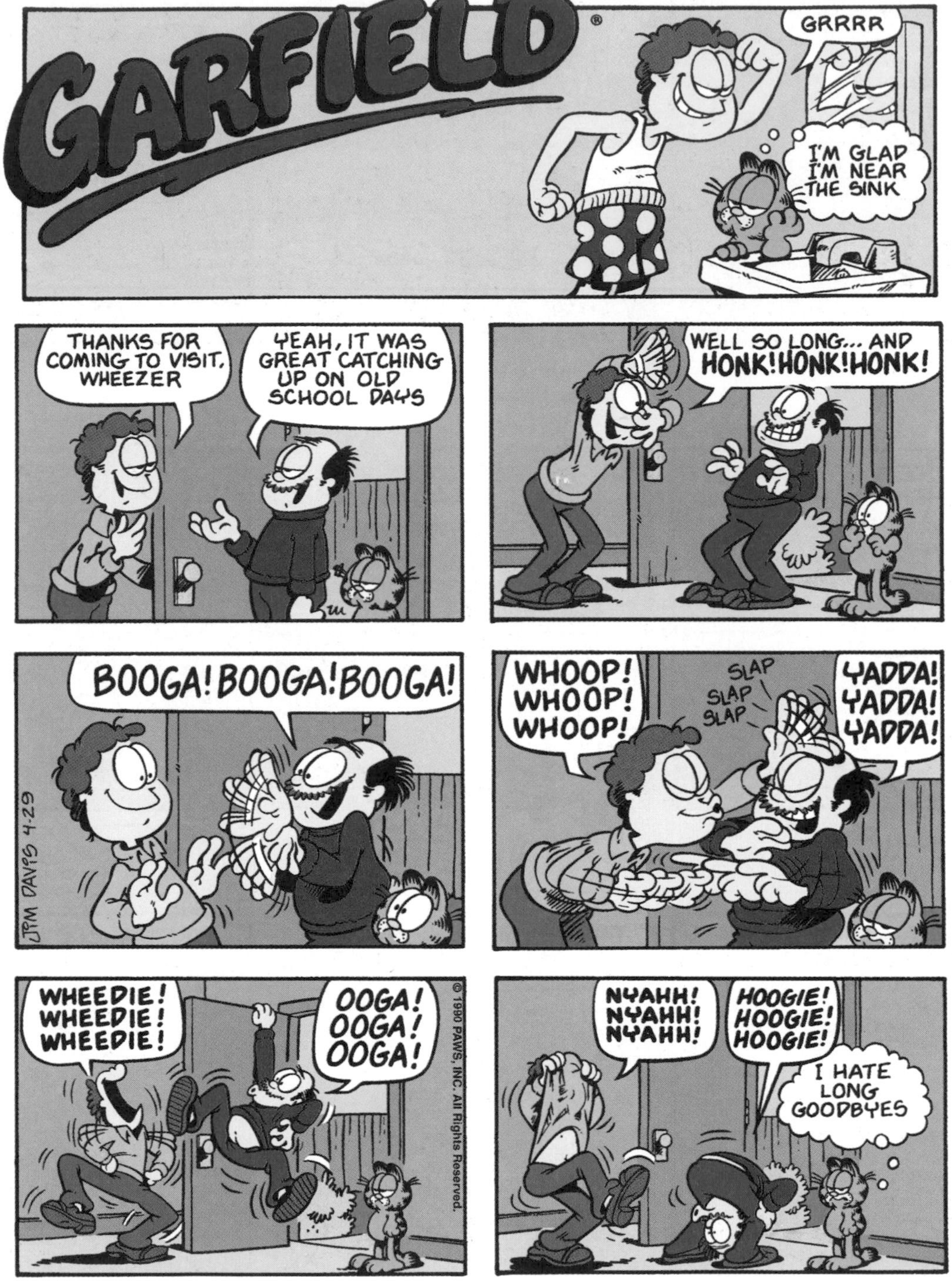
GARFIELD®
GRRRR
I'M GLAD I'M NEAR THE SINK
THANKS FOR COMING TO VISIT, WHEEZER
YEAH, IT WAS GREAT CATCHING UP ON OLD SCHOOL DAYS
WELL SO LONG... AND HONK! HONK! HONK!
BOOGA! BOOGA! BOOGA!
JIM DAVIS 4-29
WHOOP! WHOOP! WHOOP!
SLAP SLAP SLAP
YADDA! YADDA! YADDA!
WHEEDIE! WHEEDIE! WHEEDIE!
OOGA! OOGA! OOGA!
© 1980 PAWS, INC. All Rights Reserved.
NYAHH! NYAHH! NYAHH!
HOOGIE! HOOGIE! HOOGIE!
I HATE LONG GOODBYES

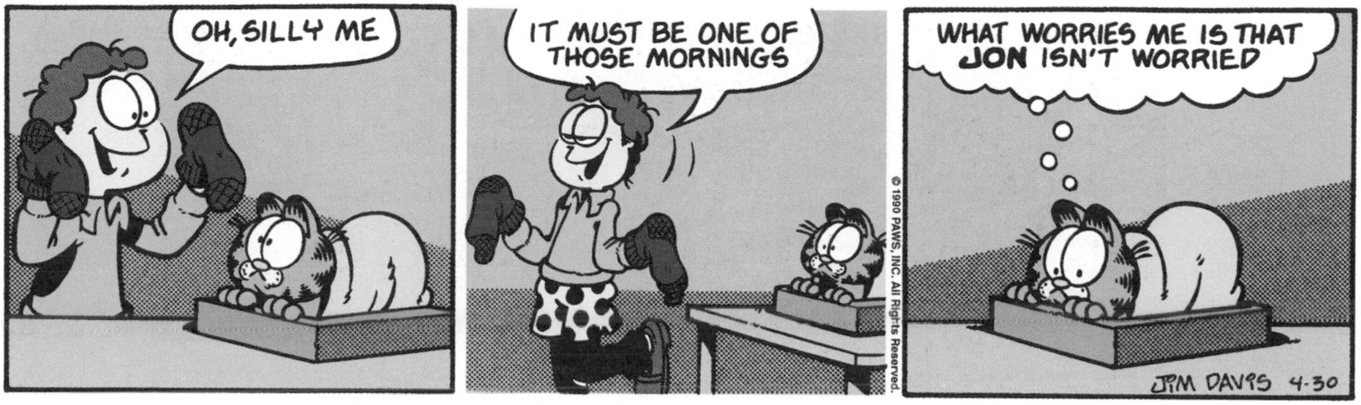
OH, SILLY ME
IT MUST BE ONE OF THOSE MORNINGS
© 1990 PAWS, INC. All Rights Reserved.
WHAT WORRIES ME IS THAT **JON** ISN'T WORRIED
JIM DAVIS 4-30

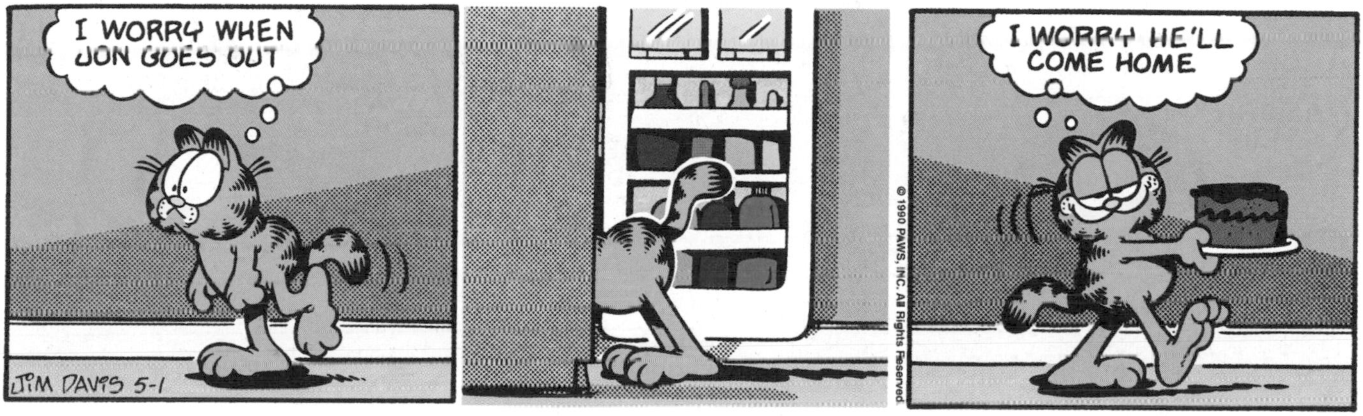
I WORRY WHEN JON GOES OUT
JIM DAVIS 5-1
© 1990 PAWS, INC. All Rights Reserved.
I WORRY HE'LL COME HOME

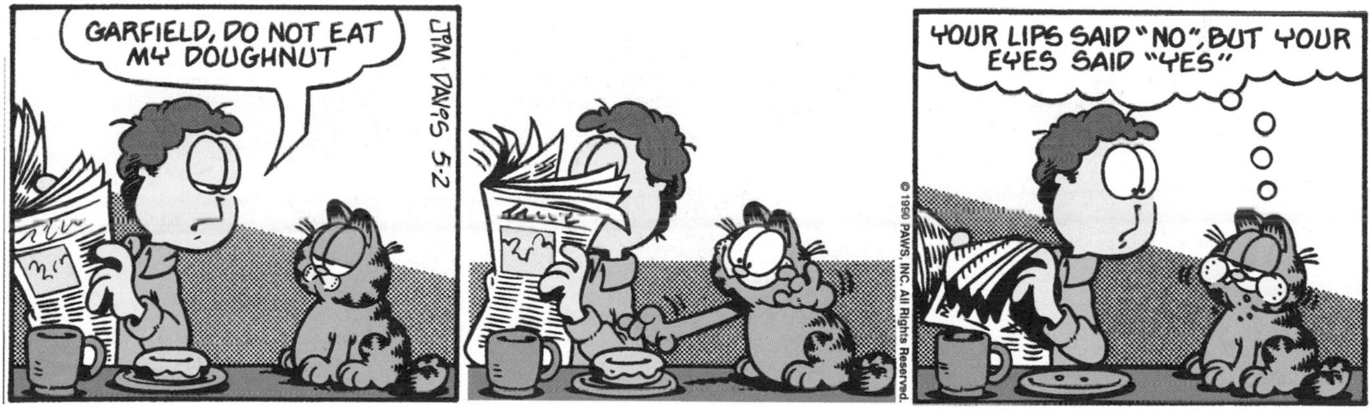
GARFIELD, DO NOT EAT MY DOUGHNUT
JIM DAVIS 5-2
© 1990 PAWS, INC. All Rights Reserved.
YOUR LIPS SAID "NO", BUT YOUR EYES SAID "YES"

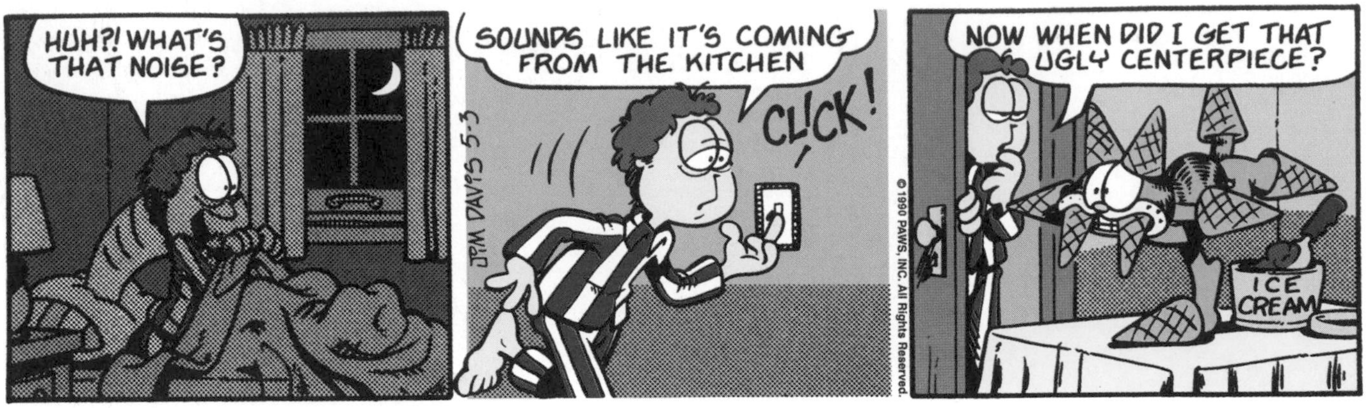
HUH?! WHAT'S THAT NOISE?
SOUNDS LIKE IT'S COMING FROM THE KITCHEN
JIM DAVIS 5-3
CLICK!
NOW WHEN DID I GET THAT UGLY CENTERPIECE?
ICE CREAM
© 1990 PAWS, INC. All Rights Reserved.

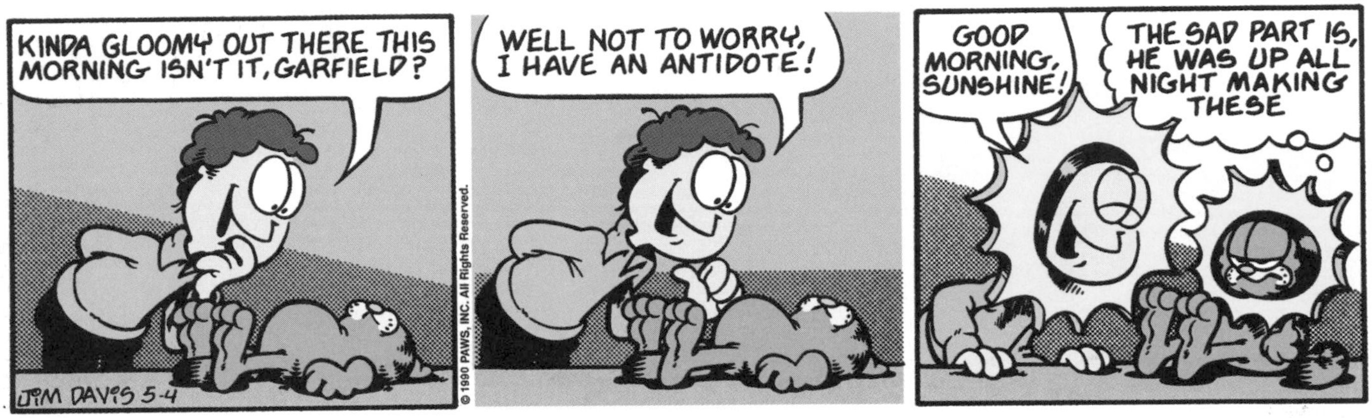
KINDA GLOOMY OUT THERE THIS MORNING ISN'T IT, GARFIELD?
JIM DAVIS 5-4
© 1990 PAWS, INC. All Rights Reserved.
WELL NOT TO WORRY, I HAVE AN ANTIDOTE!
GOOD MORNING, SUNSHINE!
THE SAD PART IS, HE WAS UP ALL NIGHT MAKING THESE

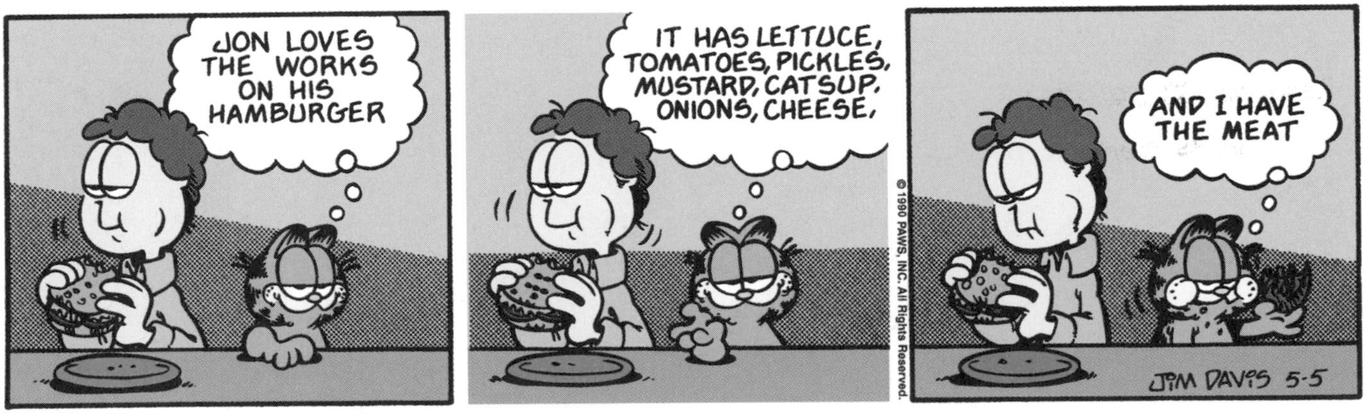
JON LOVES THE WORKS ON HIS HAMBURGER
IT HAS LETTUCE, TOMATOES, PICKLES, MUSTARD, CATSUP, ONIONS, CHEESE,
© 1990 PAWS, INC. All Rights Reserved.
AND I HAVE THE MEAT
JIM DAVIS 5-5